CW00405928

Kerrie Eyers is a psychologist, t
experience in mental health. She
Black Dog Institute, Sydney, ar
(UNSW Press, 2006).

Gordon Parker is Professor of Psychiatry at the University of New
South Wales and Executive Director of the Black Dog Institute. He
is a renowned researcher with over 30 years' experience with mood
disorders, and is author of *Dealing with Depression: A common sense
guide to mood disorders* (Allen & Unwin, 2004).

Tessa Wigney, Kerrie Eyers and Gordon Parker are co-editors of
*Journeys with the Black Dog: Inspirational stories of bringing depression to
heel* (Allen & Unwin, 2007).

www.blackdoginstitute.org.au

MASTERING BIPOLAR DISORDER

DISORDER

An insider's guide to managing
mood swings and finding balance

Edited by
KERRIE EYERS & GORDON PARKER

ALLEN&UNWIN

First published in 2008

Allen & Unwin
83 Alexander Street
Crows Nest NSW 2065
Australia
Phone: (61 2) 8425 0100
Fax: (61 2) 9906 2218
Email: info@allenandunwin.com
Web: www.allenandunwin.com

National Library of Australia
Cataloguing-in-Publication entry:

Mastering bipolar disorder: an insider's guide to managing
mood swings and finding balance/editors, Kerrie
Eyers; Gordon Parker.

ISBN 978 1 74175 546 6 (pbk.)

Bibliography.

Manic-depressive illness.

Eyers, Kerrie.
Parker, Gordon, 1942–

616.895

Text and cover artwork by Matthew Johnstone
Text design by Lisa White
Set in 10.5/14 pt Bembo by Midland Typesetters, Australia
Printed in Australia by McPherson's Printing Group

10 9 8 7 6 5 4 3 2 1

CONTENTS

FOREWORD

I begin to wonder
if I'll soar too high and break like thunder
through the sanity barrier.
Or will I plummet in the other direction
and be buried in the ground
till resurrection? (62)

This book takes the reader into the world of those who have bipolar disorder. In their stories, they have shared their wisdom about managing this most difficult condition, wisdom that can be summarised:

> Like most illnesses, bipolar disorder affects people from all walks of life; it is free of prejudice and merciless in its execution. But that's not to say it cannot be managed successfully. (127)

Bipolar I Disorder—once termed 'manic depressive illness'—affects up to 1 per cent of the population. Left untreated, it is a severe and chronic condition defined by oscillating episodes of mania ('highs') and depression. During the manic episodes the individual can become psychotic and experience delusions and hallucinations.

Bipolar II Disorder has gained increasing recognition in the last decade. It is often seen as a less severe expression of bipolar disorder. The individual experiences non-psychotic highs ('hypomania') that oscillate with depression. This disorder has a much higher prevalence than Bipolar I Disorder, affecting up to 5 per cent of the population over their lifetime. Hypomania often goes unrecognised, as most individuals enjoy the mood elevation and only seek help for the depression that so often follows. This can, unfortunately, lead to many years of misdiagnosis and under-treatment.

What are the causes of bipolar disorder? The bipolar disorders are not just personality 'styles', but biologically-mediated conditions, reflecting genetic factors underpinned by changes in brain neurotransmitters. While we once used the term 'cyclothymia' to describe the personality style of individuals whose general mood alternated from cheerful and vivacious to glum and mildly depressed, the bipolar disorders are more than this: they are categorically abnormal mood states.

What are some signs? In general, during a bipolar 'high' the individual experiences enhanced energy and mood: feeling 'wired', creative, and extremely confident and elated ('I am privy to a God's-eye view of the world' (173)), although for many, feelings of anger and irritability may dominate. There is little need for sleep; he or she is tireless. They talk more—and over—people, are loud, rash in conversation and behaviour, buy whatever takes their fancy, and are often sexually disinhibited. Previous anxiety or shyness melts away.

Mugged by 'happiness', one writer observes:

I actually believed that no-one on earth could be as happy as me . . . Tears streamed from my eyes as I began each day. (112)

But then . . .

If there is an upside to mania—and there is—there is absolutely no upside to depression. None. Depression is very often fatal and it causes untold suffering. For that reason alone, everything possible should be done to prevent mania. (54)

The depression usually follows as the elevated mood ebbs away. Feelings now are the converse: low mood, low energy. Self-worth evaporates, people feel black and hopeless, lose motivation, avoid others and have a profound sense of 'anhedonia'—an inability to experience any pleasure. Good news or happy events cannot cheer them, and they lose the 'light in their eyes'. Concentration is painfully impaired and, for most, every movement is slowed, particularly in the morning. Many are wrung by agitation during depressive episodes, and wake early with a churning feeling, tortured by restlessness.

Reaching a diagnosis of bipolar disorder involves clinical review of symptoms over the years. The individual will often report a distinct onset (usually in adolescence or early twenties) which differentiates the condition from 'personality style' diagnoses, or from other clinical conditions such as Attention Deficit Hyperactivity Disorder (ADHD). The accuracy of the diagnosis is greatly helped by corroborative information from an observer, be they friend or relative.

Advice on how to manage bipolar disorder has been disseminated by professionals for more than two thousand years. The most definitive current information about Bipolar I Disorder is to be found in Goodwin and Jamison's 1990 book, *Manic-Depressive Illness*. Kay Redfield Jamison, an author of that classic work, has also evocatively described her own experience of the illness in her very readable book *An Unquiet Mind* (1995). In addition, many psychiatric associations have published 'treatment guidelines' for managing Bipolar I Disorder. However, while many research papers have been published about Bipolar II Disorder, the first book considering this condition alone only appeared as recently as 2008 (Parker, 2008).

Professional recommendations for managing the bipolar disorders generally see medication as a 'given' to stabilise the condition and regain balance. Additional benefits are added by education about the disorder, counselling and support strategies. Advice from health care professionals has the authority of evidence that is gathered from scientific studies and clinical trials. However, mental health literacy studies indicate that the best tactics for management are not necessarily agreed on between professionals, consumers and the general public. Thus, in addition to 'outside in' professional advice, we also need and benefit from 'inside out' advice. Sharing the often painfully acquired wisdom of those who have bipolar disorder and who have trialled all sorts of strategies may be of use for others to weave into their own personal safety nets. Hence this book.

In 2007, we published a companion book (*Journeys with the Black Dog*) that reported ways of gaining control over depression, with hundreds of individuals recounting their path to diagnosis and how they had subsequently kept the 'black dog' at bay. We adopt a similar model in this book, selecting material from 260 people with bipolar disorder who responded to our invitation to share their 'getting of wisdom'—how they learned to gain their balance on the highwire of mania and hypomania. Each contributor is acknowledged by the number assigned to their entry in the Black Dog Institute Essay Competition.

Some important issues arise in this compilation—particularly for those readers who may have only recently been diagnosed. The extracts collected here do not capture the more usual course of this condition. They are, rather, more from individuals who have written about their illness at its worst or those who have experienced the more severe expressions. In response to the question about managing the highs of bipolar disorder, people have presented the more memorable and extreme times in their life. However, there are many people who, subsequent to their diagnosis of bipolar disorder, and provided with basic education and medication, have had their condition under complete control for decades. Bipolar disorder can be tamed. People with this condition can be assured that when they find and implement strategies that are effective for them, they can look forward to a settled life.

Our learning curve has been quite steep, and we were initially unprepared for the trials which the illness presented to us. But I am increasingly hopeful about my future given that I have now received a diagnosis, and have found a good team of mental health workers to help me understand and manage the illness. (10)

While most people with bipolar disorder will never require a hospital visit, the high rate amongst our contributors indicated that many writers had the more severe Bipolar I expression, and experienced psychotic manic episodes rather than the less severe and less distressing hypomanic episodes. Also, these accounts mainly portray the high periods rather than the writers' depressive episodes (the focus of our previous book).

As editors we have tried to weight views that showcase the writers' discovery and increasing mastery of their strategies. We have also avoided an exclusively 'medical' framework—medical management is only one part, though important, of the platform of skills necessary for the successful management of bipolar disorder. There is a 'spotlight' section at the end of each chapter that focuses on views from medical professionals.

What do we learn from the people who have invited us into their world and shared their wisdom so generously?

First, the vibrant description of their highs enlivens the often dry, clinical accounts provided in textbooks.

Second, we are taken into a world of dilemmas. To continue with medication or not? To court a high and experience the world through 'rose-coloured glasses' but then reap the depression concealed in its slipstream? To accept or resist the seductive invitations that are the hallmark of a high? To inform family, friends and workmates or to go it alone? To resist medication as it might compromise creativity? These are high stakes. Many describe how they had to crash numerous times before they were motivated to 'surmount' their condition:

> The true getting of wisdom may only come after several bouts with the bipolar bully. (10)

> Extremely tempting to let High take over, but life is too, too short to spend three months alone in the deep gorge of depression that always follows High. (130)

Third, we observe the snakes and ladders pattern of bipolar disorder—the high that advances the individual up the career ladder, followed by the blighting effects of a slide down the depression snake.

> I'm usually involved in ten times more projects than any of my friends: I'm strongly motivated to achieve instant solutions and I can comfortably initiate tasks far beyond my capability . . . Some things go according to plan and you experience the sweet scent of success. Other times you crash and burn in a spectacular fashion, and at great financial and emotional cost. (11)

Fourth, the writers illustrate a plurality of management techniques—education and self-awareness of the condition; the search for and discovery of a supportive therapist who will be there for the long haul; trialling medication to find drugs that work; regulating daily rhythms; minimising stress; avoiding alcohol and other drugs; and developing a wellbeing plan.

> This is not the time to stand proud and alone in silence. When one lives with chronic illness, silence is *not* golden. (27)

In trying to reach a central metaphor for the experience of bipolar disorder we considered many options. Our colleague Stephanie

Webster provided insight. Her contention (captured in the following section) that it is all about 'balance' provided a rich overarching metaphor and her suggestions are woven through the text.

Elizabeth Weiss and Clara Finlay of Allen & Unwin have employed their alchemy again to polish the text to its best sparkle, together with the inimitable skills of Susin Chow. And Matthew Johnstone, with his inspired whimsy, has produced a wonderful, evocative book cover.

While bipolar disorder can sap the soul, and is a challenging condition that requires constant self-monitoring, the contributors share sharp humour and whimsical observations, and their resilience is an inspiring springboard. The famous comedian Spike Milligan judged that bipolar disorder has no redeeming features, a view put by some of our writers:

> As you know, living with bipolar is all about living between two extremes—mania and depression. Neither of these two 'poles' is a comfortable place to live. The weather's foul. It's lonely. And the days are either desperately long or painfully short. (163)

But, in contrast, several of our writers explain why—if there was the option to relive their lives—they would choose to have their bipolar disorder again.

> Were I to live my life over, I'm not sure that I would cancel that three-month trip into the Other World. Or the other trips that I have had over the years. Don't get me wrong. I'm not trying to belittle the pain, struggle and stigma that goes with this bipolar condition. But when we attempt to throw the dirty bathwater out, just remember that there may be a baby in there somewhere. (12)

Their reasoning goes to the heart of what it means to be human. Such spirit underlines the triumph and quiet dignity of the everyday hero. We thank them for demonstrating that it is possible to regain one's feet and find balance.

> I find my rainbows in every day and knowing that you are all out there, struggling sometimes, but surviving each day. That's what keeps me going. (5)

Kerrie Eyers and Gordon Parker

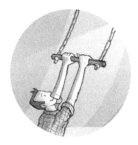

On balance
Conjuring the metaphor

Balance (metaphysics):
In the metaphysical or conceptual sense, balance is used to
mean a point between two opposite forces that is desirable
over purely one state or the other.
Wikipedia

The 2007 Black Dog Institute's Writing Competition topic was 'The
Getting of Wisdom—Managing the "Highs" of Bipolar Disorder'.
In response, writers shared their vivid and diverse experiences.
Most importantly, they provided an array of personal strategies for
managing the upswings of the illness.

I warmly thank Gordon Parker and Kerrie Eyers for building
on my suggestion that *balance* is the quintessential word to use
when talking about managing bipolar disorder. Balance draws our
attention away from the opposing forces of mania and depression
and makes us think about *the middle ground*—and the lifestyle choices
and treatments we use to get there.

Balance also conveys a sense of the very real trade-offs people face when trying to master their bipolar disorder. After my own diagnosis ten years ago, the 'work hard/party hard' lifestyle became outdated. Next, a degree of privacy was surrendered as friends and family learnt how to detect my early warning signs. Then I worked diligently with my psychiatrist to find the right sort of medication, at the right level, with the fewest side-effects.

Since then my psychiatrist and my general practitioner have worked together to ensure that my lithium levels stay in the desired range—not unlike fine tuning an engine. *Engine balance*—to ensure that the engine runs smoothly—involves design and tuning to improve the performance, efficiency and reliability of the engine. It therefore has an amusing similarity (and outcome) to the medical process involved in managing bipolar disorder.

Even now, my personality and my bipolar disorder regularly pull me in different directions. My love of spontaneity has to be *gently balanced* against the need for a certain amount of routine and plenty of sleep. My enthusiasm for work *has to be tempered* against the need to wind down at the end of the day. Stimulating friends are visited for lunch on the weekend, rather than for coffee in the evening. My psychologist helps me dismantle my old 'all or nothing' attitude.

However, life events, seasons and sleep disruption can still tip me *off balance*. More modest changes, like receiving sudden good news or having a frenetic week at work, can also destabilise me. Sometimes this illness just has a life of its own. Whatever the cause, I then have to do some *re-balancing*: cancel various social plans, get some extra sleep and make a medication adjustment.

Fortunately for most people, expertise builds with each episode. Friends and family learn too. We begin to recognise our own unique warning signs and triggers. Books are read. Websites visited. For many, bipolar disorder really is something that is *mastered* over a lifetime.

Bipolar disorder may convey an image of a somewhat precarious *balancing on the highwire*. The *high* has an obvious connection. The *wire* reminds us that many people living with Bipolar II Disorder experience their *highs* as periods of feeling energised and *wired*, without the experience of full-blown mania. Unfortunately, they are at greater risk of misdiagnosis.

The *circus* theme expands. Highwire acts are dramatic, compelling and sometimes dangerous. Trapeze artists, jugglers, daredevil feats, losing and recovering balance are all on show in the spotlight. The safety net is either there or not. Such images also invite a discussion about creativity and its connection to bipolar disorder. Finally, skilled performers demonstrate that being *balanced* doesn't have to mean losing your *sparkle*.

Of all the acts, I keep returning to the acrobatic teams who *balance in formation*. That brings to mind family members and friends. Some members of the team carry a heavier burden (spouses, partners and parents) but everyone in the formation (children, friends, neighbours) plays their part in the team's *performance*. *Acrobats* have to be supple (able to look after their own health and wellbeing) in order to be strong (resilient) enough to support those above. They improve their flexibility (ability to respond to variations in the illness) through trial and error—and practice. I can tell you that the 'acrobats' in my team have improved their agility and fitness in ways that they would never have thought possible.

This collection of stories provides a wonderful glimpse inside the experience of bipolar disorder. Wonderful, because in reading the stories of others, we can *better separate the illness from ourselves*. Much of the writing makes me smile and think to myself: 'I could have done that'.

Stephanie Webster, Black Dog Institute

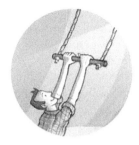

1. Triumphs and tumbles
Ups and downs of bipolar disorder

I was a light bulb in a world full of moths.
Carrie Fisher about her mania

This chapter is an overview of the experience of bipolar disorder. Seen through the eyes of those who have had the disorder for many years, these accounts capture the exhilaration, richness and seductive nature of the 'highs'. It also presents some of the varied techniques that individuals have perfected during their quest to best manage their mood swings.

The following account vividly depicts the seductive and irresistible trapeze swing into an elevated mood. The writer recounts her first episode of bipolar disorder, and her unwitting ascent into the vortex of a manic phase. She has since made excellent use of these experiences and has achieved ongoing stability.

Dancing with the Devil

I've always found the word 'high' to be a little misleading.
Sure the bipolar 'dance' begins with self-assurance and
delight with the world. However, I'm immediately paired with
an uncomfortable restlessness that I can't shake. It's pure
agitation. I can't relax. My eyes widen. I make simple errors
in my daily tasks, I miss birthdays and struggle to organise
myself. Pretty soon, I can't remember what day it is.

If I let the dance with the Devil continue, you really see
some interesting moves.

Next comes the sensory overload. I see colours more
vividly, have the urge to express myself in stories, and can lose
myself in music for half the day. In fact, I'm not just listening
to the music. In this state I have the sensation that I can
somehow breathe it in. The music is all through me.

Then the romantic mood spills over into life. Everyone
is fascinating to me, and I am to them. It's amazing how
contagious this dance is. Only, things get out of hand.
I dance too fast, with too many people, or with the wrong
people. I get no sleep. I miss job interviews, or worse still,
I show up for them. So now there will be consequences like
embarrassment, ruined friendships and lost opportunities.

It becomes a devilishly expensive dance. I lose control
over the purse strings. I need a new outfit; it must be black
and sultry. I love it so much I don't take it off for days. And
always, the music. I have been known to buy twenty CDs at a
time whilst high. All bought randomly, for their cover or some
weird connection to something else that I can't remember in
the end. I love books too. And don't the booksellers love me.
I choose books on colour or because they contain quotes I like

or maybe they just smell good. I am unable to stop at just one or two. The only thing that distracts me in the bookshop are all the men. All these gorgeous men seem to be shopping with me. I am admiring eyes, necks, beautiful hands, and even their glasses or the way their hair is parted. I have truly become part-woman and part-werewolf. Finally, I am browsing for magazines, luscious magazines with beautiful people and things. Nothing with any connection to my life. Nothing that will help distract me when the bank statement arrives.

The rest of the dance speeds up and is not for the faint-hearted. In fact, I have only continued once. My first dance. My terrible first dance.

Mildly spiritual feelings emerge. I'm suddenly reading star signs and buying books on astrology. I feel a bit unusual and decide to buy a book on the matter. It's called, *Are you getting enlightened or are you going out of your mind?* I'm so out of my mind by then that I decide I am getting enlightened. Soon after I am having messianic delusions with a feminist twist (why wouldn't God come back as a woman?). These are intermingled with delusions of reference (everything in the newspaper is about me), romantic delusions (a married man is in love with me), and grandiose delusions (I'll be moving to New York to set up a management consulting company). I was having delusions about bombs going off, about people I love getting hurt and eventually persecutory delusions (people are out to get me).

By now I am completely disoriented and terrified. I can't dance. I can only run. And run I do. From two hospitals, one public, one private. I am on the missing persons list for a time. I sleep in parks, in 'new' friends' houses. I have two trips in the back of police cars, the final one to hospital, where I belong but do not know it.

Having danced 'all the way' with my first bipolar high has actually made it easier for me to intervene medically when I sense a high coming. I know how dangerous it can be. I know not to let the high run its course. These days I intervene as soon as I notice changes. I will enjoy one afternoon of mild mania by putting the music on and letting myself 'breathe it in'. I'll also let myself buy a couple of CDs, knowing I will probably give them away in a few weeks when my normal taste in music is back. As soon as I take medication, the wonderful effect of music is gone, but I am happy to give that up to stop the dance progressing.

My major warning sign is a change in my sleep pattern. If I start waking up earlier than normal with a feeling of wanting to start organising something, it's time to act. I might get up at 5 a.m. and sort through paperwork, or re-arrange my photos. My friends joke that I am welcome at their places to organise them when I have this energy. As things progress, I become more talkative, possibly even talking over people or dominating the conversation. I also notice the agitation and a big drop in my ability to concentrate very early on. I can be a bit more hot-headed at these times, and I have to remind myself not to get worked up over small things. These days, this is as far as my mania gets. I feel secure having learnt how to recognise symptoms and intervene early.

The other benefit of intervening early with mania is the effect on the depressions. I am someone who has had four cycles, each with a high and a low. It is true to say that the size of my depressions has basically matched the severity of the high I experienced. Each time, I have learnt how to intervene with the high quicker and each time my depression has been less severe.

Once an episode has started, I will reduce my social activities for a few weeks. I'll concentrate on gentle, calming activities like swimming or walking. I'll book a massage or two. I'll tell friends that I am a little bit high. That way they know I might be more talkative or a little less sensitive, but that it will pass soon.

I protect myself financially by only having access to small amounts of cash. I don't run credit cards. I protect my friendships by letting everyone know that they have permission to tell me if they notice changes. I do my best to explain the illness to everyone. Sometimes this hasn't been enough. I think it's genuinely difficult for some people to separate illness and behaviour, especially those times when you are dealing with a mild episode. I have lost one friendship. I eventually had to accept that bipolar disorder is a devilish illness and sometimes there is mischief made in my life that I cannot undo.

I am not someone who will say that I would choose to have bipolar. There was sizeable damage done by my first episode in particular. It has also taken me eight years and three further episodes to finally feel that I can intervene as required to avert an episode. There were so many times when I wanted to wish the bipolar away.

Then I read a little on bipolar disorder and personality traits. It seems just possible that the things I most like about myself (sociable, lateral thinker, good at linking ideas, verbally confident, ability to see the big picture) are connected to the bipolar genes. So I will say that I can't really wish away the bipolar disorder, because it's possible the best bits of me would be wished away with it.

And as for dancing with the Devil, I'm just happy to remember the music. (185)

The following story cleverly conveys the unremarked onset of a mood elevation. Mania or hypomania may approach by stealth, and the individual, caught off guard, can quickly lose insight. The writer has accumulated a repertoire of strategies. Her self-observation and resulting self-management tactics ensure that she is now in control.

Of strategies, paradox and wisdom

Mania (*n.* mental derangement marked by great excitement and (freq.) violence; craze, passion *for*)

Becoming manic, learning that one has been manic, is not something that happens quickly. Kay Redfield Jamison (1995, pp. 68ff) explains that she did not wake up one day and just find herself mad but, rather, gradually became aware that her life and mind were going at an ever faster clip until spinning absolutely out of control. She found the acceleration was 'a slow and beautifully seductive one'. At first everything seemed normal, but 'the more I tried to slow down my thinking the more I became aware that I couldn't. My enthusiasms were going into overdrive as well, although there often was some underlying thread of logic in what I was doing. One day, for example, I got into a frenzy of photocopying.'

For me, it didn't start with photocopying, but looking back that was one of the indicators. I was planning a party for my son's eighteenth birthday and decided it would be very creative to display large photographs of him in a continuous border at eye height around the room. I chose the photos I wanted and took them to work. Every day after my colleagues had left the office, I enlarged, copied and laminated photos, 200 of them in total, in what I recognised later (after reading Jamison's book) as a 'frenzy of photocopying'.

Warn (*v.t.* give timely notice of impending danger or misfortune, put on guard, caution against; give cautionary notice or advice with regard to actions, conduct, belief, etc.)

Early warning signs of mania include: difficulty falling asleep; racing thoughts; increased activity; increased productivity, energy and rate of speech; talking over the top of people; spending sprees; heightened libido; and irritability.

I waited until the children went to bed. Then I did the folding and the ironing, put a few loads of washing into the machine, hung a few on the line (in the dark), tidied the house and mopped the floor. At ten o'clock I went to bed, but I couldn't sleep so I got up again. I went to the computer and logged on. When I looked up it was midnight, then 2.30, then 3 a.m. I forced myself to go back to bed, not because I was tired, but because I had to get up at six to get the kids off to school and go to work. It was strange, after weeks of this I should have been exhausted, but quite the opposite, I had lots of energy.

As mania gathers momentum, early warning signs intensify and additional signs emerge, such as obsessiveness, sexual indiscretion, unusual and inappropriate behaviour, risk taking and psychotic thinking.

Insight (*n.* mental penetration)

Insight is lost.

My birthday was approaching and my husband asked what I wanted for a present. I said I wanted a lime-green Holden Monaro

*and if I couldn't have that then I wanted a tattoo. A big one with
beautiful flames of red, orange and yellow, flaring up my right
arm from my elbow to my shoulder. My husband assumed I was
joking but I wasn't. He said 'no' to the Monaro and 'NO' to the
tattoo. It didn't matter. I would talk him around, if not about
the car then about the tattoo. I had made up my mind. It didn't
matter what he said, if I couldn't talk him around, I was going to
get a tattoo anyway.*

Recognising the warning signs means there can be earlier
and more effective treatment, harm minimisation, self-
management, awareness, understanding, communication,
reassurance and relapse prevention. An action plan can also
be developed.

Mood (*n.* state of mind or feeling)

Personality and behaviour when mood is stable: when mood
is stable, people usually have regular appetites, sleep patterns
and energy levels. They have reasonable decision-making
skills, and planning and organisational abilities. Their actions
and reactions are appropriate. They feel comfortable with
themselves, in their own company and with others. They
don't have obsessive thoughts and, in fact, they are usually
not even aware of the state of their mood.

> We don't usually notice how little control we have over
> the mind, because habits channel psychic energy so well
> that thoughts seem to follow each other by themselves
> without a hitch. (Csikszentmihalyi, 2002, p. 119)

Personality and behaviour when mood is manic: when
someone is manic, they usually don't sleep for more than a few
hours a night. They are irritable, hyperactive and restless. They

can be angry and aggressive. Their behaviour is disinhibited and impulsive. They spend money on things that are expensive or things they don't need. They argue persuasively and passionately rationalise every decision and every action.

When I'm manic, I say . . .

'Of course I'm not manic, I'm fine. In fact I'm better than fine. I feel fantastic.'

When I'm manic, I think . . .

'There's absolutely nothing wrong with me. I'm not ill. This medication is going in the bin.'

When I'm manic, I can't . . .

Stop moving, sit still, slow down, relax, watch TV, or read a magazine or a book.

When I'm manic, I appear . . .

Articulate and coherent, logical and organised, persuasive, and determined.

When one is riding the high of bipolar disorder, there comes a point of no return. The mania destroys everything in its path and, when its fury is spent, it is inevitably followed by depression. If there is an upside to mania—and there is—there is absolutely no upside to depression. None. Depression is very often fatal and it causes untold suffering. For that reason alone, everything possible should be done to prevent mania.

Strategy (*n.* art of war; art of planning and directing larger movements and operations of campaign or war)

Strategies when mood is normal: *when my mood stabilised, I found a doctor I had total confidence in. He was the fourth one I went to. I established a good relationship with him, and made and kept regular scheduled appointments. I took my medication religiously. Together we documented a detailed and specific management plan so that my preferences could be respected if I was ever in a situation where I could not advocate for myself. I established a support network of people who could help me when my mood was becoming elevated. Now I maintain regular daily rhythms and routines and am strict with myself about sleep, diet and exercise. Well, I am strict about sleep and diet most of the time and I exercise on the odd occasion.*

Strategies when mood elevates: *when my mood is becoming elevated, I contact my doctor straightaway and check my medication. I make sure I get enough sleep. I decrease my activities and reduce sensory stimulation. I stay away from shopping centres and other busy, noisy places that have lots of people and fluorescent lighting. I quarantine my credit cards. I see my counsellor and I use the cognitive behaviour skills I learned in group therapy.*

Paradox (*n.* seemingly absurd or self-contradictory though possibly true statement)

Kay Redfield Jamison believes that there is strong scientific, biological and historical data to support the thesis that the mania of bipolar disorder is intrinsically linked to artistic and creative expression. She cautions, however, that this issue is fraught with clinical, ethical and philosophical considerations. While mania can be an 'exhilarating and powerfully creative force', it is more often 'a destructive one' (Jamison, 1996, p. 240). As another writer says:

> . . . the best treatment for [the] 'wound in human consciousness' lies in music, painting, literature, and, at its finest, philosophy. Art, unlike 'the swooning egocentricity

of closed-off uncaring hedonism . . . from which we awake
to bitter solitude', opens us to reality. This . . . encourages
us to find, awaken and employ our latent creative powers.
(Farrelly, 2006, p. 28)

I used to write short stories and enter them in competitions.
I spent hours at the computer, sometimes not doing anything else
for days and nights on end, hardly eating or sleeping. I approached
publishers and agents and attended courses.
  I was desperate to be published, to have recognition, to be
famous. After my first high I wrote nothing for a very long time.
My biggest challenge was to read a book rather than to write one.
Then, one day, out of the blue, I sat down at the computer and
wrote a short story. Not to be published or for recognition; this
time I wrote for the sake of it, because I felt like it, for the love of
the words and the beauty of creative expression.

Wisdom (*n.* being wise; soundness of judgement in matters
relating to life and conduct; knowledge, learning)

There is great value in specific kinds of adversity. None of
us would choose to learn this way . . . We go forward with
courage and with too much wisdom but determined to
find what is beautiful. (Solomon, 2001, p. 437) **(54)**

Most individuals enjoy their bipolar high, immersed in the gush
of ideas, zest for life and supreme certainty that it confers. The
question implicit in this: is it possible to access the energy of an
elevated mood without being dazzled by the spotlight? Those with
the more severe manifestations of bipolar disorder think not.

The author of the following piece considers that there is no
harnessing the energy of mania once it gathers in intensity. He argues

(creatively) against bipolar disorder's reputed link with creativity and thinks that people have to control their bipolar disorder if they are to be productive. It can be a case of how much you can handle without losing your footing.

Halcyon days

When we are charging in that ferocious vortex, I mean *really charging*, there is no place for 'strategy'. To us, when we are on fire, that word is as effective as telling an addict to 'Just say no!' It's not a word for us. It's a word for you. A word for them. A word to give structure, security, purpose and direction to the listless worker bees. For those who can bask in the heady glow of monotony. The glow of stability. Strategy is bullshit.

You don't 'manage' it. Not when it's got your balls clenched tightly in its vice-like grip, or when its swooping, screeching talons tear every good instinct from your defenceless, child-like mind. You flail at its eyeballs and rip at its flesh. You cover your head and tuck your knees to your chest and scream an eight-octave howl that makes the world turn up their televisions to muffle the discomfort.

It can't be 'harnessed'. You can't skydive without the speed. It's a fucking racehorse and you're taking that ride and any notion of control is distorted in a blur of emotional velocity. You find yourself in Boston because you wanted to see the Sox play. The next week you go drinking in London for three days, because nothing can slow you down. How the fuck are you going to harness that energy?

Go down to the water's edge and bring me back a fistful of foaming seawater and we'll talk about 'harnessing' a little more.

I thought we were discussing a mental illness but instead I'm breaking out into a cold sweat. Recalling mangled memories and abhorrent flashbacks triggered by discussions of strategy, management, reliability, and harnessing that vitally important 'upside'. I'm reminded of a previous life when holding down a mundane office job was easy. Bipolar II isn't so bad after all.

These days I make wine for a living. Or, in adhering to the frame of reference governing the compilation of this piece, I strategically and reliably harness nature's most stunning combination of elements to romantically create delicious 750-mL packages of upside for the worker bee population. It takes me all over the world. It can be solitary. I love it.

I chose it for a reason. You may call it strategy. I call it 'A Fighting Chance'.

Talking about wine, drinking it, sharing it, growing it, enjoying it however it comes puts my mind at ease. It offers a lifetime of learning for someone who, when on a sleepless high, has got a lot of time to kill. Freezing cold, soaking wet, working 'round the clock' with your mates during harvest and all you want to do is scream to the heavens how good life is. Then there's the flipside to that coin, on those other days when the 'black dog' is snarling and gnashing and chilling you to the core. These are the days it becomes about nature. Solitude in the vineyard, beauty in every direction. A Fighting Chance.

My point is this. Managing our highs can't be done once they take hold. *C'est impossible.* It's less about the highs and more about those fleeting moments of normality. It's about giving ourselves a fighting chance to get through it when that seductive son of a bitch starts whispering in your ear. It's about putting ourselves in a place so that when high times are calling, we have somewhere to fall back to, to take ourselves out of the game, and out of harm's way. For me it's Margaret River, or the Clare Valley, or the South Island of New Zealand. Remote. Isolated. Safe.

We prefer not to 'romanticise'. For me it's the mythical notion that a winemaker spends his days swirling claret in a cave by candlelight. Or that a bipolar-suffering winemaker is somehow potentially capable of creating some earth-shattering blend never before considered by those not afflicted. Let's focus on the cold, wet concrete and steel, the flesh-corroding caustic soda and the deadly CO_2. Let's focus on not being able to do your job some days because the depressing effects of alcohol might make the difference between living and dying. Let's focus on the fact that there's no mental health professional within 300 miles. This is the gritty reality of daily life that we all go through. Let's not put added pressure on ourselves by subscribing to this coincidental clash of circumstances, that bipolar disorder is a guaranteed ticket to the fifteen minutes we all apparently crave.

A huge amount is made of prominent artists, comedians, writers and captains of industry, commerce and politics who had symptoms of bipolar disorder. How these successful people were somehow able to 'channel' or 'harness' their highs into an avenue that facilitated the advancement of the worker bee population. Google 'bipolar disorder' and the first response you get is a list of celebs who suffer.

We, the everyday sufferers of bipolar disorder, piss down the throat of this assumption. There is no link between the two. It is a loosely correlated statistical blip that creates a warm and fuzzy glow for the newly diagnosed. A seven-second soundbyte for the evening news. A tree branch to cling to for a drowning man when he's swept off his feet for the first time into a torrent of high times. A trigger for us hacks to go scurrying to our word processors, trying to tap into a lyrical high that will earn us a place next to Hemingway or Kerouac.

How many people, diagnosed or not, suffer from these highs? And how many great writers are there in the world? Or accomplished artists, admired comedians and venerated politicians? Why this focus on one-in-a-million achievement? You can't throw Picasso's name up there and expect the common bipolar sufferer to relate. Hundreds have sat in the House of Lords since Churchill. The average bipolar sufferer is getting off the train in front of you at Central Station. We are family members, we are friends and workmates. We tile floors, we drive taxis and we process insurance claims. And some days we are in a knock-down prize fight for our jobs, our partners, our families and our lives.

The creation of great things rarely takes place in the vortex of a bipolar high. Picasso didn't have one hand on his mistress and the other on a brush and, hey presto, two sleepless weeks later let's call this one *Guernica*! On second thoughts, that's a poor example. Bipolar highs do give us time—hours in the day the worker bees don't have, to hone our skills to a savage, deadly point. Time to practise, time to research, time to read, time to get on a roll, time to see it through, time to refine. But it's not enough.

It gets back to the individual. Who they are and what they are made of. What interests them? A bipolar high doesn't stop us wasting time, we just have more time to waste. It doesn't stop us being lazy, it doesn't give us direction or skill or insight

if we didn't have it in the first place. I find myself coming back
to the halcyon days, the calm between the storms. There is
no doubt that a bipolar high can give us an edge few others
possess, but we need to make the most of the stable times
to truly capitalise. We need to lay the groundwork to make
success possible. We need to live our entire lives. We need
to give ourselves A Fighting Chance.

In a creative writing competition that used words like
'strategy', 'reliable' and 'upside' as the cornerstones of its
content, it's only fitting that I should conclude with a wise,
well-worn Management 101 quote: 'There is always room
at the top, but there's never room to sit down.' Sometimes,
luckily, we can stand a lot longer than others. (187)

The following narrative is from a woman who looks back over
her early life in the company of a mother who had severe bipolar
disorder. The account fondly commemorates a courageous individual who, in the days before effective treatment, did her best by
her daughter. She, now a mother herself, is the upside to her mother's
illness. She displays resilience and tolerance. And the legacy of this
groundedness continues in her daughters and granddaughters.

A family story

Resilience is about facing adversity with hope. We inhabit
one world in which we are all deeply connected.
Anne Deveson, *Resilience*, 2003

My daughter sits across the table from me hugging her
coffee cup. Outside the kitchen window her two daughters

run among the plum trees, chasing the hungry birds from Grandma's summer fruit. 'You need to write this,' she urges. 'You need to go back, remember and write it.'

She's right, although it's never been a secret between the women of our family. My mother, cousin Helen, Aunty Elsie, and all the others who went before and who will come after us.

The women of our family are prone to bipolar disorder. Some of us have less severe symptoms (bipolar II) but others are more acutely affected. My mother was hounded by the bipolar swings and the black dog from the time she was nineteen and yet it is her story that we, the women of her family, take courage and comfort from.

I was an only child with a distant father who worked at a power station in another state. By the time I was eight I knew two things for certain. The first was that it took two trains and a bus to get from where we lived to Mont Park Psychiatric Hospital. The second was that I would have to make that journey at least three times every year.

My mother's warning signs were subtle and in my child's mind they were signals to a game we would play together. My mother's fingers would clench and unclench, the soft skin on her top lip would shine with sweat, her eyes would cross slightly and she would begin to talk to herself. These were my cues. I would climb onto a chair and haul her hospital bag down from the top of the wardrobe. Then I would take her hand and tuck Rosa between the handles of the bag and we would walk the track to the railway station. If my timing was right, we would finish our journey before my mother had descended into the nightmare of full-blown psychosis. A game, like avoiding cracks on the pavement.

Rosa was a jointed walking doll. In one of my mother's good times we had picked her out in the toy shop window and I had watched her every day after school until my mother had saved enough money to have her lifted out over the trucks and train sets and into my arms. On the way home that day, my mother's eyes were straight and calm as we tried out names on our new 'baby' and finally settled on Rosa.

I guess now that Rosa was a strategy before the word had ever been used in relation to mental illness. Outside the psychiatric ward where my mother was housed was a pool of water from a broken pipe. It was a ritual that every time I visited Mum we took off Rosa's pink dress and bathed her in the pool. No matter what state my mother was in, the rhythmic motion of the water running through her hands and over Rosa's small body somehow gave her flashes of clarity. Rosa turned into me. 'Rosa needs a haircut,' she'd whisper to the doll. 'Rosa can get money out of the post office account.'

As I got older I hid Rosa away at the bottom of Mum's bag so that no-one would think I still played with dolls. But Mum's illness continued through my teenage years and on into my children's lives. Sometimes it caught me up and whirled me around, winding me as if I'd been dumped by a freak wave at the beach. But my mother was always stronger than bipolar, and I learnt to be that way too. I pause while writing this to smile at some of the 'creative escapades' we lived through—bedrooms 'redecorated' to resemble darkest Africa, with gigantic black poster-paint gorillas looming off yellow walls; Mum playing Gilbert and Sullivan operas flat out all night while she cut up boxes and boxes of tomatoes and onions to make chutney, and set the kitchen on fire instead.

Tragedies or comedies? Depends on whether you see the

mud or the stars out of your prison windows, I guess.

My daughter's voice cuts across my thoughts, 'Don't forget the Garden of Lost Children'. I laugh. How could I forget? My mother leading my daughter and a group of her friends around the streets of our town on the day of the council rubbish collection. By this time in her life, Mum's mania had modified a little and presented as an over-the-top exuberance not usually seen in little old ladies of seventy. She danced the kids through the piles of junk like a grey-headed Pied Piper, collecting the detritus of old dolls and toys and, it seemed to me, anything brightly coloured and useless. Next she and her band of enthusiastic followers placed headless legless and armless Barbies and Cabbage Patch orphans in a circle of old bassinets and prams under the poplar trees in my usually attractive back garden. Then my mother, bless her, sat in the middle of the circle and created beautiful haunting stories of unwanted and lost children who were rejected because they were broken or different.

I watched from my back veranda with tears welling, quietly looking out at the intent faces listening to her. The creative blip in my mother's life changed hearts and minds that day and the garden of lost children stayed long after my mother had gone.

So have I romanticised my life with my mother? I don't believe so. I think life gets messy for all of us and living with bipolar disorder or with someone who has it can make life messy a lot of the time. What's the upside? My mother lived a strong life and loved and raised a child in a time when bipolar was feared and the sufferers punished with punitive and useless treatments. She left more good memories than bad and she will always be a matriarch to look up to. I am the upside to my mother's life: I have learned to be resilient and tolerant and to celebrate difference, not fear it. I have taught my children to accept that, like people living with diabetes and asthma, we, the women of this family, can achieve and strive for anything we want. My daughters and granddaughters have learned that along with their defective genes they have inherited something much stronger, the knowledge that the bipolar black dog can lie at their feet and be tamed. (64)

• •

IN THE SPOTLIGHT
What is bipolar disorder?

- The term 'manic depressive illness' is now less commonly used, replaced by the concept of a 'bipolar spectrum'.
- The 'bipolar spectrum' comprises:
  — Bipolar I Disorder, with oscillating manic (extreme 'highs', often with psychotic features) and depressive periods
  — Bipolar II Disorder, with less severe 'highs' (i.e. hypomania) oscillating with depressive periods
  — Bipolar III states—when an individual experiences a hypo-manic episode that is induced by commencing, ceasing or increasing the dose of an antidepressant
  — Bipolar IV states—describing mood oscillations in individuals who have a 'hyperthymic' (or excessively exuberant) temperament. This 'category' risks falsely diagnosing those with certain personality styles as having a bipolar disorder.
- Those who have four or more episodes of highs and lows (or highs by themselves) within a twelve-month period are

classified as having 'rapid cycling' bipolar disorder. This is probably the norm for those with Bipolar II Disorder. Some people have multiple episodes within a single week, or even within a day.

- A 'mixed state' is when an individual has both a depressive and a high mood at the same time.

- There is wisdom in restricting the diagnosis of bipolar disorder to those who experience Bipolar I or II conditions—which are viewed as mood disorders with a genetic underpinning and with disturbance in brain neurotransmitters. The pattern of mood swings is unique to the individual: some people have an episode of mania once a decade, others have daily mood swings.

- Bipolar I Disorder may be experienced by up to 1 per cent of the population over their lifetime (there being no gender difference). The lifetime risk of Bipolar II Disorder is up to 5 per cent (with rates higher in women). These rates may be increasing: large-scale community studies identify the highest rates in adults under the age of thirty years. Over time, the two conditions, bipolar I and bipolar II, are equally impairing.

- Early onset of bipolar disorder in childhood is rare. The most common risk period is in mid to late adolescence, with most individuals able to report a 'change' when their mood swings commenced. For most, the average interval from first mood episode to diagnosis is ten to twenty years. During that period of undiagnosed and untreated mood volatility, considerable damage can occur both to the individual and others (e.g. marital break-up). Some who have a bipolar disorder are more likely to have significant problems with alcohol and illicit drugs.

- As detailed in the next chapter, highs are reflected across four arenas—mood and energy elevation, disinhibition, mysticism and irritability. Misadventure and damage to one's reputation is increased during high phases. During depressed periods, the converse is evident, with low mood and low energy, as well as an inability to experience pleasure or to be cheered up. The risk of suicide is increased dramatically during a depressed phase.

- There is no ultimate test for diagnosing bipolar disorder. Our Institute's (www.blackdoginstitute.org.au) self-report screening measure has some 80 per cent accuracy, but confirmation (or rejection) of the diagnosis is best reached by clinical assessment of the individual (and, ideally, information from a family member who has observed them over the years).
- At present, the bipolar conditions cannot be cured but can be well controlled via medication, education and the development of wellbeing plans (see Appendix 2).

2. Dazzling and daredevil
The spiral of mood elevation

I recall taking my clothes off and standing in an empty
dustbin in a back alley in the moonlight to dance my
interpretation of 'The Dying Swan'.
[in response to being 'dropped' by her boyfriend] (7)

The excerpts in this chapter illustrate some of the many expressions
of the highs of mania and hypomania. As a high gathers momentum,
there are some early warnings. One of the first signs is a disruption
in an individual's sleep patterns—a sharply decreased need for sleep,
accompanied by a surge in energy and optimism. Both are staging
posts on the way to euphoria. Initially, family and friends may be
carried along on the rising seductive swing, enjoying the surge
of good spirits, particularly if the individual is recovering from a
depressive episode. Later, as their mood elevates more obviously,
family and friends may be disinclined to label their companion's
exuberant high spirits as a psychiatric disorder.

Like toy shop wonders who come alive after bracing the first alpha wave of dreams, we surf coffee mugs to the tick of the 2 a.m. clock. (25)

My pen transformed from metal to feathers. (106)

I found it very difficult to relax enough to get to sleep because my mind was buzzing with positive thoughts, and when I did manage to get to sleep it was only for a few hours, at which point I was wide awake and keen to begin writing, feeling I was on the brink of discovering an important truth. This pattern was repeated until I found it impossible to dream and my behaviour and thinking became quite bizarre—I was hallucinating, finding coded meaning in simple statements from those I spoke to, and leaving the house to walk very late at night. (6)

As my mood elevates my strongest sense is that I am being watched and my every move recorded—for recognition and appreciation and companionship are what I crave above all else. I pick up all the litter, sing in the street and hope to collect my halo before I die. (7)

The following accounts illustrate how difficult it is to be aware of, and to control, mania (or hypomania) once it has taken hold. The euphoric upswing is usually swift, and a person's insight—the capacity to stand back from their feelings and perceive them as out of the 'normal' range—can be rapidly lost.

I am hell: all thunderbolt and lightning for those around me when I'm hypomanic. A bit like Phaeton and the carriage in the early days—before taking lithium carbonate for twenty years and becoming Apollo.

If I walk in the sun I shall melt. I am an I-cycle made of

lithium carbonate: a pillar of salt, the finest trace element; a body salt. People make rockets with it to fly to the moon. I could save them the bother: I am a lunar-tic. (7)

While a lack of perspective means that you can tackle the biggest projects with confidence, that same lack of perspective causes the biggest headaches. Of course, the worst of these is failing to recognise that your personality is operating outside the boundaries of a normal playing field. Perspective is difficult to acquire when it's only via hindsight. (11)

The euphoria of a high is impossible to match. It is a wonderful happiness, a feeling of knowing everything, with a special emphasis, in my case, of heightened religious awareness. When high, everything made sense, beautiful sense, and I was anxious to share my insights with anyone who would listen, or to type on my manual typewriter day or night (I was on holidays), insisting that what I typed was my 'soul' and not to be read without my consent, especially since feeling Christ-like was considered blasphemous at worst or crazy at best by those nearest and dearest to me. (6)

It can become very awkward trying to convince your partner's father that you have been telepathically communicating with his deceased wife. (143)

Take a photograph, pass it around. Guaranteed all will get a good laugh. But it's not funny. It's 3 a.m., and, clad in nothing but bra, G-string and stilettos, I am perched up the ladder pruning a rose bush in my front yard. My then-boyfriend stirred, rolled over and found me once again not in bed, and his search began. The entire house was illuminated, piles of paperwork, linen and knick-knacks were strewn throughout the house but still I was nowhere to be found. Upon opening the front door he is confronted with the aforementioned. When he asks what the hell I'm doing, I simply reply, 'Pruning the rose'. Then, to the question of why, my response seems so logical to me and plainly put: 'It needs doing.' I cannot be persuaded or coerced to stop, to go inside, to get dressed, or to go to bed. I am flying. (141)

She was 'wired' with visionary plans, and glossy eyes. Up to this point you could not tell her anything. No manner of reasoning helped—my wife was in her own world—the bipolar world where she hung on to Tarzan's vine, swinging from thought to thought, looking for the Divine. Nevertheless it was her creative reality: being the Queen, or a major ambassador on a spiritual quest to save the world. Great things, but they were 'just around the corner', about to actually happen in her world, the world on the swinging vine—creativity that would never really land on this earth. (20)

I arrived home one night to discover that my forty-year-old husband was now a professional skateboarder. My heart sank. He'd bought a top-of-the-line skateboard and all the kit to go with it. I sat down with him that night and asked how he felt. 'Wonderful babe, just great.' I knew then that he wasn't taking the pills. I said, 'I think you're a bit high.' He thought about it for a bit and then said he couldn't understand why people kept saying that to him. He felt great. And he wasn't going back on those pills. They dulled his thinking and made him tired. (56)

I have only ever loved one man with all my heart. Receiving a phone call from him on his mobile at 30 000 feet in first class, informing me that he is Neo from the *Matrix* and that I am to arrange a Porsche to collect him from Heathrow Airport is not a call I wanted to receive, nor could have ever anticipated.

The love of my life's slippery slide into mania seemingly took a few hours, but with the cruel gash of hindsight I realised that he had been headed for this moment for months and months.

The fundamental components of his ending up in a north London mental institution were a yearning desire to be wealthy and successful, a burgeoning disappointment in his chosen legal career, a vastly negative 'I'm better than that' attitude, followed rapidly by a period of unemployment, and burying all these dissatisfactions in smoking marijuana.

I was flying over from Australia when he was released to his parents' care. During an unsupervised shopping expedition at this time, he clocked up an extra $3000 (on top of the $15000 he had already shelled out pre-hospital when he was en route to his £400-a-night suite in London's Park Lane). Unwittingly, they also allowed him access to email, unattended, which sent him straight back into attempting to develop a network for his reality TV idea, and enabled him to denigrate many colleagues for their lack of support, via a global email in which he also lovingly included many a personal detail about our relationship, and espoused our love story as the ultimate in blockbuster epics. (179)

One precaution I am very happy to have taken was to cancel my credit card. After one of my manic shopping episodes, my mother coined the term 'buypolar'. I bought in bulk. My mother had casually complained that for some time she had not seen any redcurrant jelly to use in cooking. I made two separate orders from two online stores and bought out their stock. I even branched out into redcurrant blends with other fruits! I tend to buy big at night online, but where possible, I cancel orders the next day on more level-headed reflection. (158)

One morning my seventy-year-old husband awoke saying he had a dream in which he had to stop taking his medications. The consequences of this changed the course of our lives. His behaviour altered dramatically. He began inviting people he hardly knew to our home, pouring out his life story to neighbours, driving with no regard for traffic rules and he grew too familiar with people, particularly some of my women friends. In a week $5000 was spent on presents, T-shirts, a felt beret, collections of jazz CDs and kitsch lamps and candles. Someone he met on the street invited him back to smoke dope. On impulse he emptied his study of his valued possessions. Chaotic piles littered the living room floor, the dining table and the chairs. 'How long are you leaving these here?' I asked, dismayed. 'Forever! It's my Installation!' he told me, laughing madly. (106)

My aunty's highs would include really silly obvious things like surprise visits from her in a clown outfit or giggling and spontaneous farting competitions, which are fun but tiresome. My experience of her highs when I was younger was very exciting. I thought my aunty was so crazy and cool and generous . . . Sega drives and impromptu parties with tons and tons of lollies that we got to shop for ourselves, holidays at the beach and generally a good time. Her highs usually resulted in spending, and eventually the plan would change and she would give away the expensive stuff she had acquired. My dog we received after she decided to move to another state and couldn't keep her in a flat; we also got the spa she had purchased. (23)

I was on a high, and drove to Sydney to go to a concert. On reaching the harbour city, I booked into the top waterfront hotel, views to mountains and water, put on my new after-five outfit, and caught a taxi to the entertainment centre. How was the concert? Unfortunately, I have no memory of it. For the next fortnight I bought beautiful clothes, stunning ornaments and crystals, and put a deposit on a unit, sight unseen, from a plan. Sounds fantastic—well, think again.

On waking in the psych hospital, approximately three weeks later, I had no comprehension or memory of my actions post receiving my medical retirement letter a month before. It wasn't until it was explained to me that I had disappeared for three weeks, made no contact with family or friends, and had been brought into hospital by ambulance, that reality set in. (5)

Bilateral negotiations

I'm planning to become the Secretary General of the United Nations by 2027. I feel energised. Confident. So sure I'm the woman for the job. I'll fight for social justice with integrity and passion. Good over evil. Like Superman. No wait, Wonder Woman.

I am experiencing my first 'high' but I don't know it. I don't need to sleep. There is so much to do. I find it intoxicating staying up to the early hours of the morning. It is quiet and serene and provides me with respite from the grinding noise of the city to which I travel to work by day. I feel like a rebellious freedom fighter challenging a restrictive patriarchal system.

I've no desire to cook a meal for myself. Hunger is not my friend anyway. Peanut butter on toast becomes my staple diet. I start to lose weight. A small sacrifice, I reason, for my commitment to a higher good. I consider a future world where war between nations continues ever bloodier, and I shall lead the negotiations for peace and stability.

> I undertake to repair a broken electronic keyboard I received as a gift years earlier but rarely played. The truth that I have no knowledge of electronics does not elude me but I continue on steadfastly. I pull the keyboard to pieces but I'm unable to reconfigure the many minute parts back to their original home and connection with each other. The war in Iraq continues and my keyboard is discarded to a lonely corner of the lounge room floor.
>
> I haven't washed up in a week, and plates, cups and cutlery lie dour and dirty on the kitchen sink and surrounding benches. Will North Korea explode nuclear bombs? That could be difficult. I stop putting my clothes away in the wardrobe and build unceremonious piles around the floor of my bedroom which bleed out to the living area. Soon it is difficult to walk a straight line in my small home due to my reluctance to now put any clothing or household item away in its rightful place. I revel in the chaos where once there was order. (125)

For others, the highs can be distressing—even in the midst of their seeming exuberance and good cheer. Some are affected with an underlying 'thrum' of agitation. For some there is the realisation that they can't get 'out of' their elevated mood: that they are in some way captive rather than in control of an experience that can accelerate to breakneck speeds, especially when they begin to get physically 'shredded' from exhaustion.

> This is a positive essay but I have to point out that hypomania is not a happy state. It describes a cluster of symptoms, only one of which is euphoria. Singing was a symptom for me, not as

a celebration, but as lamentation and a way to breathe enough oxygen. Hypomania was often a state of being desperate, communicating with others and inappropriately asking for forgiveness as if death was imminent. (118)

For me the highs can only last so long before the body of my being starts to feel shredded and overworked and overwrought with all that has come before and what is to come. By then the sleepless nights, the irregular or skipped meals, the go go go, the need to write and write and write to fill my heart's desire, have an accumulated debt that I must repay. I ride the high for as long as I can and then if I'm lucky it drops away and that is all. The ride is over. If I'm unlucky the irritations set in. The fatigue and lack of food causes me to want to rip off the head of the nearest person. I can't take it and after a while I cry and cry because I feel that I am so horrible and bad and mean to everybody. (47)

And the further downside: what goes up and up must come down. The downswing, the depression that follows a high is usually savage. While sometimes an individual will court a high when it arrives as an escape from the black hole of depression, ultimately, for many, as shown below, the memory of the ensuing ugly lows discourages flirtation with the highs.

It takes a length of time to recognise and forsake the highs, and even longer to see the connection to the lows. (132)

For those with bipolar disorder, mania returns a sense of feeling 'alive' to a numbed, depressed or labile mind and I find it is easy to want to over-compensate for this regained energy by being caught up in its web of temptation, the overwhelming impulsive need for stimulation. It is easy to believe that mania with all its energy, increased charisma and euphoria, is generating all this added lust for life and the belief that one can achieve whatever one puts one's mind to. This is a very stark contrast to the lack of motivation, inspiration and enthusiasm that have been lost in days gone by to depression. This is so apparent, that there is almost a desperate need to hold onto the mania, as the heightened mood makes everything far more satisfying and life is now less lacklustre. (159)

If only I could stay 'up'

I was Queen of the World. I would drive to work each morning as if on 'speed', zooming along Basset Street, believing I could do anything, be anything. In my most extreme euphoria, I actually believed that no-one on earth could be as happy as me. I was simply bursting with happiness. Tears streamed from my eyes as I began each day. And I could hardly sleep at night as the joy for life, beating in on me, kept me from switching off.

During this period I survived on three or four hours of sleep every night. However, in the daytime this lack of sleep never showed in my appearance or presentation. My energy levels were up and people commented: 'You look so well' or 'What are you on?'

I wasn't 'on' anything and I had no idea what was happening to me. I only knew I was happy. I don't understand what triggered my bipolar but my sense of satisfaction did skyrocket into RIDICULOUS HAPPINESS, and I never saw it coming. I just took off. Up. For two years.

My brand of the disorder seems to be an elevation of feelings rather than actions. I'm Leo(nora) di Caprio on the bow of the ship but (fortunately) I'm not going to jump or fly. My euphoria does not translate into mad exploits. I feel invincible but I don't gamble my savings away, or stay up all night painting the house, or fly to Rio on an impulse. I'm just madly happy, soaring, cartwheeling, freewheeling through my life. There *was* no downside. The only management strategy I had to employ was to get sufficient sleep to restore my body. I was in my forties after all and was at risk of burning out physically.

Then came the FALL. From this great height, I came crashing down. I was no longer Leo. I was Alice, falling helplessly down a bottomless well. When I crashed, I really crashed. At first I became irritable and erratic in my moods— overreacting to small things. Tense and overwrought. But this period didn't last long. Very soon I had sunk to the bottom of the well. There was a bottom and it wasn't very pleasant there. This depression, in contrast to the euphoria of several years, was almost unbearable.

Many people have described their depression and I don't need to add to their words here. In my misery I yearned for the euphoria. I longed to experience that elation again—and indeed still do. Sometimes I feel the source of my sadness is having known that elation and possibly never experiencing it again. And if I can't experience that elation again, then at least I want to know that sense of ease again when I was 'placid, even Kate'. (112)

• •

IN THE SPOTLIGHT
Identifying the upswing of bipolar disorder

- In making a diagnosis of 'highs', the clinician needs to distinguish bipolar disorder from normal mood swings and from personality 'style' and from other conditions such as ADHD (Attention Deficit Hyperactivity Disorder), where the individual may have periods of disruptive and distractible behaviour.

- A useful clinical probe question to uncover highs (after establishing that there have been episodes of clinical depression) is: 'Do you have times that differ from depression and your usual mood when you are more "wired" and energised?'

- If this is affirmed, further questions might check whether, at those times, the individual:
  — talks more—and talks over other people
  — spends more money, buying things that are not really needed
  — becomes disinhibited—speaking out too frankly, and doing things that might be regretted later (e.g. having a tattoo, gambling excessively, or engaging in one-night stands)
  — needs less sleep but is not tired
  — feels very confident and able to realise their dreams
  — feels more creative and 'one with nature', often finding coincidences in every event, and describing mystical experiences
  — finds that normal day-to-day levels of anxiety disappear.

If such features are confirmed, further support for the diagnosis comes from the report of a clear onset (mostly in late adolescence), and this preceding or following a distinct depressive episode. And, further, that episodes are not restricted to times when the individual has taken stimulant drugs or alcohol, or when starting or stopping an anti-depressant drug.

- While official classification systems state that a high should last for at least several days, in reality those with bipolar I or bipolar II can experience highs that may last only minutes or hours.
- If highs are diagnosed, the clinician will next seek to differentiate manic or psychotic episodes from hypomanic episodes (by asking whether there have been delusions and/or hallucinations), as each condition is managed differently.

• •

3. Sparkling in the spotlight
Creativity and bipolar disorder

Many people say that they do their best art and writing when
they are high. But it is hard to harness this energy without
it becoming out of control. I've thought maybe it would be
grand if we could all be manic together . . . but then, who
would pick up the pieces? (137)

This chapter considers an issue contemplated by many with bipolar
disorder—can the 'highs' be harnessed, and the creativity and energy
accessed productively? Some with a milder form of the disorder
suggest that they can use their heightened moods to advantage; others
refuse to court any elevation of mood, convinced that it is too easy to
lose insight and spiral out of control. It is an issue that provokes fierce
debate. Ultimately, it is the individual's decision. Alongside the advice
and feedback from partners, friends and health care professionals, they
learn the shape and trajectory of their particular disorder, and whether
it can be entertained or whether it quickly slips all restraints.

In the following extract, the writer ponders a way of reframing
her bipolar disorder so that it fits into the sweep of her life.

Being better than manic: Creating colour in a grey scale

In managing mania what is it we seek to achieve? Is it worth the effort and the sacrifices to 'get better'? What does 'getting better' mean? These questions deserve more than a clean-cut academic regurgitation of statistics. Both mania and depression can be seductive, and the links between disorder and identity often run far deeper than a chemical imbalance.

We know that it is possible to live a 'normal' life with bipolar disorder, but why aspire to 'normal'? Why interfere? The immediate benefits from a manic episode may include supreme clarity, creativity and productivity. The obvious downfalls, such as unpredictability, and the high cost of burn-out are not the whole story. Before we can assess the costs and impact of these episodes, we have to ask what the person stands to *lose* by giving up their mania. Long-term sustainability is the ideal to which we aspire, and this can be considered on a multidimensional scale, including each individual's life satisfaction as much as their neurochemistry. A life of major mood oscillations may be essential to an artist's creativity and their functioning within the lifestyle which their community considers 'normal'. This takes us beyond the question of 'What is normal?' and highlights the need for every person to be considered as an individual case.

Looking back over old journals to read what I have written in various moods is the strangest feeling, almost dissociation. Like I have been kicked out of, or quit, my own life. Like it was a bad habit, an addiction that I was trying to beat out of myself. I guess it's like this for a lot of people, not just with bipolar, but with any disorder. Identity and disorder become one and the same, and the thought of living without the disorder is far more terrifying as we approach the idea of 'normality'. There is so much uncertainty in the grey. While manic, everything makes sense and has a purpose. Being depressed, there is meaning attached to almost everything. The middle ground is dead boring. It is hollow. Taking meds, censoring my thoughts and fighting natural mood swings, I feel as though I have dumped my oldest and dearest friend. Although the rest of the world is reassuring me that I'm doing it for all the right reasons, I'm struggling to forge a new path for myself alone, often questioning if it was really worth the fight.

Treating mania can feel like amputating a higher self and wasting potential. Even when the mania manifests as something uncomfortable and dysphoric, it still feels more significant than feeling numb and hollow. To manage mania, an amount of 'ordinary' must be seen as valuable in an individual's life. It must be desired to be attained. We have to ask and answer: 'Why change?'

Reframe dealing with mania as 'management' rather than 'treatment'

Living with mania can be reframed as an experience which can be empowering as well as challenging, rather than as a symptom of an illness which needs to be negated. Thinking in terms of 'management' rather than 'treatment' allows a totally different and more achievable set of goals. After riding the rollercoaster long enough, my mental health management has come down to sustainability, meaning and satisfaction.

There needs to be a balance and a lot of middle ground between the highs and lows of normal life. A manageable and sustainable life will include up and down times. Compared to untreated bipolar disorder, these moods may seem somewhat uninteresting, so it is important therefore to be constantly mindful and appreciative of the stability achieved. German philosopher Nietzsche said: 'If a man has a *why* to live by, he can bear almost any *how*.'

In treating bipolar disorder, it may be that the focus of treatment should be directed towards the person's own reasons for wanting to 'get better' and their adjustment within a more stable, *meaningful* lifestyle, as much as it may be towards the prevention of mania or depression. It is not enough to pharmacologically cut out the mood swings for someone whose identity has been determined by their bipolar disposition. I can't just plug the source and clean up the oil spill. To simply cut out the technicolour of a previous life would leave a person static in the boredom of all grey scale. Discovering the true colours already within each identity should be of paramount importance, as it will support the individual's management and compliance. Rather than a sacrifice, change can then become an opportunity for growth, for getting better and for the getting of wisdom. (55)

The following extracts convey a little of what people feel to be the benefits of a high. Many, when in a hypomanic state, feel very generative and that they can channel the current of creativity into productive activity. Perhaps this is more a characteristic of those with bipolar II, who may not experience such a frenzied high, and/ or for the more experienced 'survivors' of bipolar disorder who have weathered enough episodes to have learned to manage their mood elevations, directing the creative sparks to fuel performance rather than freefall.

Are there upsides to being on a high? Are there ever! When you are on a high, you can leave the pack behind and get way out in front. You get innovative ideas. If only one in ten becomes a winner, you gain the right to be considered a 'creative' person. In fact, not only do people accept you as a leader in a cause or an initiative, but you can become its champion. All successful causes and initiatives need leaders and these are generally elected, but they also need champions who are not elected. They just appear and, by their enthusiasm, carry the day. (131)

Should the highs be avoided altogether? How could we deny our mother the enthusiasm, excitement and passion that she showed when moving into a 'high'? We would never have received the 55 000 words that Mum, in residential aged care, wrote in the last February and March of her life. (114)

It seems cruel to limit oneself in one's finest hour, before the shades of grey wash over us again. Like a drug, this added momentum of mania can be misused and taken up to a speed where mania is not functional and can be dangerous. So where does one draw the line in this balance of lust for life and normal productive functioning?

The upsides of mania are invigorating, with its renewal of energy and exuberance for life. The freedom of creative thought and being entertained by your own wit and wisdom. The surge and passion for endeavours that are few and far between in normal mood states. It is euphoric, as one feels all of one's capabilities are running like a finely tuned machine, capable of anything. Mania is a state of being that is extraordinary to experience! Unfortunately my experience is that mania is unsustainable at a productive, functioning level. (159)

I feel that if I can control my impulsiveness adequately, the highs do have their positives. They leave me totally exhausted, but in that time I have usually started some new hobby, which keeps me occupied for some time, and I have painted and written, things that I find fulfilling and calming. My mind works faster, the connection between things seems obvious, the implications clear. I work feverishly, inspired, easily completing many more tasks than usual. I have amused my colleagues (normally I am rather quiet and reserved), entertained my husband, kissed and hugged the dogs countless times, and, with any luck, kept myself from explaining to the boss how things should be done! (9)

Till I knew better, I loved being manic. I could do and feel things that normally felt so out of reach. But harnessing the creative energy has been difficult for me. The type of bipolar disorder I have means that my moods cycle rapidly. If I start to indulge my mania in any form, I become so involved that my moods just escalate. One thing I can do safely and I enjoy is writing. I take myself into a room without stimulation and put my thoughts down. Sometimes I write poems. If the writing turns into 'To Do' lists, I put the paper down and remove myself. (53)

Some people say that you can 'channel' manic energy for creative purposes, but not in my case. I do feel very creative. I believe that I am as gifted as Sylvia Plath or Vincent Van Gogh. But it's akin to the confidence of twelve beers. (65)

I have had 'mystical' experiences during hypomania, instead of the bleak orderliness of materialism. Amassing phenomena occur, coincidences in song lyrics, newspaper, radio, TV; synchronicity; feeling I was being enlightened. Other upsides to hypomania are having lots of ideas, being able to cry watching early morning TV, offering to help more around the house—and it gives a perspective on the periods of depression: something to contrast them with. (118)

The intensity of emotion experienced during mania often makes it a seductive force. What can surface during these times is an increased desire to engage in creative activity. How far this can be said to be an 'upside' is open to debate. Eugene Bleuler (1924), perhaps best known for his coinage of the term 'schizophrenia', wrote of the heightened creativity in what was then known as 'manic-depressive psychosis': 'Artistic activities are facilitated even though something worthwhile is produced only in very mild cases and when the person is otherwise talented in this direction.' This raises the question of whether or not the Hemingways, the Robert Lowells and the Virginia Woolfs of the world have been unusually talented despite their tragic illnesses. In my view, people who suffer from bipolar disorder are frequently highly sensitive, and this sensitivity often converts into an asset in artistic pursuits. One sufferer has written that because of her illness, she has 'felt more things, more deeply; had more experiences, more intensely'. This does not necessarily convert to creative achievement, and oversensitivity can certainly be a hindrance. (108)

A 'brilliant madness'?

Can we be so bold as to suggest an 'upside' to an illness? A 'brilliant madness'? In the case of bipolar disorder, it is tempting to entertain the thought. History is dotted with exceptionally creative individuals who suffered from this unique illness and who have concurrently transformed their field of endeavour. John McManamy (www.mcmanweb.com) has pointed out that this list of high achievers reads like an 'honour roll', but that in acknowledging this we run the risk of glamorising the tragedy that bipolar disorder leaves in its wake. Bipolar disorder is therefore something of a double-edged sword: while there may be a creative outpouring in the early phases of the illness, the severe depressions or rapid cycling of the illness often throws sufferers and their families and carers into extended periods of despair.

Some have claimed that hypomania promotes heightened creativity. It is unlikely that this high can be sustained (though there are rare exceptions to this rule)—to use a crude metaphor from the world of physics, 'What goes up must come down.' Nevertheless, the high of this illness is indeed seductive, particularly once it begins accelerating. Swift treatment remains the most humane response, however, and the getting of wisdom is in learning about one's 'self' in growing beyond the confines of the illness.

Hypomania seems to be particularly conducive to creative endeavour, with its increased drive, flight of ideas and focused energy. It is said that during one year of intermittent hypomania, the composer Robert Schumann completed a staggering twenty-seven opuses. This is in comparison to six completed in 1852 while he was euthymic [an even mood, neither elated nor depressed], and none during a severe depression of 1844. However, as mania intensifies, there is more likely to be disjointedness, distractibility, and an extreme restlessness which hinders the creative process. Robert Schumann spoke of a persona with a 'head so full of ideas that I cannot actually form any of them'. Writing of the impetus behind Spike Milligan's creative output, the psychiatrist Anthony Clare (1994) has said, 'Beyond the level of hypomania, with the onset of mania itself, Milligan lost the ability to mould the material into humour and lost his own power to control his day-to-day life and feelings.'

Mild depression may promote a reflectiveness that is favourable to creativity. Again in the case of Spike Milligan, he has documented his inclination to write poetry only when he is depressed, never when euthymic. It is therefore my contention that the more severe the mood state, the less likely there is to be creative output from an individual with bipolar disorder. A hypomanic condition may be valuable in giving the artist increased energy and focus for pursuing a project, but this usually breaks down under 'pure' mania. The intensity of feeling that I experienced during my most recent exacerbation of mania was so intense that I simply sat back and let the euphoria flood my system—nothing of any artistic merit was about to be achieved in that state. (10)

Thoughts on writing without a safety helmet

I'm weighing the pros and cons of harnessing the creative surge of bipolar highs in order to write. It's made me look back over twenty-plus years of writing. Most of this time my bipolar was undiagnosed, so it gives me a bit to draw from. Last year I started on lithium and that and a careful lifestyle has helped keep those highs mostly away. Did I need those highs to write? I was ambivalent. What I've figured out is quite different from what I imagined.

That creative surge held a lot of promise for me at the start of my writing career. A small but clear idea would seep into my consciousness. It would be something tangible—a line someone said on a bus, a memory from childhood. That something would stoke the little coal fire in my artistic belly, my pulse speeding. The next moment I'd have a character, a place, a full chapter unfurling with definition. The growing relationships between the fictional people would seem interesting, complex but understandable. By the time I was home, I'd have the plot line of a book mostly thought out. I wouldn't need much more than a darkened room and a word processor—I'd have the first 200 pages down before breakfast. Or so it felt.

I'd then write like a steam train. Once I've gathered momentum, there's no end until the coal runs out or someone pulls the brake. Pages and pages. Friends envied my productivity, but much of it was out of sight, nothing was ever 'there' yet.

Wrapped up with my manic phase were not only large ideas and speed of execution, but also overlapping thoughts, agitation, and inability to judge the value of what I produced. The quality of the prose was pretty ordinary at best and sometimes plain unintelligible. The truth was I couldn't keep track of what's called the 'narrative thread', otherwise known as the 'story line'. Writing in a manic phase was causing me to lose the plot.

I then stopped caffeine and alcohol and started lithium.

Now, in role reversal, my writing has a role in monitoring my bipolar. One of the early warning signs for me is whether I'm writing coherently and steadily or whether speed starts to gather and I aim for volumes in one sitting. I check with myself. It's something that I watch. If it starts to feel like the old days (15 000 words written over a weekend), I go to the wellness plan developed with my doctor. In this way that creative surge and my writing will always be linked.

Full stops are only little fellas. They're small round dots employed to sit at sentence ends to stop words slipping away. Words are restless things; they often hang in groups connected by an idea. When the full stops have been left out, words start to creep in a convoy along the line. Runaway words, like mania or hypomania, can gather speed and be impossible to stop. Inevitably they crash. It's not nice. Lowercase figures scatter across the page and an editor has to be called out to salvage sense. It's better to write without the crazy speed of mania. (172)

Although I am wary of the sheer explosive power of a high, the energy and creativity a bipolar high brings can be a relief from depression and viewed positively if mood elevation is recognised early, managed to minimise risks, and channelled productively. (31)

Tips for fellow metaphorical sailors

Go with the flow and not against the rip when only low to medium 'out of control'. Do not revel in your magic wonderfulness, eyeing the crow's nest for a possie. Do not be dispirited when you find yourself adrift again. Coast along and try to be assured by these measured manoeuvres that you *will* arrive safely.

Balance the stigma of not keeping 'normal hours' against what you've created or achieved. Not a wasted journey, then.

Call for professional back-up when the medium level threatens to swell hazardously.

Do not deny these 'high seas', nor attempt to keep navigating solo. The idea is to come out alive, not get a purple heart for foolish bravery. Your friends and family will not thank you for refusing help or ignoring warning signs.

Avoid pressurised speech. A dead giveaway. Distil those unruly thoughts into telling one-liners. However, don't become an audience-reaction junkie, striving for overkill cleverness, pointing out synchronicities to which most are not so highly attuned.

'Act normal and people will relate to you likewise' is the best line my psychiatrist ever said. Embracing the pirate can be quite liberating. Use your not-so-accursed creativity as an escape route on occasions. (25)

When everything seems to be 'Upsides Down', something fantastic happens. I find myself taking pleasure in small wonders. After eighteen years, and counting, of living with this brain chemistry, the joys of nature, the joy of music, great art, great literature and the simple pleasure of a great conversation, everything seems to mean a little bit more. I wisely invest in my health in order to experience another eighteen. I would never advocate inducing a manic episode, but at the age of twenty-five it chose to induce me; I can look back over the years since and even slightly understand, appreciate and smile at my non-conformity.

With work, I am sometimes the ideas person, always the trouble-shooter, having developed a sixth sense for planning. I find myself living with honesty and integrity, and I am not afraid to say, with respect, what I think. I have grown accustomed to the pace. I have put the brakes on the driven demeanour and am learning to not second-guess or question myself too much. I *can* differentiate between the normal and the abnormal.

If we did not take risks, albeit calculated, our world would be much poorer. The highs can allow us, when monitored safely, to do this. As von Goethe wrote: 'Daring ideas are like chessmen moved forward . . . They may be beaten, but they may start a winning game.' (110)

Bipolar disorder: An owner's manual

Are there upsides to being bipolar? You bet! You know that feeling—that 'hyper' feeling, when you're hyper-sensitive, hyper-generous, hyper-friendly, hyper-passionate, vengeful, aggressive, creative and competitive. It's that iron-clad confidence, that silent pervasive sexual predator feeling and that less-than-favourable opinion of other people and their monochrome ideas of what they think is 'good advice'. How good is that high while it lasts?! From a woman's viewpoint, the most obvious benefit is that you seldom have to worry about your weight, insurmountable obstacles are merely temporary challenges, you have energy to burn, you are unfettered by traditional social constraints or other people's opinions, and a lack of perspective means you can tackle the biggest projects with confidence. There are many advantages to the hyper-intuitiveness, limitless energy and confidence. The trick is to somehow harness the power.

What are some reliable strategies?

The downside to hyper-sensitivity is that it can interfere with relationships. This isn't such an issue where personal relationships are concerned because people who love you have great tolerance. But work colleagues are not necessarily so understanding—nor should they be. Therefore, unless you like job-hopping, it's up to you to adopt relevant strategies.

The experts say that there are four stages to every team-building exercise: **forming**, **storming**, **norming** and **performing**. The first stage, forming, is the honeymoon stage; storming is the inevitable in-fighting and bickering that occurs when people sort out the team hierarchy. Then there's the norming where members settle down into a cohesive team; and finally, there's the performing stage, where the benefits of long-term relationships kick in and create significant productivity benefits.

It's a challenge for bipolar personalities to progress further than the first two stages. For example, during the forming stage, I intimidate team-mates when I fall in love with them and want to be their instant best friend. Then, during the storming stage, I irretrievably burn bridges with my passionate sparring. When 'normal' people meet or argue, they seem to know instinctively where the line is. Being immune to traditional social constraints, I tried to rely on visual cues but often by then it is too late, and the only way out is via another job.

I overcame this trend by working for myself as a consultant and outsourcing my services for a year at a time. I would join a company, achieve pre-established objectives, then leave exactly one year later by longstanding agreement. It was long enough to get the job done, but not long enough for people to really get to know me well. Having energy to burn most of the time meant I had no trouble achieving results, which translated into no trouble getting the next contract.

I've since discovered another successful strategy—working

in a virtual team or telecommuting, both of which involve working part-time from home. I now work as part of a virtual team whose members are scattered throughout the world. Our sole form of communication is email (or online instant chat) and the occasional telephone conference. It is very difficult to be perceived as anything else but 'traditional' through either of these mediums. Any overfriendliness that does slip through is attributed to a cultural difference and I have a five-minute delay on any emails I write which is enough time for inappropriate responses to be retrieved. Testimony to the success of this strategy is that I've worked for the same company for seven years now.

An over-abundance of confidence is not so easy to manage. One benefit is that I'm usually involved in about ten times more projects than any of my friends: I'm strongly motivated to achieve instant solutions and I can comfortably initiate tasks far beyond my capability. Maybe because you play the numbers game, maybe because you're lucky or maybe because you're a natural genius, some things go according to plan and you experience the sweet scent of success. Other times you crash and burn in a spectacular fashion, and at great financial and emotional cost.

Balancing creative and destructive tendencies takes perspective. Let's not beat around the bush. Perspective is probably the single most difficult thing to acquire. The only really reliable way to develop perspective is through hindsight. Unfortunately, not too many of us have time machines.

An alternative is to use time forwards, not backwards. For example, pick a suitable delay period you think you could live with, and delay making any big decisions until after that time elapses. It might be a different time period for different things. If I get a great big 'business' idea, I generally sit on it for at least a week. If it still seems like a good idea after that, I'll pursue it. For less grandiose ideas, I wait for at least a day and a night before making a decision to implement. But in the area of personal relationships I force myself to wait for three months before sex. That's tough, and I have to admit I cheat sometimes.

Harnessing the power

The point is that if you want to live medication-free, you can try these alternatives. The first step is to recognise when you are operating outside the 'normal' band of emotional limits.

The next step is to be aware of your particular idiosyncrasies caused by your bipolar disorder. Do you relate to that hyper feeling? Do you have problems maintaining relationships, or do you find your robust self-confidence is an issue?

Develop strategies for each of these idiosyncrasies and live by them. What other people might view as a weakness is your unique strength when managed effectively.

The key is active participation and persistence—you're bipolar, so you're good at that! (11)

• •

IN THE SPOTLIGHT
Do 'highs' hamper or help performance?

For those with bipolar disorder, the highs are a welcome relief after episodes of depression. But do they truly increase creativity?

- Many individuals argue for a true increase in creativity—as do many of our writers. For example, the American Producer Joshua Logan (1976) once reported to an American Medical Association meeting that it had taken him eighteen months to produce the musical *South Pacific* when his mood was stable, but only three days (during a high) to produce *Charlie's Aunt*—and to critical acclaim.

- There is an over-representation of eminent creative people with bipolar disorder, as first detailed in 1889 by Cesare Lombroso in *The Man of Genius*. In Kay Redfield Jamison's 1993 book *Touched with Fire*, she provides an appendix of some 200 poets, writers, artists and composers who experienced a mood disorder (bipolar disorder principally), while her own study of British poets suggested a rate of bipolar disorder some thirty times higher than in the general population. Similarly, Nancy Andreasen (1987)—who compared thirty writers with matched controls—quantified a rate of bipolar disorder four times higher in the writers. In her 1993 book, Jamison drew parallels between this 'artistic temperament' (i.e. periods of fierce energy, high mood, quick intelligence and a sense of the visionary, oscillating with darker moods) and the experience of bipolar disorder, which, in combination, could become a unique forge for creativity.

- In a 1995 *Scientific American* report, Jamison noted individuals when hypomanic were better than a control group at speech components such as forming word associations and listing synonyms, and so rated high on tests of creativity. Jamison has documented how, in hypomanic states, there is an increase in ideas and mental speed, sharper and faster perception, mental fluency, cognitive flexibility and an increased capacity to reshape old ideas into new and original ones—all elements promoting creativity.

- The famous comedian and principal writer of *The Goon Show*, Spike Milligan, had Bipolar I Disorder. The text for many of his sketches exemplified the circumstantial, over-inclusive and loosened associations observed in hypomania and mania. Such processes also underpin divergent creativity.
- The link works both ways. A 'high' can drive creativity—and, for some people with bipolar disorder, being engaged in a creative task can 'trip' them into a true high.
- The association between mood elevation and creativity is not a straight line—it has more of a curvilinear pattern. Creativity increases initially with mood elevation and then falls away as mood becomes more severely elevated. So, at mild levels of mood elevation, the individual may be truly more creative and profound—but at higher levels such creativity gives way to pseudo-creativity (and with the bipolar individual often quite unaware that their seemingly brilliant thoughts, plans, works and writings are opaque to others).
- In contemplating the link, many writers note the positives, which in some cases could support an argument that a creative individual should embrace and take advantage of their highs and not seek to have them treated. However, two key caveats are: (i) in the long run, the highs can be more damaging than they are productive; and (ii) any distinct high will very likely be followed by an enervating and disabling depression.
- Many creative people with bipolar disorder are concerned that mood-stabilising medication will dampen or take away their creativity. To the extent that their highs contribute to their creativity this is a theoretical risk, although mood stabilisation will also reduce the fallow periods associated with uncontrolled depression. A seminal article addressing this concern was published in the *British Journal of Psychiatry* in 1979 by the Danish psychiatrist, Mogens Schou. Twenty-four

artists with bipolar disorder who had benefited from the mood-stabilising drug lithium were questioned about their subsequent creative power. Fifty per cent reported increased productivity, 25 per cent lower productivity, and 25 per cent reported no change. In this and other studies reviewed by Schou, those reporting increased productivity had found that the lithium aborted 'long and barren' depressive periods, and said that not only was their creativity retained but that they 'produced more and better work than before' (1979, p. 97).

- Each creative individual with bipolar disorder needs to undertake a cost–benefit analysis, examining the impact of medication on the creativity experienced during highs—and medication's correction of their painful depressive lows. For those who experience only milder hypomanic episodes, the final paragraphs of the essay 'Bipolar disorder: An owner's manual' (pp. 48–51) offer some very good suggestions.

• •

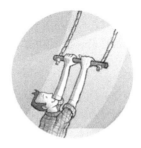

4. Damage control
The fallout from a bipolar high

Emerging on the other side of ill-managed highs is akin to
emerging from a storm shelter and being confronted by the
flotsam and jetsam of an emotional cyclone that was you:
collateral damage is often high, self-esteem invariably low. (111)

I once read that 'divorce is the death of a small civilization' . . . so
is the devastation and blindness of the psychotic experience. (8)

In this chapter are stories of the aftermath of mania, the subsequent
clean-up, and the attempt to make sense of the experience. It is also about
the writers' evaluation of their experience of mania—the dilemma:
what is 'me' and what is 'it' and what one can trust as 'oneself'? What
is 'reality' after a psychotic episode? There is distress, and sometimes
shame, for what occurred when the mood swing removed inhibitions
and judgement and family, friends and workmates were reduced to
spectators as the trapeze swung wildly and dislodged the rider.

A cruel irony is that this 'time of reckoning' arrives as the
high ebbs away (or has been precipitously halted in its tracks by

medication). While still physically and mentally 'shredded' by the episode, the individual has to marshal the resources to repair any damage caused to self and others, while avoiding the recoil—into depression.

> See look at me now. I don't always think I am Jesus, and sing songs all day long. When I explain what it is to experience mania, most people tend to be polite, offering reassuring glances, and undercurrents of 'Are you completely mad?' It is one thing to explain behaviour from last weekend in the wee hours of the morning under the influence of something—that is seen as 'cool' and often encouraged. Consider an explanation of often similar behaviour: this is what happens to me when I'm sober and get stressed. My brain needs only a few environmental factors to be a bit out of whack and, hey presto, I suddenly start talking faster, see the world in vivid colours, become super-confident, have no fear . . . It sounds quite appealing actually, except when you lose your job, spend all your money, offend family and friends, and end up living for a while with a group of strangers in your nearest public hospital who have their own sets of 'issues'. (121)

> My wife and I are rediscovering our relationship but there isn't enough fat in it to take anything for granted. She has suffered and although she knows my illness was the culprit, it looked and sounded like me at the time. (143)

> During my first manic episode, I got so high I lost myself. Then reality comes crashing back. You survey the wreckage of your life and despair. This is why bipolar sufferers have such a high suicide rate. Before my episode I had numerous acquaintances. After, I had maybe two friends, who remain best friends today.

When I was relegated to the psych ward, they asked if I was pregnant. I was so ashamed . . . I didn't know. I was so lucky. For a female bipolar sufferer, mania leads to high-risk situations, promiscuity and unwanted pregnancy. I had totally lost any inhibitions, was grieving, and dropped to under 50 kilograms in the course of two weeks. I couldn't eat, couldn't sleep. I was burning the candle at both ends. I was initially misdiagnosed as suffering speed psychosis. This was sent in a letter to my GP. I phoned lecturers at my uni while I was in the psych ward, thinking them responsible for driving me mad with useless knowledge. My honours thesis supervisor, with whom I had been quite close, visibly recoiled from me when I saw her a year later. (189)

I was asked to leave work, having become a risk to my own reputation, and in spite of the mania it was, and still is, a source of great shame. (105)

There are many individuals with bipolar disorder who would prefer to live a more ordinary life, and feel that there are, for them, few benefits in the exuberant heights of mania. Their approach is to monitor themselves carefully, and act fast to extinguish the first sparks of mood elevation. Here are some of their views, including those of a wife who is keen to 'put to death' the 'creative myth'. On the whole, these writers judged that the creativity that is potentially unleashed during the highs is neutered by the release of the brakes on all other parts of the individual's functioning: too much speed and too little concentration leads to a fall, and the cost of the injuries is too much.

The draw card is being empowered to choose when a mania or 'high' is coming—do you let the sparks of euphoria and grandiosity sweep you up and warm you, letting the creative urges soar as you fuel the flames and roar into the fireball; or do you choose to douse the flames to save getting burnt?

In the past I've become so manic that I have been hospitalised. Most times, I was scheduled and I came very close to life-threatening situations occurring. The scares and hardships I have given myself and the pain of putting myself back together after a mania means that I now choose to avoid my triggers and be aware of early warning signs to combat heading into an uncontrollable manic state. I believe that the behaviours we experience when manic are directly linked to mania and that they therefore are manageable and not just inherent behaviours of oneself. (159)

Some see it as emerging from a cocoon to the beautiful light of a new dawn. For me, I seem to be catapulted head first into a frenzy of overexcited butterflies, which in turn become commonplace old moths. (161)

Bipolar disorder is unique in that it is the only illness which attracts the proposition that there may be an advantage to being unwell. Though the madness of artists is not entirely mythical, this 'brilliant madness' has been overstated at the cost of neglecting focus on the less dramatic and more painful aspects of bipolar illness—the protracted depressions, for instance. Therefore in this regard it is just like any other illness: best treated as early as possible, though the true getting of wisdom may only come after several bouts with the bipolar bully.

The clinical DSM-IV descriptions of mania don't account for the trail of destruction that is usually leftover after an episode has been resolved. By the conclusion of my most recent episode of mania, which somehow did not see me hospitalised,

I had quit my job, quit university, quit on an important, loving relationship, and was encountering suicidal feelings for the first time in my life. Then there were the 'intangibles' to contend with: the utter loss of sense of self and of confidence; the desire to hide away and resurface at a more convenient time. Mania is a little like a seductive elixir which delivers short-term pleasures at the cost of medium-term harm. My psychiatrist assures me this harm is 'completely reversible'. I choose to believe him. (10)

My experiences in hospital with manic episodes have been traumatic, with high levels of anxiety, thinking and talking at a rate too fast to comprehend, whilst concerned with various scenarios of childhood, adolescence and adulthood that had caused me some grief and sorrow at the time. These hospital experiences seem far too overwhelming and complicated in a delusional way to think about, even now. I noticed that I was often in a childlike state, looking around at others' faces trying to work out whom I could trust. I would avoid loud, boisterous people and befriend those who took time out for themselves, and would listen to me. (175)

It never ends, you never know what is coming and when. I haven't seen a controlled positive surge from this disease— perhaps it can happen. The highs I have lived with have always been fraught with hazards, pain and stress. I guess the upside is that you find what you are really made of. What your philosophy of life is truly grounded in. What love means: *till death do us part*. (20)

In my experience, the most benefit from a creative urge is achieved in the first two weeks of a high. After that, insights tend to be meaningless and the need for dreaming sleep greater. For instance, I saw the phrase 'Chasing rainbows' in a cartoon, decided it was an anagram of 'brainwashing' and began to sing 'This is the way we wash our brain so early in the morning', much to the bewilderment of my husband. At one stage in the middle of a three-week high, I felt that I was being urged to remove all my clothes and walk down the street naked. I fought the urge again and again and did not strip off, but in hospital I shared a room with a woman who had succumbed to the feeling while on holiday with her husband and was deeply ashamed and afraid he would leave her. (6)

The Casino Bipolar—the house always wins

I myself know the feeling of being 'The One', and of feeling chosen. Everything made sense; there was no anxiety. Ecstasy pervaded my whole body: all my thoughts, emotions and actions were heavily influenced by it. The symbols that ignited my imagination were everywhere. Walking to the pie shop seemed like a creative experience and, quite honestly, a spiritual one. Associations between scenes that crossed my path would form in my head, questions would then be asked and answered, and I had no way of keeping up with all the information. Later, when depressed, I discovered that what I was mourning in my depression was really a *feeling* of creativity. There was no work to show for the effort of losing my mind, no masterpiece to present to the world and confidently say: 'It was worth it.'

Some say that a lot can be achieved by someone in the first stages of a manic episode. This is true, up to a point. But if you approach it from a purely mathematical position over a period of months, and add up the time lost in hospital, the time taken off work through depression, the missed

opportunities when you have to leave employment, and
the relationships you can destroy with friends, family and
workmates, it is actually an extremely unproductive way of
accomplishing anything. If I wrote just one page a day for six
months, remaining stable, it would be far better than trying
to write a book in two weeks without sleeping and then
ending up in a mental institution.

You think it's all going to be fine. But it's not fine. Things
get very dark, so dark that you never want them to be like
that again, so dark that people can, and regularly do, kill
themselves. (60)

Navigating the bipolar rapids

I have been living, for twenty-four years, with a man who has
bipolar disorder. If I am wiser for the experience, it has been
hard-won wisdom. The lack of honest, straightforward, easily
accessible information on the subject continues to be a source
of annoyance and frustration to me. The only information
our local hospital had when I enquired was a Department
of Health brochure which blithely stated: 'With the right
medication you can live a normal life.' The lack of wisdom in
that phrase probably can only be appreciated by those with
bipolar, and those who suffer with them.

First, let's put to death the 'creative myth'. People on a
bipolar high are not creative, they only think they are. They
are full of great ideas—unfortunately, an even better idea
arrives before the last one can be captured, and so it goes.
Perhaps if you are a creative type in the first place and have
the skills necessary to follow through on your ideas, you

might actually benefit in the short-term from the high. I have no doubt that in the long-term exhaustion and confusion will defeat even the most creative.

This creative myth is usually the first thing you read about when you do find information on bipolar. Churchill, the poet Shelley, the artist Van Gogh are among the usual list that's trotted out of famous people who have had the disease. That the disease has contributed to their talent is rubbish, if you ask me. These people would have succeeded despite the disease. What is not usually mentioned along with this list of great achievers is that they were all drunks and/or drug addicts (not to mention sexually adventurous) and usually died young. What I'd like to know is what their family and friends thought about their illness and their self-medicating habits. History doesn't spare a thought for them. I don't think it helps anyone to have this list of high achievers with bipolar constantly brought up; it tries to glamorise what is truly a horrible illness and encourages sufferers to think that they too can be as creative as these people just because they have a disease in common.

Now I've got that off my chest, let me say that one of the key factors in determining whether my man is getting a high *is* the creative impulse. As soon as he mentions his 'project' in a positive way, I get that tight knot in the pit of my stomach again because I know a high is on. No amount of argument will convince him that someone who normally can't even write a shopping list isn't suddenly going to produce a fabulously successful screenplay. (Never waste your breath arguing with someone on a high!)

The hazards of being on a bipolar high are well-documented. Sufferers are a danger, mainly to themselves, when this powerful disease takes over their body. One of the big hazards of a high that I don't think gets enough attention is the damage it can do to your relationship with that person. While the very high divorce rate among sufferers is often cited, any advice on how to curb this is usually totally lacking. We all know that people say and do outrageous things when they are on a high and if you take those words and actions on face value, why would you stick around! I've found that I have to keep reminding myself that it's the disease talking, not him. You know that when the disease finally releases its grip, you will have the same old person back again and they probably won't realise what havoc they have caused in their 'absence'. I think you have to try to forgive them, because they have no control over it—they don't want to have the disease, they didn't have a choice in it, and they are not responsible for what they do and say when on a high.

The one thing I have learned above everything else is that you cannot tackle the problem alone. Mental illness is very isolating, not just for those who suffer from it, but for those who have to care for them. The stigma of mental illness is alive and well in the community, so be careful who you confide in. It's probably better to tell as few people as possible; try to explain the disease to them and ask them to respect your privacy. It will certainly sort out who your real friends are.

Having said that, there are people out there who can really help you. Our turning point came when I finally made an appointment with the local mental health unit at our hospital. My man had resisted this for many years for no logical reason, but I was at the end of my tether. Years of inadequate treatment or no treatment at all had meant that he was now

rapid cycling. He was either up or he was down; there was
a week or two of 'normal' and then the rollercoaster would
start again. A year of proper care was quite transformational
for both of us. I can still see the highs and lows happening,
but they aren't extreme anymore. He isn't cured, he recently
had quite a major high when a new GP carelessly took him
off a drug 'cold turkey' that he had been taking for the pain
in his broken neck (two of the hazards of bipolar—the broken
neck and the GP who doesn't understand the complexities
of bipolar disorder), but we are both now enjoying a much
better quality of life. He misses the highs—he enjoyed them
and he admits they can become addictive—but I certainly
don't miss them.

We are lucky that we live in an age where there are drugs
that can really help people with bipolar disorder. These drugs
aren't perfect, they aren't a cure and they probably will cause
side-effects, and the optimum regime for each individual is
different, so you will probably have to persevere for quite
some time before you find what suits you best. Of course,
drugs have to be taken religiously to do the job we want
them to. This is my main role as a carer. I put his various
drugs out morning and night for him to take, make sure
his prescriptions are filled and make appointments when
necessary to see the psychiatrist and accompany him on these
visits.

He relies on me to tell him when I think he is starting to
get high so that additional medication can be introduced. I
think it's important to step in and make this suggestion early
while he is still rational enough to accept my advice. It is
tempting to hold off and let him enjoy the high for a while.
He certainly has to endure a lot of 'lows' and it is appealing to

see the high as some sort of compensation, but the longer you wait the more difficult it's going to be. I always try to keep my role as carer as low key as possible. People don't want to be constantly reminded that they have a serious illness. They know.

I strongly believe that people with bipolar disorder (and other serious chronic psychiatric disorders) need someone to keep an eye on them on a daily basis to help keep them well and to be able to intervene in the early stages of a high so that the potential hazards of the high can be avoided. Carers should automatically qualify for the carer's allowance/ payment, but they don't. The seriousness of the disease just doesn't seem to register with the bureaucrats. If you can talk your way into a carer's allowance, you will certainly earn your $47 a week. ('Of course, we'd love to be able to pay you more, but we simply can't afford it,' said my federal member, after the government announced a multibillion-dollar surplus.)

Having bipolar disorder doesn't mean that you will be creative. It does mean that you will almost certainly not live a normal life. You will be on medication all your life, and you are likely to be hospitalised more than once for the disease. You will have the stigma of having a psychiatric illness. You will have a better than average chance of going to gaol, getting divorced and being financially insolvent. You are unlikely to have a permanent job and you'll probably injure yourself seriously at some stage. You may end up killing yourself accidentally or intentionally.

Is there an upside to bipolar? Well, I can't think of one, but then, I don't have the disease. So I asked someone who does and he said, 'No, I can't think of one, I just want to be normal.' (45)

One legacy of bipolar disorder's mood swings and their effects on behaviour is that individuals question what is their core, their 'true' self, and what is their disorder? What *is* a 'normal' mood for them, what is this 'euthymia', this not-depressed, not-high state referred to by the medicos? How much can they trust the evidence of their own senses? How much have they to be ever-watchful, vigilant that simple feelings of pleasure aren't the beginnings of a bipolar trapeze ride?

It may take practice to find the balance between excessive self-observation and failure to spot the onset of a mood swing. Until a person with bipolar disorder becomes more used to spotting the early warning signs of a high (or a low), family, friends and health care professionals can provide valuable feedback. (See Appendix 2.)

I must be prepared to respond to that niggling suspicion that all is not quite right. It's hard to describe but there is a quiver, a moment of recognition that things look and feel just a little strange. It might be the beginning of that glow? Whatever it is, it must not be ignored. I must confront it, articulate my worry, ring my doctor . . . It might be nothing: it might mean a blood test to check my levels, an increased dose of lithium, some help to ensure some soothing sleep—and it might mean avoiding being dragged through a full-blown and life-interrupting episode. (43)

On many occasions I have asked my psychiatrist about making the distinction between personality traits and characteristics of mental illness. Invariably her response is that 'it is probably a bit of both'. Obviously there is no cut-and-dried answer when examining what goes to make a human psyche. (113)

The moments of clarity were more frightening than my hallucinations. (48)

I spent sixteen years denying I had bipolar disorder. Instead, I enjoyed the highs, ignoring the chaos I caused and convincing myself that it was only depression that was the problem. It took me even longer to realise that if I didn't have the extreme highs, maybe I wouldn't have the extreme lows. People fear if they give up their highs they will give up the best part of who they are, and that is scary. When I gave up the extreme highs and lows, I discovered the *best* part of myself. The highs are fun, exciting and addictive, but also draining, demanding and destructive. I loved the great happy feelings, the confidence I felt, but I chose to ignore the people I hurt through my rudeness, and the damage I did to my reputation through my risk taking. (132)

There is a mopping-up operation after a high that has got out of control, but it can still take some time before a person with bipolar disorder and those around them come to recognise the behaviour within the mood swings as part of an illness. Many individuals have quite a few episodes before they hear about 'bipolar disorder' and realise that help can be sought for their symptoms. As a result, people can lose years of their life, and much collateral damage can happen at the workplace and in relationships.

My father—through his love for my mother—was able, usually, to discern what was my mother and her behaviour, and what was bipolar disorder and the behaviour which it caused in my mother. (114)

The muse sweeps in and pushes everything else out of my view . . . that terrible beauty . . . my music bursts from me . . . my vision explodes . . . never was the world so tangible as now. A feeling of power comes with what my doctor and other professionals call 'mania'. I like to think of it as the source of power. If I could just tame it, I wouldn't need to take tablets every day. But, when I survey the wreckage that this power brings—strings of broken relationships, debts and damages, days off work, confused messages, the ties of family frayed—I know that the power is too much at once and all too fleeting.

I was diagnosed with bipolar disorder three years ago. Apparently I am bipolar type II, meaning that I have some grip on reality still. I doubt that reality sometimes when I'm convinced that my food is poisoned or that the best course of action is a fast drive towards oblivion on a cocktail of speed and gin. (59)

When a management plan has been adopted to protect against the risk of future episodes of mania, hypomania and depression, there is still a danger—self-sabotage. Long periods of routine and regularity, or the sense of an encroaching depression, can provoke the urge for a change, a hankering for the bright lights. The highs are addictive and seductive, and many people regret having to trade them in. The temptation can be to—consciously or subconsciously—'court' an upswing by seeking excitement, skipping sleep and routine, and/or forgetting to take the prescribed medications. The individual usually becomes aware of such temptation, sometimes after the damage and jolts of further highs. Any such ambivalence needs to be recognised to enable the best mastery of this disorder.

I really believe everyone should be privileged enough to feel the intensity of joy, happiness and pleasure of a bipolar high at least once in their lifetime. It really is indescribably fabulous. The world becomes flawless and beautiful and every moment brings joy and colour. It is quite magical, which is why I think it's so difficult to let go of. (105)

Risks escalate if your cocktail includes recreational drugs and an abundance of stress in your job or your lifestyle. With any form of mental illness, recreational drugs equal disaster. There is no middle ground in this one. I researched every bit of information I could find regarding the link between the use of marijuana and bipolar disorder. The word 'joint' has, thankfully, reverted back to anatomy in our household. (179)

Sometimes you can physically feel the headlong rush into that bittersweet energised state. Do you recognise these traits? It's that condition that's negatively referred to as bipolar disorder. Apparently it's bad because what goes up must come down, meaning that after every high, there's the possibility of free-falling into a low that can sometimes be impossible to resurface from, at least without medication . . . But how good is that high while it lasts?! Unfortunately, that same lack of perspective causes the biggest headaches. (11)

I recognised at an early point that I was back on the rocket, and that it was time to do some seatbelt fastening. My psychiatrist, no doubt, would have said, 'Return straight to Earth. Do not pass "Go!" Do not collect $200.' Which is probably why I didn't contact my psychiatrist. It was too damn exciting. After five years of depression, the chance to blast out of the rut and into the wild blue heavens was an expedition I could not abort.

What I *did* do was to up my dose of antipsychotics. I had discussed this with my psychiatrist previously and, all credit to her, she had granted me the latitude to self-medicate when I felt it necessary. Wherever I go, I make sure I've got an emergency supply. Step two, I told my wife how I was feeling. Actually step two, in all honesty, was only do-able thanks to at least two years of preparation. Following my 'official' diagnosis, my wife and I educated ourselves thoroughly about bipolar disorder. And that's why, when I said to her, 'I'm worried that I might be getting a bit hyped-up and out of touch with reality' she didn't phone an emergency team, but stood firmly by my side and helped fight off the demons—Ground Control, as it were. Nothing fuels paranoia more than all of those around you starting to panic. (173)

• •

IN THE SPOTLIGHT
Gracefully regaining balance

- Bipolar highs are associated with 'driven' and impulsive behaviours and lack of judgement. Driving too fast, dramatic overspending, sexual indiscretions, as well as anger and irritation, can damage reputation and safety. The 'hypomanias' of bipolar II are less severe than the manic episodes of bipolar I, and less likely to be associated with personal and social damage. However, it is more the individual's own trajectory over time (rather than their bipolar sub-type) that better predicts the risks to them of an elevated mood state. If highs are non-productive and/or associated with a trail of destruction, individuals should seek to control them and resist the seductions offered by memories of their short-term pleasures. Counselling, and drawing up a 'profit and loss' ledger when the person is 'euthymic' (well/normal), can combat the ambivalence about 'giving up' their highs.
- The 'Who is the true me?' question is not readily answered. For some people, a high is an extension of their normal personality traits—expressed without any brakes or respect for social conventions, rather like a caricature of their normal self.

For others, perhaps the majority, ideas and behaviours emerge during mood elevation (or depression) that are categorically distinct from the individual's usual personality style, judgement and moral code.

- A second 'Who will I be?' question perplexes many people when medication is recommended. Individuals accustomed to mood swings wonder if they will lose their intrinsic identity and personality. This concern is readily answered—no. Successful management will bring mood swings under control—and the individual will lose some of the positives of their highs—but it will not compromise their identity.

- Few people 'glide down' from a high to a normal mood state. Most swing from an 'up' down into the horrible black maw of depression. This is the other key reason for bringing mood elevations under control—the risk of depressive episodes is lowered. And good management reduces the chance of the common 'screw-ups' that compromise relationships and careers.

• •

5. Down to the wire
Responses to diagnosis

At first there was the initial shock of *having* and *accepting* the mental condition, but I was also *relieved* to finally understand what was going on with me and that *bipolar is treatable*. (134)

My mother had bipolar, not that it would be diagnosed until twenty-three years later. (144)

This chapter is about diagnosis and its impact. Bipolar disorder may take some time to evolve, often being preceded by other conditions—such as anxiety or eating disorders—before the characteristic pattern firms. This lead-up can be very perturbing, creating many 'wobbles' and setbacks, and some individuals with developing or full-fledged bipolar disorder 'self-medicate' with alcohol and drugs, which further obscures symptoms. Even when the bipolar pattern is clear, many individuals still fail to receive the correct diagnosis, particularly those with bipolar II. And, even for those who are diagnosed, the interval from onset to firm diagnosis is commonly ten to twenty years.

After the swirl of reactions to his diagnosis settled, one writer posed the question to himself: 'Am I a manic-depressive [older term for bipolar disorder], a mentally ill, unstable, erratic lunatic? Or do I simply have a mood disorder that, when medicated, lies dormant in the rivers of my mind?' (162).

As the following excerpts illustrate, giving a name and a rationale to troubling and confusing behaviours and moods confers some power to understand and gain control of them.

The getting of wisdom in bipolar disorder establishes itself over time, largely through learning from past experiences with the illness, as strategies for identifying warning signs of a relapse emerge with growing self-knowledge. In many cases, the management of bipolar disorder becomes easier over time as the individual and their support network learn more about the particular vulnerabilities. An accurate diagnosis may become the turning point in an individual's life, ultimately changing them from 'victim' to 'victor'. One Australian study (Access Economics, 2003, p. 6) found that the average time between the onset of the first symptoms of bipolar disorder and its accurate identification was more than ten years. This time-lag builds, in effect, to a cumulative mass of hardship. Diagnosis is the first step in helping the individual and others to identify symptoms and begin to learn about the disorder.

If the illness is familial, there is some precedent for further illness within that particular family, but if it is isolated within an individual, the learning experience becomes rather more ambiguous for those involved. I am the 'bipolar black sheep' of my family, so our learning curve has been quite steep, and we were initially unprepared for the trials which the illness presented to us. But I am increasingly hopeful about my future given that I have now received a diagnosis, and have found a good team of mental health workers to help me understand and manage the illness. (10)

I was hospitalised in my forties. It was the first time I had been told I had bipolar disorder, though, on reflection, I have had episodes of mania since my young adult years. (124)

I felt troubled as a teenager, but somehow I knew this was beyond 'normal' troubles. I could spend hours painting, play-ing music, writing and, equally, hours staring into space, uncomfortably numb. No one seemed to notice much. I man-aged, as I have always been able, to keep up some sort of functional face, appearances in no way betraying the darkness I could feel eating away inside.

When I left home at seventeen, I thought I had found some relief. I took to drinking with a vengeance, and the possibilities of the different recreational drugs that entered my sphere proved a convenient escape. I stopped feeling and it felt good.

Next, I was treated for depression, with my part-time alcoholism and heavy marijuana-use the supposed culprits then. At age twenty-two, I took six months off drinking and taking drugs, with a whole lot of antidepressant pumping around my system instead. I seemed to be getting on with things—working, going to the gym, painting, playing music, the regular things. However, as previously, a niggling doubt began—something not quite right. My mind began to cloud, nothing I thought was fast enough. Then I'm convinced that I'm really OK, I don't need medication, besides I can't think straight on it, I'm going to write a book, I'm going to form a band, no . . . go to London, no . . . have a solo exhibition, quit my job, buy a new car, buy a new guitar. I'm drinking again, and I'm shouting everyone (let's go out!!!), having a party, sex with a stranger, then a friend, then a friend's boyfriend. Everything is going so fast until the inevitable crash.

Finally I'm diagnosed with Bipolar II Disorder. (159)

My daughter Sandra probably had bipolar disorder from her early twenties or late teens. However, it was only at age thirty-nine after the psychotic attack—*I want to thank you for being my birth mother. You have been specially chosen. I'm here for a reason. I always knew this, but now I know for sure. Jesus is my brother and I'm from another planet, and Jesus will be coming soon to join me . . .* —and admission to hospital, that she was finally diagnosed. (69)

I had unfailingly supportive parents who loved me and loved each other. They had built a warm and stable home and provided me with a blessed life. I felt guilty about wanting to end it all—what did I have to complain about? But that would be rational thinking. And that's one thing depression robs the mind of.

After two bleak years came the upside: the high. Moving from my home in Yorkshire to London, I loved the anonymity of the big city where nobody knew me—I could leave the past behind and begin again. But then I didn't understand the hyperactivity. I didn't understand the crazy binge drinking. I didn't understand how I could party all night, wander the streets until dawn and still not need any sleep. I thought I was having a great time. But that would be irrational thinking. And that's one thing the high provides plenty of.

A couple of years ago I was finally diagnosed with bipolar disorder and life became about how to live with it rather than run away from it. I was experiencing rapid cycling and my mood shifted three or four times a day, which was exhausting not only for me but also for my husband, who never knew whether saint or shrew would greet him when he came through the door. (138)

I crashed downwards from my first, unrecognised 'high' to land hard in the unwelcoming lap of depression. 'I've got you now,' it said with venom, dragging me exhausted and fragile back to my GP. I felt hopeless. A referral to a psychiatrist resulted and so began a series of tests including a CT scan to check that the cause of my behaviour was not related to brain damage. Thankfully it wasn't, but I was diagnosed with Bipolar II Disorder soon after.

This period was lonely and filled with uncertainty about all that was happening to me. I told a few family members about my experience but I didn't feel it was something I could share more widely. I was in shock but trying to remain calm. Only other people had a mental illness, not me. I cried the first day I took my medication. It was Good Friday 2006. (125)

The muse sweeps in

I began writing songs when I was fifteen. I've always been surprised at how quickly they came, almost as if they wrote themselves. When I left home I started playing my songs to different audiences. Their reaction was so positive. Every experience came to be a song, every broken relationship, every moment of self-doubt, all of my thoughts and confusions. The words and music poured out of me. I was prolific, at some points writing two or three complete songs in a day. I did some recording. People were excited, and I had an offer to work up a full demo.

But then I played a gig after smoking a few joints. This was a huge mistake. I was feeling bad already and I wasn't sure if I could do it. A friend convinced me I'd be fine. I just needed to relax. I started to play. I started to hallucinate—my voice felt like it was failing me, my words seemed empty. I had to leave . . .

I didn't play music for three years. I'd be stopped on the street, 'When are you playing again?' The very thought of reliving that experience was painful. I threw myself into work, and heavy drinking. I vaguely remember going to work drunk, and more than a few times. I had a string of infatuated entanglements that would ultimately end in some form of violence. I decided to leave town, through the haze of burnt bridges.

The move turned out to be a new beginning. I returned to study. I made new friends, and more importantly, I found my music again. I began to experiment with noise and vocal effects and my music started to reflect the real complexities of my emotional states. I played a few shows, to some success. Then a depression hit and my music was stolen along with my wellbeing. I started to see a pattern—periods of intense creativity and feeling hyper-well, punctuated by a more constant depression. This led me to seek treatment. (59)

As the excerpts in this chapter show, the diagnosis is a shock to most but there is also relief in the wings. There is now a name, and a 'handle', on the disorder. This gives the individual an opportunity to educate themselves about the condition and its management, and to begin to assemble strategies and back-up to outflank what were, previously, unpredictable and overwhelming mood swings.

The keys lie in self-conceptualisation; how to emerge intact from the barrage of derogative terms swirling in the newly diagnosed head. Am I a manic-depressive, a mentally ill, unstable, erratic lunatic? Or do I simply have a mood disorder that, when medicated, lies dormant in the rivers of my mind? (Stigma = the Ebola of ignorance, of the inability of the average person to sedate their incessant urge to categorise in order to try to make better sense of the world and the kaleidoscopic enigma of human behaviour.) (162)

Saying 'I have bipolar disorder' is an important step; it never goes away—the diagnosis—but the symptoms do, if you treat them. (60)

Bipolar is under my skin. I can't deny it. I can't ignore it. I try not to dwell on the negative aspects, but it has infiltrated the essence of who I am. Accurate diagnosis came mid 1999, amidst feelings of utter despair and relief—and some thirteen years of previous misdiagnosis. Then began a new chapter in 'managing' the disorder, and here, seven years on, is where I'm at. Managing the highs of bipolar disorder is about empowering myself with knowledge, being hungry for more, and continuously updating information. It is equally about managing the lows. (146)

Filling in the blanks

Apparently my presentation is not uncommon, but being diagnosed with bipolar disorder in my thirties wasn't easy— not for me, my family nor my work colleagues.

I think I lived with an undiagnosed depression throughout my teen years and into my twenties. I managed this the way many others do—I self-medicated. It doesn't help that I have by nature a personality that always needs to have everything right now, if not before. Instant gratification is pure pleasure for me. I've travelled a lot, and often in countries experiencing civil disorder and with dangers for travellers. I survived two days aboard a yacht in gale-force winds with a captain who couldn't sail and a first mate who couldn't swim. I've been bungy jumping. I've been gliding. I nearly died in a white-water rafting accident. I've flown in helicopters. I've ridden a motorbike way too fast. I've been skydiving, and I've been to hell and back in a drug- and alcohol-fuelled blaze. But none of this could have prepared me for my first manic episode!

I've made friends, I've lost friends, but I really believe that my diagnosis of Bipolar I Disorder has added to the jigsaw that is me. I am not my diagnosis, it is simply another facet of who I am. Now I control it instead of it controlling me. I will always fantasise about the joy of being high, but the cold hard truth is that it gets in the way of my other life. The life that provides me with stability, happiness, strength and security. (105)

Goodbye Hollywood (Part 1)

High! Who's high? I feel fantastic. I ooze with confidence. Relate to anyone. Life's a breeze. I leave my loving partner, my cosy and welcoming home, and take off with my two-year-old daughter to begin a new life in a different state, in a town where I thought I knew everyone, when I actually knew no-one.

It doesn't take long to crash heavily into reality once luck and life's high energy runs out of fuel. The severe depression that accompanies this reality is totally debilitating, and all the while life is ticking by, though I'm not functioning.

In the early years I had parents to run back to, to hide me away, cook meals for me and my daughter. Perplexed by my new persona, which was empty, lifeless and uncommunicative, my parents rode through the frustrating depressive months, until I simply woke one morning, and everything was 'normal' again. I'd have a new job, a new flat and a new boyfriend in the first week of being 'on top' of things once more.

Depression? That is never going to happen to me again!

Unfortunately, however, this episode wasn't a one-off and I had no idea how to live with the highs and lows that continued to rule my world. I attempted visits to psychiatrists and welfare officers, but to no avail. The professionals would take one look at me and simply tell me, 'You're good looking, just go out and get a job. You'll be right then.'

But I couldn't file ant under 'A'. I couldn't wash myself. I felt completely alone, trapped in a waking nightmare of extremes. Eventually, there were no parents to hide me away and I was institutionalised as each episode became worse.

Yet again, there were no follow-up programs that were successful, because a correct diagnosis hadn't been forthcoming.

Another crippling episode hit when I was fifty-three. My 'Ground Zero'. As witness to my debilitating lows and the not-so-obvious highs, my now-adult daughter became my advocate, my voice, my saviour, and at the round table of doctors I finally had someone who could speak for me. She attested to my mood swings which she had witnessed and persevered with her entire life. There *were* highs! What a breakthrough! Through her input she helped the doctors to get a clearer picture of my situation, and therefore, a preferred diagnosis.

All these years—thirty in all—I had been unable to relate my feelings to the doctors. Electric-shocked out of my depression, I would leave the facility with very little to back me up. Anyway, I didn't need anything, I was well again. Ha! Ha! It was always only a matter of time—a stressful job, a relationship, a family matter, a general build-up of stress and I was back on the roundabout.

I can see now that there is always a high before the low. For some, these highs are Hollywood melodramas, glamorous and grandiose, exciting and violent. For me, it was brushes with the law, a youthful fairytale wedding, divorce court, promiscuity, top jobs, hanging with the movers and shakers: life was a party and I was the life of the party.

Life is different now. I no longer live with the dark institutions of years gone by, where ECT [electroconvulsive therapy] was the weekly activity and 'pills for dills' was the daily roll call. Many of my fellow inmates were the 'high rollers', locked up while still waiting to come down from their Peter Pan adventures—walking, pacing; talking, babbling; sleep a stranger to them; and cigarettes their constant companions.

I now have an understanding of my illness. This balance and awareness allows me confidence in myself and my future. My medication is correct and I monitor this closely with my doctor, along with regular blood checks. I get a certain amount of satisfaction and confidence as I read my levels every few months. I'm now involved, taking action and responsible. (178)

The next challenge concerns disclosure—whether to share the diagnosis of bipolar disorder with partners, family members and employers. Will it then assume centre stage in everyone's mind? It takes courage and good judgement to decide whether to disclose any illness. Chronic and recurrent illnesses, more especially if they are mental illnesses, are particularly challenging. Even those quoted in these pages sometimes thought twice about putting their story into print. When embarking on an intimate relationship, most individuals did choose to disclose their bipolar disorder upfront, and were gratified by the ready acceptance from their potential partner.

There was more reluctance when it came to disclosure in the workplace. The consensus seemed to be that if bipolar disorder is recurrent and manifest (for instance, requiring time off work), workmates' cooperation and acceptance is needed. Indeed, some writers noted that a trusted colleague can provide the best 'outside insight' for spotting early warning signs of a potential episode of bipolar disorder that may have slipped past their own radar. Other contributors, however, found that too-ready disclosure dashed their chances of securing the job. Others described how disclosure in the early weeks of a new job had been followed by swift dismissal—particularly if the disclosure had been required because of time off work. Many others decided to inform colleagues only after they secured a position of value within their team.

'You are only as sick as the secrets you keep.' That phrase slapped me in the face about a year ago. It changed shape over the months and over the episodes. (Don't you love that medical terminology—an episode—as though you are part of a soap opera you can't get out of?!) And for the longest time I took it to mean the secrets that you keep from others. But it is the secrets we keep from ourselves that make us the sickest. (57)

I do not share information about my bipolar disorder with many people as I will not risk the stigma that is attached to mental illness, especially in the professional arena. When I don't have to consider being compromised in the workplace, I will certainly wish to share my experiences with others if it can help them manage mental illness. (113)

Coming to terms with the bipolar mood disorder has meant acknowledging and accepting the condition, and trying to be honest and open with my friends, workmates and peers who are my everyday support group. I'm getting better at knowing when to disclose and when not to disclose; sometimes the knowledge burdens others or, worse, is titillation. Sometimes no matter how much you explain, people will never understand. After explaining the condition to a young friend, she said, 'But I don't see you that way.' If people don't understand after explanation, it is not my problem. Quite frankly, most people are ignorant and misinformed about mental illness. I remember a poster series in the psych ward showing people with bipolar out in the world working. The slogan was something like: 'X doesn't care that Y has a mental illness.' Someone had graffitied under it: 'That's right. They don't care at all.'

When I started a teaching diploma, I thought there would be negative repercussions if I was honest about my condition. When I realised that secrecy wasn't helping, I contacted the university's disability officer who showed me how to negotiate academia without disclosing too much. For a while I began to see my mental illness as my defining feature, but I don't feel like that girl anymore. (189)

IN THE SPOTLIGHT
Setting the stage for diagnosis

- Bipolar disorder can be difficult to diagnose unless there has been an unambiguous high. Sometimes true bipolar disorder is triggered by an antidepressant prescribed to treat a depressive episode. Sometimes an antidepressant (on starting, or because of dose raised or ceased) can cause a 'high' that is purely drug-related ('Bipolar III Disorder') and not reflect true bipolar disorder.

- Bipolar 'highs' usually have a clear and identifiable onset—often in adolescence. This can be elicited from the individual by questioning or the highs may have been observed by a family member. Mood swings may, however, be masked by 'self-medication' (drugs, alcohol) or misinterpreted as merely risky behaviour—and the diagnosis therefore 'missed'. Such mood instability may be misdiagnosed as personality disorder; or the impulsivity and distractibility might be mistaken for Attention Deficit Hyperactivity Disorder (ADHD), or other features lead to an incorrect diagnosis of schizophrenia.

- Bipolar 'lows' are usually melancholic or psychotic depressive episodes, although young people may show 'atypical' features, such as particular food cravings, weight gain and excessive sleep ('hypersomnia').

- The interval of ten to twenty years between onset and diagnosis (if a diagnosis is made at all) reflects many factors:
  - First, bipolar disorder may initially present with mainly depressive episodes and few or no highs for several years.
  - Second, most people with bipolar disorder seek help for their depression and, usually enjoying their 'highs', do not complain of them or seek treatment for them.

— Third, if the assessing clinician does not ask the relevant 'screening' questions, or if the condition is mild, and/or if the clinician is unaware of the existence of bipolar disorder, the diagnosis will be missed.

— Fourth, co-occurring disorders, such as substance and alcohol abuse, obsessive compulsive disorder and eating disorders can obscure the primary bipolar diagnosis and complicate the illness course.

- Thus, clinicians should screen all people who present with depression for symptoms of hypomania. If the condition's onset occurs later in life, screening for any organic or medical cause should be undertaken.

- If the possibility of bipolar disorder appears fairly firm, it is best to inform the patient about the possible diagnosis. While such a diagnosis is stressful, it will generally demystify years of perplexing behaviours and disturbed mood states, and bring relief in the wake of uncertainty. If diagnosis is followed by a practical management plan—providing the individual with strategies for bringing the condition under control—the stage is set for progress.

- In terms of disclosure, it is usually better if a relative or friend sits in at the diagnostic and management discussion, as this will also inform them about the 'cause' of previous inexplicable or bizarre behaviours, signal their encouragement to the individual and often lock in ongoing support. While the newly diagnosed individual may wish to tell some family members and close friends, it is generally wiser not to disclose the condition more widely unless there is particular need— unfortunately, the stigma associated with bipolar disorder is still prevalent.

6. Perfecting balance
Acting on early warning signs

> My psychiatrist suggested I write out a plan for early warning
> signs of elevation (as well as depression) and to give a copy to
> my family and close friends including myself. It was important
> for me to know who to call, and self-assuring to know that
> help was at hand if I wasn't coping alone. (134)

This chapter highlights the vital significance of the early warning
signs and triggers that herald the arrival of more problematic
symptoms of bipolar disorder. Identifying any individual's 'relapse
signature' can be the key to early intervention and control of the
disorder.

The writers inform us that there is no one reliable portent—
more commonly there is a 'soft cluster' of signs and symptoms. Also,
there may be changes in the early warning signs over time, or even
differences for each episode. For most individuals, however, there
are characteristic and indicative signals, with the most commonly
cited—and most powerful destabiliser—being a disturbed pattern
of sleep.

Steven Jones and others in *Coping with Bipolar Disorder* have written about 'individual relapse signatures', which surface in the person from episode to episode. Common ones are lack of sleep, irritability, restlessness and flight of ideas. And then there are specific relapse signatures with which each person becomes familiar. As my most recent episode was gaining momentum, I stood on the sands at Coogee Beach and gazed at the horizon, enraptured with my newfound appreciation of the overarching synchronicity of the universe, whilst lines from the poem 'God's Grandeur' by Gerard Manley Hopkins darted in and out of my thought traffic, awing me with their truths. This was odd for an atheist who had never read any Jung! I now know that if I start obsessing about unlikely scenarios, if everything feels 'profound', as though I am seeing it for the first time, it is a sign that I require urgent medical attention. (10)

Learning the early warning signs

Dr Meg Smith, President of The Depression & Mood Disorders Association of New South Wales, provided some wise observations in a talk given at the Black Dog Institute in 2006.

Over time, Dr Meg Smith has become very attuned to her mood changes: she has read everything she can about the disorder, she has given permission to her friends to give her feedback, and she keeps a journal so that she can spot mood swings. She feels that patient confidentiality is a luxury that one can't afford in this situation, so, as a back-up to her own self-management strategies, she has given permission for various of her friends and relatives to access the professionals that monitor her if they need to, and for all to share relevant information.

There are particular times during the year that hypomania, or the constellation of symptoms that signals hypomania, occurs; for her it is generally at change of seasons, particularly spring into summer. When she first experiences the 'early warning signs', she takes the following actions—as she knows she only has a day or two before she loses insight into her disorder:

- She sees her GP. She used to see her psychiatrist, but now she is well-versed in the disorder, and has checks in place (such as vigilant friends).
- She and the GP take steps to normalise her sleeping patterns—the strongest sign that she is in for a 'bout'. While sleeping tablets might seemingly normalise her sleep, those that are benzodiazepine-based do not, for her, operate on the neural circuits that are going askew—the wrong type of sleeping tablets merely mask the mood disruption, which will continue to develop underneath. For her particular bipolar condition, she needs to be treated with antipsychotic medication for her sleep disruption.
- She 'cocoons'—she cancels what commitments she can, and reschedules others.
- If she is in imminent danger of an episode (and some episodes are worse than others), she takes some days off work.
- She studiously avoids coffee and alcohol and any other stimulants.
- She keeps away from excitement (including talkback radio or the evening news on TV). She can get any news she needs from the newspapers.
- She has a written contract with her GP, her psychiatrist,

a friend at work and a friend at home. This specifies what actions she has agreed can be taken when she is unwell. She has been in hospital and is determined that she won't go there again! She is also *very* aware that she could damage her reputation at work and, while her students consider the lectures that she delivers while 'hypo' are entertaining, she herself says that they are verging on the disorganised even at a 'low' level of a high so she ensures minimal involvement with the more 'exposing' parts of her job while she is fragile.

- If she *has* to fly (disrupting her circadian, or body clock, rhythms is really dangerous for her even when she's euthymic), then she ensures that she does short hops with overnight stays, takes sleeping tablets each night, and preferably has a rest at the other end and avoids wall-to-wall activity.

- She says that one survival strategy is to know where the boundaries are and be very firm about not crossing them when you feel like it. One of the positive things about bipolar disorder is that the moods can be very elastic—it is possible to hold onto a set of behaviours for short periods of time. So an effective approach is to decide what is important and what you need to do to retain your reputation. For example, your work identity might mean a particular set of clothes and a particular set of tasks. If you want to hold on to the job, don't get creative with that role.

- While hypomania is fantastic for deciding that great changes must be made, it goes along with poor judgement, general inability to weigh up the consequences, and feelings that things are wonderful when they are, in reality, often far from wonderful. Most people learn the hard way that decisions made during periods of hypomania are not always the best decisions.

- Crucially, the most successful self-management occurs when people have a strong sense of ownership in relation to their strategies. This is only possible, of course, when they are well or fairly well, and they've had the foresight to put these strategies in place as self-protection. They are not merely 'following doctor's orders' but assuming responsibility for the overall management of their illness, including accepting the diagnosis, taking medication, seeking appropriate help, and remaining mindful about the presence of the illness in their lives so that they can act decisively when early warning signs appear.

- The most-used strategies included a commitment to getting adequate sleep, being aware of warning signs and triggers, keeping stress to a manageable level, taking appropriate medication, and making use of compassionate social and professional supports.

- Make use of any supports that your employer might provide. Access the employee assistance program at your workplace. They often have discrete support and advice to keep you productive and stable. Very often the sessions are covered by Medicare.

- So, as emphasised by Dr Smith, it is best to decide ahead of an episode what is important to you and to put in place what has to happen to preserve this part of your life.

When I'm off the planet, reality alters. It's not like there isn't a reality, it's just different to the one normally experienced. As the senses heighten, I never get much warning that I'm about to become full-blown. My emotions don't feel different, my thoughts seem like my thoughts always. Then it hits. The first time, I didn't eat or sleep for more than a week. I've learnt to pay attention to poor appetite and sleeping disturbances. Sleep has long been difficult for me. I can't afford to go more than three nights without a decent sleep. I always have sleeping tablets on hand. I've learnt to take notice of other things—suddenly spending up big, or becoming more interested in the opposite sex than was good for me. I had to take note of major stressors. One, two in a row I can handle, but throw in a third and I'm gone. I'm easily disturbed by aggravating spirits. By this I mean the people who court chaos and want to share it, or the people who enjoy stirring the emotional pot. I make a point of avoiding them. It's easier for all concerned. I'm very fond of what I call strategic retreat, and I use it. (38)

A few signs that I need to keep an eye out for now include: an over-the-top interest in spirituality, including going to spiritual talks by so-called 'gurus', doing spiritual courses, seeing 'signs' and experiencing untoward synchronicity; meditating too deeply; writing too much; becoming too excited; shopping extensively; buying shiny pretty things; staying up late cleaning my room; an inability to get to sleep because I am buzzing with excitement; and racing thoughts. Also, I have become very good at reading people's looks of concern and taking those looks on board. If they are concerned, maybe I should be concerned too! I can now sense when I am becoming too high. It feels as though I have a lot of energy pulsing through my body, and my eyes are really bright and intense. It is almost as if I can feel a flame burning behind my eyes, and I need to calm myself down until the flame recedes. I have been told before and I have felt that my eyes 'glaze' over. Whenever I see even a few of these signs, I need to tell someone, pull back, stop all 'stimulating' activity, and bunker down at home until I calm down. (104)

The first sign of an imminent high for my mother is the time of the year. Twice a year Mum knew she was headed for a low. Lows coincided with the anniversaries of the deaths shortly after birth of her first two babies, and the loss of the family farm when she was eleven. She would alter her medication to create a heightened mood leading into these periods. Packaging and sending parcels was another indicator. It was only when the puzzled recipients rang that we realised that something was amiss. The contents would be a mix of Mum's most valuable possessions, as well as items which were worn out plus an occasional brand-new item, like a shirt of my dad's. One way of working out whether she was high was to ask her to repeat what had just been said to her. Another indicator was frequent and repeated high intensity activity. For Mum, this seemed to centre on washing. She would do the family washing, then re-do it, then wash clean clothes, then wash anything she could find! However, our skills in detecting when Mum was becoming high were considerably less than her skill in concealing what was happening! (114)

My bipolar can be seasonal: a little spring fever and summer madness. I watch for an increase in my activity, energy, ideas and religious beliefs; a decrease in appetite and concentration; agitated moods, anger bursts; and a sense of the unfairness in the world; coupled with feelings of being extra well. (120)

Others around me help alert me to my early warning signs (usually my too-rapid speech). I watch their reactions. (130)

Warning signs include higher morning and evening heart rate than usual; feelings of stress/anxiety; a second bowel movement in the afternoon; urgency/raciness; more mobile phone use; an increase in goal-directed behaviour (e.g. weight reduction); increased energy; an inability to sit still and relax; lack of normal chocolate cravings; dressing better and feeling attractive; a decrease in concentration; absentmindedness; cleaning things; need to write; and more self-confidence. (147)

Just as Hawaiian scientists constantly monitor seismic activity, I am always on the lookout for symptoms of mania. The most obvious indicator is my need for sleep (or lack thereof). A sharp rise in libido is another warning sign. In my heightened perception, I'll feel bombarded with pick-up lines wherever I go. When I'm manic I believe myself irresistibly attractive (I am not) and misinterpret everything as a come-on. I have innumerable ideas, all of which seem terribly profound (they aren't). Each idea sparks others and my thoughts fragment down limitless tangents. It feels as if my skull is exploding with more thoughts than I could ever express. This shows in my speech. I talk fast, jumping from idea to disjointed idea. I am annoying. I'm also quick to flip from joyous to angry—easily frustrated because the thoughts overwhelm me and everything else seems painfully slow. (65)

I find that I develop a fine hand tremor, and I can become excessively itchy in the days preceding the onset of a high. I also notice speeded-up metabolism, which results in extra visits to the loo. (28)

Common triggers for my highs are changes to everyday rhythms such as sleeping and eating, and stressful life events. Possible early warning signs include destructive or impulsive behaviour after being sleepless or irritable, looking haggard, speaking in a caustic manner, telephoning friends indiscriminately regardless of the time, stopping medications and impulsive self-destructive threats and gestures. (32)

Ironically it can be the biggest challenge to look after myself when more of my triggers are present that make me less able to do so. It can become a juggling act. Change, which can be perceived as positive or negative, requires energy. Sleep, exercise, relaxation time, and pleasure such as from seeing friends, can restore this energy. It is the same for everyone except that if I get run down, I don't get a migraine or a cold sore, I become hypomanic.

The hypomania might be knocking at the door during times where I am not as resilient and it may be tempting to go out late as a quick stress release. To those not as close to me, I may look like I am just having fun. However, good friends and family especially start to notice my behaviour becoming a little more over the top than usual. Simultaneously, in the past, I have taken up painting, bought a guitar and a keyboard, and started learning French.

Even though the warning signs start to become obvious during this hypomanic lead-up, I believe it is too late at this stage to arrest the process. It is far earlier that the much more subtle signs, such as irritability, appear. Detective skills need to emerge. It is difficult sometimes to look through the magnifying glass at myself, and this is when the value of carer figures becomes obvious. (121)

Episodes can be sparked off, or made worse, by a combination of stresses. Thus, for example, a wedding is the cause for celebration and excitement. However, follow this stimulation with further stressors (stressors can be both good and bad events) such as bad news about a loved family friend, and then a busy business trip or holiday away, and the combination will be potent fuel to fan a fire of energy and inspiration. I find

I can manage, for example, two stressors, but a third is often the 'last straw'. Other triggers for me can include over-the-counter medications for cold or flu, the time of the year and, of course, the bipolar's bugbear: sleep disruption. I go very easy on alcohol and caffeine, too. (187)

MANIA—mental alertness not in alignment

I have identified the following warning signs and written them into a contract with my counsellor. Sometimes I experience these singly, sometimes as a cluster.

- Rapid thoughts. Everyone else seems on 'go slow'!
- Fingers, or a finger on my right hand, moving spasmodically
- Talking loudly, saying inappropriate things, butting into conversations (it's all about me)
- Paranoia—becoming overly sensitive and emotional
- Starting many projects at the same time
- Wide pupils
- Getting irritable quickly, for no apparent reason
- Developing a very short attention span, and difficulty concentrating
- Needing less sleep
- Thinking other drivers are in competition with me, and driving fast
- Spending even more on gourmet food in the supermarket.

To slow down, I read the contract, and because of what I have written it tells me to:

- Talk to my fiancée or ring my friends—talking about it out loud makes everything more real
- Stay away from busy social situations

- Minimise stimulation and background noise
- Remove the money and credit cards from my wallet
- Write down my thoughts, write poetry
- Avoid caffeine
- Go to bed early—even if I can't sleep, I tell myself it's OK, I'm still lying there relaxing
- Think about something else and take the dog for a walk
- Go to the beach or be near water
- Call my counsellor
- Find an outlet in writing—if it's 'creative' it's OK, if it degenerates into 'Lists' then I stop! (53)

My Bipolar's Hitchhiker's Guide to the Galaxy

What I like to call my 'Bipolar's Hitchhiker's Guide to the Galaxy' is my own compilation of a survival guide to prepare against extreme mood changes. It has three main components:

- Know your triggers
- Devise your strategies, and
- Maintain your inspiration.

I use my Guide as a shield to combat the rapid incline into a manic state. It has repeatedly been effective for me. Each of us have individualised 'red flag' triggers that can alert us that the tornado of mania is well on its way. Not having a regular sleep schedule, misusing alcohol or drugs, stopping your medicine, seasonal changes, disagreements with family or friends, problems at work, or the death of a loved one. It is imperative to know your own red flags or triggers and choose to take action early before an upward spiral takes hold and mania sweeps you away on its turbulent ride to being unwell. Of course, we can't avoid life's stressors, but at least we can be somewhat prepared when facing them.

All of these triggers I've had. Most times these triggers have left me so manic that I have been hospitalised. Most of those times I was scheduled and most times I was close to life-threatening events. The scares and hardships I have given myself and the pain of putting myself back together after a manic bout means that I now choose to avoid these triggers and be aware of early warning signs to combat heading into an uncontrollable manic state. I believe that the behaviours we experience when manic are directly linked to the mania and that they are therefore manageable and not just inherent behaviours of oneself.

Regulating your moods seems to be a key ingredient in protecting oneself against going too far into the manic phase. Once things are seeming the slightest bit irregular in behaviour (like unsettled sleep, racing thoughts), those individualised warning signs that deep down we all know too well, then we have a choice to act to douse them or to continue on the up, up and away into mania.

Seeking the best advice and support for you is vital for maintaining the best health. Find specialists, friends and family who become your confidants, your therapeutic listeners and who are proactive in respecting your sense of self and judgement. This is your journey, it comes from behind your eyes, so you are the platform and they can be the stilts that hold you up when things become shaky.

It is documented to keep as healthy as possible to maintain mood stability. Exercise, healthy diet, routine and reduction or cessation of alcohol. The use of illicit drugs is a big 'no-no'. My hand is raised, I can certainly vouch for the effectiveness of such methods. Helpful techniques to dampen the highs include meditation and relaxation, as well as activity and social interaction to avoid isolation.

If you can look into yourself and know what gives you peace and enjoyment and makes you feel good about life, it is important to give yourself this gift. Create a life that's going to be good for you, not harmful. A social worker once said to me, 'Look after yourself as you would a pot plant or a pet, keep it well, happy and loved.' I've always remembered that analogy. (159)

. . . .

IN THE SPOTLIGHT
Acting on early warning signs

- Pre-emptive strategies for walking the fine line to avoid bipolar mood swings include protecting the sleep–wake cycle (as sleep disruption is both a contributor to and a consequence of bipolar mood swings) and imposing steady routines. Also keeping a mood chart can help identify the build-up of a mood swing.
- Triggers that can put a person at risk of an episode include: skipping medication, stress and frustration at home and work, life changes and taking drugs and alcohol—or other stimulants such as cough suppressants or too much coffee. Late nights or changes to circadian (body clock) rhythms can also be a stress. In this regard, the onset of spring is a trigger for many, as is changing work shifts or overseas travel.
- Individualised 'relapse signatures' can be collated from each episode to help the person with bipolar disorder and others

involved in their care to recognise the triggers and early warning signs of an impending high (or low). Many signatures noted by our writers are well-recognised: sleep changes, irritability, flighty or obsessive ideas, mysticism and profound and synchronic ideas, changed eating habits, being intrusive or paranoid, multi-tasking (in talk and at work), increased libido, driving faster and spending more.

- Other early warning signs acknowledged by our writers have either not been previously described or are rarely noted. These include feeling a quiver or glow or flame, hand and body tremors, cleaning during the night, excessive washing, increased heart rate, generalised itch, increased metabolism and more frequent bowel movements.

- If a person with bipolar disorder is faced with unavoidable life and work changes, then strategies for normalising sleep as well as self-calming techniques such as meditation and exercise are often useful remedies.

- In addition to identifying their own 'relapse signatures' and putting in place their own self-management strategies, it is also useful for the individual with bipolar disorder to appoint people that they respect to act as their 'outside insight'—to watch over them at home and work. The loss of insight characteristic of bipolar disorder means that the person affected may not be aware that they've been captured by a high or a low. Thus, they may benefit from appointing an assertive person who will firmly challenge their manic confidence that there is nothing wrong!

· ·

7. The show must go on
Acceptance of bipolar disorder

Through acceptance some peace can be found. Acceptance
is simply part of bipolar disorder. I must move on, taking it in
my stride. (26)

Acceptance of my illness has contributed to me being as well
as I can be. This is because accepting what I have allows me to
acknowledge the illness and makes me responsible in caring
for myself as best I can. (93)

This chapter presents some tricks to the successful management of
bipolar disorder: acceptance that there is a problem, awareness of the
early warning signs of an impending episode, and assertive back-up
by family and friends, together with a 'wellbeing plan', a document
written by the individual when well and shared with trusted others
who will help them to manage the disorder should they become too
unwell to manage their own treatment.

The following passages suggest that the writers were (ultimately!)
grateful to be rescued from themselves when they were in the grip

of a mood swing. This enabled them to catch up with themselves and then shape their own strategies, which included medication and putting in place the 'outside insight' provided by sympathetic and informed relatives, friends and health professionals.

My world was happening in technicolour, brilliant intense colours, feelings and movements. I drove recklessly, I spent recklessly, I engaged in reckless relationships and I treated my friends recklessly. Nothing mattered except the ongoing pursuit of happiness.

Finally, my family intervened. Visits from friends were supervised; I was never allowed out of the sight of a family member or a friend. Visits to the doctor were almost daily as we struggled to manage the rapid cycling of the disorder. However, I became addicted to the highs and stopped taking my medication; I felt that I could control the highs and enjoy the fun without medication. I lied to everyone, including the psychiatrist. Back to square one. Only with the love and support of my family was I kept out of hospital.

I was told that the longer I left the highs untreated, and the more I experienced the rapid-cycling effects, the more difficult it would be to treat the disorder in the future, and the worse the effect of this disruption on my life would be. I like working, I like being independent, I like living on my own, I like to be able to have fantastic holidays . . . Would I sacrifice this for the ultimate shame that the end of the manic episode brings? The disruption to my whole life? To relationships? To friendships? (105)

I have spent a great deal of time 'analysing' the patterns of my life; not in a scientific way, it doesn't work like that, but so that I know where I am headed and am able to manage this to the best of my ability. There are times when I wish I could wake up and not be affected at all, that my life could somehow be so 'normal', but I realise I must live with my reality. That reality being that I do suffer from mental illness, bipolar disorder. I feel I have from such a young age—and now I realise that the only thing that can change is my capacity to manage this reality. I believe my capacity has and continues to change. I rely on this to move from strength to strength in order to reach my full potential. My articulation of this experience is just that— mine—and in no way undermines any others' experience. It is my attempt to feel deeply and live courageously and have ownership over my life and illness. **(44)**

Soothing and warding off the beast, the manic, energised 'high' of bipolar disorder, has been—and continues to be—no easy task for me. Despite learning all that I can about it in my attempts to understand its peculiarities and complexities, its seductive and potentially lethal powers, I know I can never completely harness and tame it. So, at best, I implement strategies to live with, and protect myself from, it.

Psychotherapy has helped me to understand that the highs of bipolar disorder are caused by genetic, biochemical and life event factors, and not by any weakness of character on my part. I believe now that the only way to live with the illness, rather than helplessly suffer from it, is to be very vigilant and religious with taking my medication and implementing other preventative strategies.

Avoidance of the build-up of stressful workplace and family situations that can trigger manic highs and sticking to regular daily routines involving exercise, healthy diet and stable sleep schedules help to stave off the beast, or at least to curb its intensity. I must be ever vigilant with alcohol: it's a major ongoing battle for me. I must carefully monitor and control its consumption, since it can have the effect of pouring fuel on the already smouldering beginnings of an elevated mood.

Like alcohol consumption, excessive caffeine can also have this effect by causing sleep disturbance, thereby exacerbating my mood problems, particularly if I am already stressed and not getting enough regular, quality sleep. To help ensure a good night's sleep, I try not to drink coffee after 4 p.m. and to limit alcohol to one or two glasses of wine with dinner. (41)

All you need is love, sleep, drugs and . . .

High now, so I could write all night. I can write and think more quickly than 99 per cent of the population when I'm feeling like this. How long have I been writing about being bipolar? First diagnosis of mental illness would be thirty years ago. Remember the shrink's face . . . Bedside manner of a Dalek!

Do I have a strategy? Well, **I note sleeping patterns**. I monitor my sleep. I never allow myself the luxury of remaining awake for a 24-hour period. My bare minimum is five hours, or I go back to taking a prescribed sleeping tablet. If I have to take it every night, I do. I refuse to worry about developing dependency because after all these years I know that after a week or so I won't need them anymore.

I keep a journal though I write mostly while 'Down'. When High, I've too many other things to do! When I re-read my journal when I'm starting a High, it reminds me to stay on track, or I'll end up feeling like . . .

Paragraph from May: 'I gave up trying to change the world because it was killing me. I spend a lot of time trying to work out ways to kill myself without it looking like suicide. I don't want my family to know. It always passes, yes, but when it is in the present it is hard to put to one side. I've contemplated many kinds of ways. I am such a wimp, I would probably mess things up. And I worry about repercussions for the person who would find me. Sometimes I resent the people I love because I can't kill myself because they will feel bad. The bastards.' Well, that little exercise worked! Shoot! I don't want to go back there again. That depression was three months? Six months? Felt like years at the time.

What else? **I try to focus**. I'm so easily distracted when High. My action lists help. For just that day, or even for the hour, lists can help me focus and 'appear sane'. So there are little lists stuck everywhere! I'm artistic. Get over it. My 'Five' list really helps. Five things to remember before I shut the front door: keys, money, phone, prescribed drugs and lipstick!

Remember the struggle is lifelong. Highs can be good, how else would I be deemed an awesome thinker who has 'achieved so much in such a short life'—as said to me frequently by people who achieve far more. A High gives me confidence to be me. I'm not always sure when High is real. Who really knows? BUT letting High take over can be a disaster financially, physically and mentally. I recall buying a brand-new piano with a credit card when I was already terribly in debt, and once I hired heaps of recording equipment that I had no idea how to operate! My struggle to avoid hospital is worse than climbing Mt Snowdon in a blizzard (which I actually did once). Sometimes High is like a descent of an endless rollercoaster. You can't escape. It's hard to focus then on staying sane. But I do it, don't I?

Dealing with temptation to give in to High! Feels great to finally laugh out loud again! After those Down months,

I don't want to make myself sleep, don't want to stop having fun, or working on that painting, story or song just to go to bed! I'm entitled to a little fun, surely? But the pragmatic boring-old-fart in me sets the alarm clock, and takes that sleeping pill regardless. (Resent this—'cos 'girls just wanna have fun'.)

Other People. Bloody other people! It's so frustrating when there's so few around with perception to comprehend my magnificent ideas and the patience to listen. Yes, trusted friends and family are now more aware of the warning signs. I finally got around to getting leaflets on bipolar for them. I gave one to J. She was cool. I'm pissed that my family hadn't bothered to get information themselves but maybe they did. I'm working harder on helping them bring my attention to the fact that I'm becoming 'ill'. 'Perhaps you really don't need to use your credit cards to hire a stretch limo, dear sister.' I must tell them it's OK to tell me when I'm speaking more rapidly than normal (actually, it pisses me off when people say that, but it IS helpful).

Enablers on the road to High. You-know-who-they-are: people (and situations) that speed up High. Last week I had to tell M. that I couldn't handle an evening with all those arty academics, it was too much. He was really annoyed. He's got to learn that I have to put my health first or he has to get out of my life. I need 'me' time—times! I need to be alone. I have to be alone, like he needs his piano.

Happy or High? Differentiating between 'normal' happy times and the path to a manic episode? Thank God for my psychiatrist. A genius, not bipolar, I presume. I still hate that she has a family, other patients and a life outside my sessions with her.

Genius Club 'A' list. My mental list of artists, writers and other interesting humans who have been 'outed' as bipolar! Always helps remind me that it is not all hell and in some ways I'm in good company! 'A' list Genius Club folk have times for genius, we can't always tell the genuine act from the imaginary, but the reader would probably know that already? Occasionally the problem is lack of perception on the part of rest-of-world. Majority rules when it comes to declaring someone insane.

The boring stuff: medication and exercise. It's like cleaning your teeth. You HAVE to do it. I assert the right to detest the meds that make me an emotional zombie. Wow, eighteen years since I was correctly diagnosed and prescribed loathsome lithium which transformed me for a while from a lively, artistic maniac into a person with a personality akin to a grey lump of plastic. Able to function, most of the time now, without those drugs. Yes! Still use antidepressants, benzodiazepines and mood stabilisers when I need them. I work hard not to get to the state where I have to take them. Every time I take them, I go up a dress size. Now six sizes bigger than when I was first prescribed lithium. Annoying, as I was particularly, awesomely sexy! Most people taking these drugs don't end up as big as me though, the bastards.

Exercise helps my brain if I can do it alone. It's meditation.

Plan for winter! Extremely tempting to let High take over, but, life is too, too short to spend three months alone in the deep gorge of depression that always follows High. I have longer periods between having to take mood stabilisers. Management strategy must be working. Down comes after High. It's like a London winter; there is nothing good about it. See above under 'May' for further clarification about how bad Down is.

   Count blessings. Remind myself that good things can come out of life with bipolar. I'm lucky to have access to good mental health services and affordable medication, when half the world has no clean water. And my family and (most of) my friends still speak to me. (130)

After acceptance of the illness, individuals with bipolar disorder have a greater capacity to learn what safeguards to put into place, pre-emptively or following onset of early warning signs—so that an episode can be averted. Early intervention can lead to successful accommodation of the disorder. The wellbeing plan can be of immense help in this regard in providing a safety net (see Appendix 2).

   I have been formed and shaped by mania. I can never stop the eruptions but I can avoid getting burnt. Overall the greatest key to achieving stability has been my mind shift. I no longer think of myself as 'ill', just different from the majority of people, and with different needs. This makes me neither inferior nor superior. I no longer seek a 'cure', but continue to research and explore new ways of living in harmony with my natural mind. (65)

   I have found regular attendance at a weekly mutual self-help group good for a better comprehension of my own ways of thinking. I have found the group method and the program and interaction with fellow group members to be an excellent two-hour 'investment' each week in understanding, regulating and accepting my own feelings, no matter how high, low or in-between. This organisation has taught me that 'feelings are not facts' and that they can be stirred as much by imagined as by real causes. Significantly, feelings are good servants, still better friends, but terrible masters. Any feeling, no matter how elevated or beautiful in itself, if not controlled, can unhinge my mind and disorganise my life.

The first step was that we admitted that we were inadequate or maladjusted in life. I found this step to be very liberating because it meant I no longer had to be perfect, or know all the answers all the time. If 'admitting' you are inadequate or maladjusted seems too big a step to take, I challenge you to look around and point to anyone you know who is *not* inadequate or maladjusted in some way, at least at some point in their life! In my mind, it is part of the human condition that we are simple, fragile and fallible human beings, and it is on that level that we connect best and most compassionately with each other.

My own prescription for managing a high? Always test your thoughts against trusted others. Another piece of wisdom from my support group is 'Those that matter don't mind, and those that mind, don't matter'. (166)

Three understandings

Everything races and everything glows. My body is alive and alight. Energy explodes with a power that pounds. Nothing can hold it, squash it or stop it. I stride along linoleum corridors, across pathways and lawns, my bare feet skimming and thumping. The words tumble and burble, but cannot keep pace with the thoughts that race. Talk, laughter, eye-glinting talk. It's a film, and I'm the star. I bounce, laugh and dance on my stage: flirting, flying, bursting . . . skimming through the blur of light. I dance, turn, twist, flick, bounce and ping . . .

> *I'm on fire. I spin through my manic days, leaving all behind*
> *and beneath me as everything races, and as everything glows.*
> [Personal diary, 1999]

This is the magic of the manic phase of bipolar disorder. It
doesn't sound too bad, does it? To have that sort of energy
and elation, and to delight in a world filled with colour,
could well be something to envy and emulate. And there, of
course, lies the danger. The magic of the high is beguiling;
it's seductive. For me, the first step in managing the highs
of bipolar disorder was to admit just how magical this stage
of the illness feels. Only then could I move to honestly
determining that I did not want to go there; I realised that it is
not worth it, and that I'd do everything possible to avoid it.

    This determination to shun the high comes from **three
key understandings**. The **first** is the knowledge of the flip
side: the life-sapping depression that is the inevitable part of
the deal. Recalling the experiences of the low is more than
salutary:

> *I lie, curled on my side, my legs bent. My head is lead-*
> *weighted, my cheek stuck to the vinyl bench. Lank strands of*
> *hair hang between my fingers. I cannot move. I am filled with*
> *fear, of everything. I lie there, frightened and dull-eyed. I sit*
> *up, as slowly as mud, and stare. I twist my body as though it*
> *might break, and lower myself down. I curl my body, legs bent*
> *I face the wall, my cheek stuck to the hard vinyl, and touch a*
> *strand of lank hair.* [Personal diary, 1999]

I remember this and shudder. I will do whatever it takes to
ward off the months of not being able to sleep, eat, laugh or
think, or make a decision about anything; months of needing

constant reassurance about everything, from everyone. The hideous, life-sapping misery of the black dog cautions against the temptation of the high.

The **second understanding** is admitting that the fruits of the high are not what they seem. The elevated state brings surges of apparently brilliant ideas: for saving the world or for getting enormously rich and famous, and, for me, creativity flows with outpourings of apparently inspired writing. Most people know the experience: the idea that comes with a rush in the middle of the night but looks very ordinary, or just foolish, in the morning. A magnification of this is reading what I've created when manic, in the light of the reality that comes once the episode is past. If there was one small window when the mania inspired the creative juices, there's a good chance the creativity would have happened anyway— and the risk isn't worth it.

The **third understanding** moves attention away from the self, to others—to the partner, family and friends—who become caught in the whirling and the misery of the illness. Understanding what they suffer while I am dancing in my own manic world, and when I'm splayed out, lifeless and filled with fear, is essential to honestly confronting the devil that's to be being dealt with. While the egocentric nature of the illness makes it difficult for the sufferer to have empathy for those who are mustering all of their patience, forbearance and love to see it through, you must do so. You must remind yourself of what it does to them, and that you do not want them to go through it on your behalf.

This honest confrontation, and these genuine deter- minations, can be made because of the episodic nature of the bipolar condition. Thankfully there are periods of respite, of months—or years—of wellness, of clear-headedness and rational thinking, of a healthy range of moods, in between episodes. During these times I must put my pride to one side and admit that, if or when the next episode hits, I will not be the person best equipped to make decisions. During these intervals I must put things in order so that I have the best chance for episode-free living, and to give myself, and those around me, the best chance of dealing with storms when they do hit.

Warts-and-all self-knowledge means that I know precisely how I feel, and how I act during both the mania and the depression. I know that once that high takes hold, my judgement will be impaired. I will do diabolical things and the implications will be dire. Therefore, I must be prepared to allow others to take control. Between episodes I am an intelligent, independent and clear-sighted woman. I don't relish the idea of handing authority over myself to anybody. But, I know that if I allow myself to go high, I'm no longer this intelligent, independent and clear-sighted woman. Once my devil takes over, I cannot be trusted. (43)

While there's no doubting the value of a wellbeing plan, individuals can be too careful in crafting a routine. If the routine is too stern, ascetic or boring, then the temptation to go with a mood lift is very strong and there may be self-sabotage. So it's essential to create a lifestyle that allows some excitement and scope for creativity. As shown in the stories below, each person needs to find a shape for their life that gives them the best possible satisfaction and fulfilment.

Everyone is different. Just as every fingerprint is unique, so is each individual's bipolar disorder. I don't claim to know about bipolar disorder in general: all I can talk about is my version and the things that work for me. We each have to continue to work on our own strategies. (38)

Become familiar with the alertness that can be part of the bipolar disorder. It can be frightening to be, or feel, so alert that other people actually seem mentally sluggish. An understanding of this experience can go a long way to keeping the sufferer in a calm and composed state. What is also very useful to manage highs is to do activities that are 'naturally' elevating. Supplant the desire for a high with more appropriate mental stimulation; read, paint, write poetry, walk, cook and do crafts. (2)

I think every bipolar sufferer is aware of changes in themselves with the onset of mania. However, they usually lack the insight to realise that they are getting ill and instead revel in the symptoms and do not want to 'come down'. This failure blinds the person to the markers. There is no Rubicon on the road to mania. With respect to my last episode, all the warning signs were there and I also heard voices. While the voices were more exultant than persecutory, they were strange enough to make me realise that I was getting ill. (52)

Acceptance

I have a truly manic laugh. It embarrasses my children and deafens my friends. I convulse with laughter at the oddest times, and in inappropriate places. Yet I know that it is a primary indicator of my wellbeing—if my sense of humour (however strange) is operating, my life is manageable.

Imagine a chaotic emergency room. I have been lying on a bed for four hours in savage pain while a harassed registrar attempts to establish its cause. At fifteen-minute intervals a nurse asks me to quantify the pain between 1 and 10. I am either in floods of tears about the welfare of my children or earnestly telling the doctor the pain is not psychosomatic. The registrar constantly tells me he believes the pain is of gastric origin and the nurses keep reassuring me that a friend has the children in hand. Finally, a diagnosis of pancreatitis is made and admission deemed necessary: minutes later my six-foot-plus son, in full school uniform, lopes in, hurls his backpack under a bed, drapes himself over a chair and asks, 'What's the verdict, Mum?' I glance over at the nurses' bay and wonder why they all look completely pole-axed. As my teenage daughter comes in, I realise why everyone is astonished. I had been stacking on such a turn about the children, people assumed they were very young, and then, despite the pain, I laughed. I still think I was lucky to have been admitted to a general ward and not the psychiatric unit.

And that, to a large extent, is how I manage the rollercoaster of bipolar disorder. No matter how *grim* the circumstances, how severe the crisis, if there is an element of farce, life is manageable. I am a fifty-one-year-old single mother of two teenagers, wholly dependent on the generosity of the taxpayer and the gracious help of family and friends. I have been a recovering alcoholic for nearly nineteen years and have the employment skills of a moribund seagull. *But*, as I lurch from one crisis to the next, if I can tip the story on its head and share the funny side then I can stay sane.

I didn't get sane until I got sober and turned back to God. I was diagnosed with cyclothymia at seventeen but didn't have a psychotic episode until I was twenty-eight when my first marriage broke down. I used alcohol to manage my mood swings from my adolescence and, when first introduced to the psychiatric system, only stopped during hospitalisations. At thirty-one, I had an epiphany and decided that a life governed only by a desire to know where my next drink was coming from was not worth living. So I hopped on a plane from Adelaide to Sydney intent on jumping off The Gap [an infamous place for suicides]. Instead I ended up in a rehab unit, then a psychiatric hospital and started to get well.

Acceptance of my illness heralded the start of my recovery: I also had to accept that I was an alcoholic and was hugely resentful that I had to contend with both. Honesty is the cornerstone of the AA [Alcoholics Anonymous] program and it has stood me in good stead managing bipolar disorder. I am fully aware that but for the grace of God I would have been successful in one of my attempts to dispatch myself to the hereafter.

A prayer closes every AA meeting: 'God grant me the serenity to accept the things I cannot change, courage to change the things I can and the wisdom to know the difference.' Therein lies the rub—the wisdom to know the difference. Wisdom is not a virtue I claim to possess, but I have used the Serenity Prayer as a mantra for years, alongside 'Feelings aren't Facts'. I have a network of professionals, church fellowship and family who accept me as I am, provide me with priceless support and guidance, and enable me to keep myself and the children safe.

There is a dichotomy inherent to mental disorders. In order to remain sane and functioning, I need to interact with the outside world; but in order to gauge my sanity, I have to navel-gaze on a daily basis. It is all too easy to isolate, but my head dreams up unlikely scenarios within the hour. If the children's schools leave a phone message without explanation, I will be planning a funeral until I discover that I have forgotten to sign an excursion note. I am a die-hard proponent of catastrophic thinking and have learnt *always* to establish the facts quickly.

Poverty is another useful factor in my quest for sanity. It is very difficult to stay locked in my head if I don't know where the next meal is coming from. Children are very grounding— their needs are constant (they just change in nature as they get older). My psychiatrist has always maintained that my maternal instinct is stronger than my insanity and for that I thank the Lord. I must confess, the household is fairly erratic—consistency makes very rare appearances; my housekeeping skills are nonexistent; and the children can distract me off-task in a nanosecond.

Which brings me to anger management (vital in a family comprised of a menopausal mother and two adolescents— hormones ping off the walls). I have a feral temper and no impulse control. When the children were little, I instituted a strategy whereby once I had regained control (usually not having the faintest idea what I had said), each of them had to tell me if I had said anything that had really hurt, and we worked through it. I apologise a lot; the apology I consider one of the most useful parenting tools in existence. My children have always been aware of my bipolar disorder and my alcoholism. (I never had the option of anonymity—when the children were little they would approach drunks on trains and say, 'My mum can help you, she's an alcoholic', or tell teachers, 'Mum's a bit crazy in the head this week.'

Change triggers mood swings for me. I loathe change—I get miffed when the brand of coffee I buy changes its label. Irrespective of the trigger, if my sleeping or eating patterns change, I become wary. I'm an insomniac at the best of times, with decades of watching black and white movies on the ABC under my belt, so I'm careful to count how much sleep I'm getting in any one week. I try not to get resentful if I cannot sleep as I find frustration generates mania all by itself. I listen to music (not heavy metal), iron clothes, talk to the cat or get in the bath. Actually, hot baths are my universal panacea— they instantly defuse my temper. If the household is in an uproar, I repair to the bath and the children vanish to their bedrooms.

If I start forgetting to eat (relatively difficult with two teenagers), I will go and buy food I really love. If I start forgetting my medication, I enlist the help of the children. Not always a successful strategy—at the end of some very long days during which I have behaved like Attila the Hun, there will be a plaintive cry of 'Didn't it occur to anyone that I hadn't taken my meds?'

Most importantly, I stop. I subdue the urge to give in to my virulent telephone mania (it took me years to stop myself from ringing people in the middle of the night). I quell the insistent conviction that I have the answer to everyone's problems. I usually have the self-awareness to ring my psychiatrist for an urgent appointment, but the request is peremptory. Fortunately for me, her response is always swift; it may involve increased medication, but not the retribution I deserve for the rudeness my mania is inclined to unleash.

I manage my life, not just my bipolar disorder. My mood swings are so fundamental to my everyday existence that

I find it difficult to isolate a particular facet. Then again, it might just be a reflection of my life-long habit of not properly addressing the question! (154)

One of my strategies for 'red' days is to be more aware and attentive to the needs of my body, such as stopping to eat, self-imposing bed times, and reminding myself that if I expend all my energy today, there will be consequences later. Skipping meals and not getting enough sleep are common denominators of red days; I am too frenzied to eat or sleep and overlook the basic needs of fuel and rest.

Accepting the fact that this is how I am, that this is my natural flow and what makes me uniquely *me* seems to be the most successful approach so far. (142)

Fighting the good fight

The majority of my adult life could best be described as reckless, capricious and chaotic. I could never keep jobs very long, as the people around me simply could not deal with my erratic behaviour. Almost every day I would feel an intense restlessness and an incessant need to keep moving as if I were running from a ruthless pursuer. I rarely had a cent to my name, spending my entire pay cheque on alcohol, cigarettes and a vast array of junk I didn't need. I distanced myself from my family, for, through the distorted logic of my tormented mind, I blamed them for my unstable and anarchic circumstances. For a five-year period in the nineties, I made no contact with them at all. When I look back at that time,

I realise that I was truly a lost soul and that I had caused pain and despair to so many who did not deserve it. What I didn't know, however, was why I was behaving in this way. The answer was not to come until many years later.

In 2003, after a massive mental and emotional breakdown, I wound up in a psychiatrist's office. After a period of testing, he handed down his verdict. The high state that had plagued me for the majority of my life had a name—Manic Depressive Illness, or 'bipolar disorder' as he coined it. I didn't believe him of course, and left with no intention of returning. However, driven by my natural curiosity, I reflected on my past and read widely about the illness over the weeks to follow. All the pieces fell into place. As much as I did not wish to believe the diagnosis, it explained the tumultuous circumstances of my life perfectly. It was then that I became angry. Very angry! I felt that I had been robbed of almost twenty years of my life because of an accursed disorder I was completely unaware of. I thought of all the things I had wanted to achieve in my life but simply couldn't because they lay behind an invisible barrier: they were so tantalisingly close, but so impossibly far. Then and there I decided that this illness was no longer going to control me, rob me, deceive me or deny me the goals I believed I deserved. I returned to the psychiatrist and the journey towards a new life began with the first critical step—understanding the illness.

Within the context of moving towards recovery and control, it was the mania (as opposed to the depression) that I targeted most aggressively. It was the manic phase of the illness that had dictated the decisions that had led me astray over the preceding decades. The first thing I had to accept was that mania is a false prophet that specialises in mental distortion. Mania is a shadow that follows me everywhere, promising great rewards but delivering only disaster. I cannot outrun it, I cannot destroy it. I live with the melancholy fact that sooner or later, the manic shadow will reach into my mind and my soul and take control. I also realise that all I can do from now until the moment I take my last breath is face my manic opponent with total determination to 'fight the good fight'. My resolve in this must remain unwavering for, day in and day out, I must wage this battle against my insidious enemy, knowing that I will not win every battle, but by living a life of peace, happiness and quality, I will have won the war. In fact, I find that it helps to think about one's struggle with mania as a war. And in any good war, one needs an array of sound battle tactics. With this in mind, I will explain to you a set of strategies I loosely refer to as my 'self-defence' system against mania.

Strategy 1: Weaken the disorder through constant bombardment

By this I mean hit the manic-depressive beast day in and day out with medication and therapy. Every day, at the same time, I take my combination of mood stabilisers—without fail. As a fail-safe, my wife checks that I have taken them, and if not, orders me to go and do so immediately. I have discovered through harsh experience in the past that going on and off the meds intermittently can have consequences worse that the mania itself. So I must keep up with the meds, for they weaken the bipolar enemy, making it harder for it to attack and seize me in its grip.

In addition to meds, good therapy weakens the illness even further. However, this only works if you have a good psychiatrist treating you. The psychiatrist I have now is wonderful. In addition to the medications he prescribes, he carries out extensive therapy with me, discussing tools, techniques and strategies I can apply to manage my condition and live a relatively normal life. In combination, therefore, the appropriate mix of medications combined with therapy provided by a good psychiatrist who takes a holistic view of treatment weakens the effects of bipolar disorder, making it far more difficult for it to get its hooks into me.

Strategy 2: Deny the disorder the triggers it depends upon to initiate an attack

Just as a fire will struggle to burn due to a lack of fuel to consume, the manic phase finds it very hard to get its way when denied the triggers it requires to gain momentum. My manic triggers are work- and home-related stress, the consumption of stimulants, and post-depression 'rebound'. I find physical exercise to be the most effective way to keep my stress levels low and hence minimise the probability of having a stress-induced episode of mania. I do a 3-kilometre walk twice a week and hit the gym for gentle weight training three times a week. Top this off with Aikido (a martial art) training twice a week and I find that stress-induced manic episodes will occur only three or four times a year. As for the stimulants, well, abstinence is the best defence here. I will only reach for coffee or a so-called 'smart drink' when I'm absolutely desperate to keep humming along, otherwise I try to restrict myself to no more than one beverage a day. As for post-depression rebound, it appears that this is the only trigger I cannot control.

Strategy 3: Employ self-defence strategies when mania is brewing or already upon me

And then there are those times when mania gets me regardless of all the steps I have taken to prevent it. When this happens, the most important thing I must do is recognise that it has taken hold of me. In my case, the warning signs include miscues in speech and writing, surges in creativity, diminished empathy, thoughts of my own death, and difficulty with sleep. Once recognised, I implement a four-step approach to minimise its impact. I describe this approach as isolation, deferment, mental occupation and sleep.

Isolation is where I put myself in a place where I can't cause any damage by what I say and what I decide to do. This fortress of solitude is the master bedroom at home, where I have television, internet and a library. As soon as I realise that I am going under, or am about to go under, this is where I go—and stay—until the episode has passed.

Deferment means that I do not make any critical decisions whilst in the manic state, regardless of whether they pertain to my profession, my home life or my finances. This is because I know that, in all likelihood, I will severely regret these decisions later.

Mental occupation is a technique which involves keeping my mind occupied with simple, yet absorbing, tasks while I am under mania's influence. I read books, watch television and surf the internet. These things all occupy the time nicely as I wait for the episode to pass.

Sleep, in my experience, breaks the manic episode quite nicely, so a couple of good nights' sleep is my fourth strategy for damage control. To ensure that I do sleep, I take sleeping tablets as prescribed by my psychiatrist. Sometimes, just one night's sleep will do the trick.

In conclusion, let me say that there is nothing 'genuinely' positive about mania. It feels good, but it forces you to think, and ultimately to do, things that sooner or later lead to an unhappy life and a non-realisation of your true potential. Recognise mania for what it is—the enemy. And as is the case with any enemy you may face in life, be fully prepared to fight it to the complete extent of your capabilities. Know your enemy, give it no quarter and learn how to fight it when it comes knocking at your mind's door. I wish you well in your battle against this insidious foe and never forget—fight the good fight! (187)

Another valuable back-up is to appoint trusted others to act as your 'outside insight'. These people, an audience of sorts, can tackle a slip into the disorder that the affected individual may be unaware of. Studies have found that a high proportion of people affected with bipolar disorder had no insight into the signs of an encroaching episode, despite the fact that they had been hospitalised in order to receive treatment for the very same symptoms previously. Such findings indicate that many people with more severe manifestations of bipolar disorder lack the ability to recognise that they are ill and in need of medical care.

It is a delicate balance for society to decide when it is justified in curbing the freedom of an individual, determining that they have crossed an invisible line and have become impaired, and a risk to themselves, their reputation and, sometimes, to others. Mental health and associated services generally err on the side of caution before they are prepared to intervene.

Wellness begins here

Firing my psychiatrist was my first step toward wellness. But don't get me wrong. I have nothing against psychiatrists; their work is vital. And yet, it was through a negative experience with a psychiatrist that I took personal responsibility for managing my mania and mastering the principles of wellness.

Bipolar spectrum disorder crashed into my life when I was twenty, and a somewhat successful writer. I'd had a messy break-up with my first boyfriend. Rather than dealing with my feelings, I shoved a cork into the bottle and threw it away, pretending my feelings would vanish. They didn't. Instead, my freelance writing ceased satisfying me. I wanted to be so rich and so successful my boyfriend would come running back. Suddenly I saw how I could turn my writing into a big successful business. A business so big, and so successful, it would take over every other business in the world in the space of two days.

Welcome to the world of mania!

Over several weeks I stopped sleeping, barely ate, and drew a handful of people into my wake. My energy and enthusiasm pulled people towards me like iron filings to a magnet. But after a week of unpaid stretch limousines, and shopping adventures to big stores, but with neither cash nor credit, people pulled away.

I wound up in the local mental health in-patient unit. When I came out of there, my whole world had changed. You could say it had changed because I now carried the stigmata of mental illness. Despite refusing to accept that I *had* a mental illness, during my mania I'd succeeded in destroying the reputation I'd built over years—in only a matter of weeks.

I slipped into a six-month post-psychotic depression. Most painful of all was losing interest in all my regular activities. I could no longer write. When it came to sitting in front of the keyboard or with pen hovering over paper, the 'minutes seemed like hours and the hours seemed like days'.

The hospital ensured that I saw a psychiatrist regularly and I clung to the hope that my psychosis was a one-off and life would return to normal. A year later I was back in hospital—mania again—and the same happened the following year. My life was never going to be the same as it had been before I got sick that first time. And if it wasn't going to be the same, then what hope did I have of being happy?

Then a miracle occurred. A year after my last hospitalisation, I didn't get sick. Nor did I get sick the year after that. I cautiously counted the passing years, too scared to celebrate, fearing if I did that the gods would smite me for my arrogance.

At the end of 2000, my psychiatrist and I faced irreconcilable differences, so I fired him. I put my ongoing care under the charge of my GP. Through a roll of the dice, he'd been studying psychiatry before choosing to become a GP, making him a solid choice. Together, we made the decision to wean me off my medication, as so much time had passed since I'd last been manic and I was coping well.

Six months later, during a period of incredible stress, I was manic again and once again in hospital. Once discharged, I faced for the first time the possibility that this illness was something that would be with me for life. If that was the case, did I want to live this kind of life? Did I want my health and reputation to depend on the fickle gods? Did I want to be locked up? Seeking a better life, I moved interstate.

One of the first challenges I faced was setting up a medical support network. At the least, I needed someone to write scripts for my medication. At the most, I needed someone who would keep me from getting sick.

Joining the local mental health support network, I went to skill-building meetings and for the first time outside of an in-patient setting I spoke to people who had mental illnesses, I played chess in the activities room, and formed friendships—I discovered their library. As a writer, I read more in a week than most people read in a year, and I set about reading everything I could about my illness to learn what I could do to avoid getting sick. This reading led me to the first principle of staying well: **acceptance**.

For the first five years I had the illness, I was in denial. I said to myself, 'I can't really have a mental illness. People like me don't get that.' And because I was in denial, I couldn't do anything to avoid getting sick. After all, you've got to have a problem to be able to fix it, right?

If I accept I have a mental illness, not only does it mean accepting I have a problem. It means I have a problem most people don't understand—that most people are scared of. Heck, it means accepting a problem I don't fully understand that scares *me*. When I accept I have a mental illness, it means saying to myself, 'I'm sick. I'm different.' Accepting I did have a mental illness, and, just as importantly, that this illness would be with me for life, was the bravest choice I've made. Acceptance instantly gives you the power to do something about your problems.

Further reading led me to the second principle: **action**. Some of my reading was about US research which indicated failure of prophylaxis if it was with pharmacotherapy alone. Simply put, relying on meds alone to stay well is unlikely to be successful. What was working well for the majority of people they studied was a therapy called 'Interpersonal and Social Rhythm Therapy', which was based on the idea that regular social routines and stable interpersonal relationships have a proactive effect on mood disorders. Now not only did I know it was possible to *do* something, I had an idea of *what* to do.

To learn how to develop stable relationships, I started seeing a therapist. As for social routines, after a militaristic start where every moment was regimented, I've developed good habits around the time I get up and go to bed, as well as regular meal times and a set time for taking my medication. I've also created rituals to launch me into the day and to help me unwind at its end. Recently I've started paying attention to my diet and the amount of exercise I do. Specific foods have positive and negative effects on my mood, as does regular exercise.

This led to the final principle: **attitude**. Taking responsibility for my mental health finally allowed me to see a pattern. Every year I got sick, I'd focused on not getting sick. Reading self-help literature taught me that you get what you focus on. Because of this focus—sickness—my subconscious obliged me with getting sick. It was only when I shifted my focus to staying well that I began doing just that.

As I write this, it will be six years since I had a manic episode. With the principles of good mental health I've mastered, I'm confident I can stay well indefinitely.

Firing your psychiatrist is *not* your first step towards wellness. Most people with bipolar disorder need their guidance. But you, yourself, can develop the wisdom to manage the highs of bipolar disorder. That wisdom starts with learning the principles of wellness, and ends with practising them every single day. (136)

• •

IN THE SPOTLIGHT
Tactics for improving balance

- Matthew Johnstone—author of *I Had a Black Dog*—argues that we need to get MAD at mood disorders: M = management, A = Acceptance, and D = Discipline (in addressing both medication and self-help strategies).

- The right medication and adherence to it are vital basic maintenance—they provide the platform for the next management components. To help memory, lay out the tablets in a 'dosette' box so that doses and days are clearly visible, take medication at regular times each day, and enlist the help of family or friends to act as a reminder. While medication is necessary, it is usually not sufficient.

- Acceptance and coming to terms with bipolar disorder aids mastery over a disorder that can be unpredictable and which requires vigilant management. Writer 136 detailed a 'Triple A' model (Acceptance, Action and Attitude).

- Those who had developed a successful maintenance plan were consistent in resisting the romantic 'high' sirens, recognising their lethality and that they were in fact 'the enemy', and avoiding the situations and triggers that could 'trip' them into episodes. They put in their own safeguards and enrolled the support of others. They accepted the need for routine and that some of the drills—while boring—were necessary (like brushing your teeth). They did not see themselves as victims, more as 'different' and with the power to do something about their condition. They enrolled other 'troops'—health professionals, family or friends—in their 'war' on the condition.

- Keeping a record of what works, and what doesn't, is usually extremely helpful. Other specific nuances include the bipolar individual making a tape recording of their own voice when they are well, listing whatever they feel may be of practical use in helping to avert a potential high or low. They can play this back when they identify a potential mood swing, and also instruct someone to play it to them if they have started to lose insight into the need for treatment.

• •

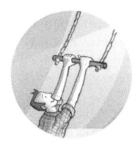

8. Handling the swings
Medication and mood balance

The highs still arrive, but they are hills, not mountains.
The lows allow my mind and body to rest. I have accepted
stability over creativity, the windows are shut. There is
a sadness in an ordinary mind. My children are the main
reason I choose medication, they need stability as much
as I do. (103)

Once the 'penny drops' that the situation is medical and
serious, the person with bipolar disorder is more likely to
cooperate with their psychiatrist at the medication and
consultative level. (2)

When in doubt, take one [in reference to her tablets] (40)

This chapter presents the role of medication in managing bipolar
disorder. While few are pleased to take medication, it is frequently
a 'given' for successful management of bipolar disorder, and is often
needed lifelong. People with bipolar, as revealed in the following

stories, come to prefer taking medication to the alternative—the chaos of unstable moods, especially depressions—although medication side-effects are common and can be troubling.

The following writers counsel that medication provides welcome respite from mood swings and a stable platform that enables some perspective.

What goes down will always go up—and up. I suggested to my doctor that it would be a great idea to work on stabilising my mood at high, and he joked that if that was possible, he'd be taking the medication himself! (9)

When doctors wanted to put me on medication, I was terrified of losing my mania. I didn't know how it would affect my life and my relationship. My boyfriend at the time (now fiancé) never knew what he was coming home to, from cooked themed dinners where I'd dress in costume and have decorated the house, to impromptu picnics, to a spotless (fanatically so) house. These were the *good* surprises he'd walk into. Then there were the days that he didn't enjoy. Hundreds of started and not-finished tasks, mess everywhere, lists and post-it notes all over the house, me having several conversations with him all at once, accusing him of totally impossible things. I wanted the uncontrollable mania to stop—I just didn't know if I would lose the lovable spontaneous ME.

I have since learnt that I am not my bipolar. It does not define me, it is merely a small part of who I am. I have an amazing life. What worked, and works, for me is being on the right medication, learning about my condition, having a fantastic counsellor, and also, I must stress, being 'clean' and sober. How can you fix your mind when you are sending it to places you don't want to go? (53)

Medication and me

In March last year, aged thirty-six, my life seemed to have hit
rock bottom when I became psychotic for the first time in
my life. It took two brief hospital admissions in two months
to reach a proper diagnosis of Bipolar I Disorder. Luckily, the
psychosis only lasted a few days. At first there was the initial
shock of *having* and *accepting* the mental condition, but I was
also *relieved* to finally understand what was going on with me
and that *bipolar is treatable*.

The first important strategy to manage my highs (which
had led to my psychosis) was to use medication. My psychiatrist
put me on 500 mg of sodium valproate twice daily, which
had an almost immediate effect of keeping a lid on the high
moods. I was also weaned off an antipsychotic drug (being
no longer psychotic) which had stopped my periods for four
months due to its hormonal content! Glad to be off it, though
I did need it at the time.

Sodium valproate can also have side-effects. For me there
was a little drowsiness at the start but after a week I felt
pretty normal. Weight gain (from sugar and carbohydrate
craving) was another, and slight hair loss. In the beginning
I was eating badly, but slowly through persistence and
awareness and a healthier diet, my weight returned to
normal. I included daily gentle exercises (walking, yoga,
Pilates, and salsa dancing).

I had been noticing my hair lightly moulting so, after ten
months, my psychiatrist has brought down my drug dose. So
far, so good. Nevertheless, I think I can handle a few less hairs
in my life more than another psychotic experience!

There are various medications out there for bipolar

sufferers and some work better than others depending on the individual's response. Finding the right type and dosage can sometimes be a matter of trial and error and can take time.

At the start of my recovery I was apprehensive to get too excited for fear of tipping into mania, but since then I have learned to trust my medication and just live my life. After hospital I was homeless so I searched for a place that was peaceful, safe and inspiring to walk, with plenty of fresh air—and I needed to live alone. Hence, and fortunately straightaway, I found the perfect granny flat close to the ocean. Also finances needed to be sorted out with social services as I was in no shape to work. It's been almost a year and only NOW I feel that I could tackle some casual work but there is no pressure! I've learned that the recovery process can be very slow and to take it one day at a time.

Using the internet and reading books and autobiographies on bipolar disorder really helped me gain wisdom on managing the highs. I found various books in my local and city libraries as well as free internet access on their computers. The most common advice I noticed was the importance to: **STAY ON THE MEDICATION EVEN IF YOU FEEL BETTER!** I've often felt totally cured until I have a really bad day. Usually a small dose of depression is a gentle reminder that I have some way to go yet!

I've been a professional musician/singer/songwriter for the last eighteen years and before my manic episode had composed many songs. Some evolved from emotionally intense and (most likely) hypomanic states of mind. Still, I wrote my first song recently (ten months after hospitalisation) in a very calm manner. Since being on medication, too, I've noticed a lot more clarity and focus and realism with the creative process of my music.

There were moments I spent in the state of mania that were quite blissful where I felt so connected with the earth and evolved and knowledgeable, and not really needing to be in a human form. The only problem was—it took a miserable three to four days of not being able to sleep, nightmares, stress, despair, exhaustion and suicidal depression to get me there! I can remember times of mania when I'd talked to my friends with such loud conviction and confidence that after a while my brain just simply physically hurt! Hence, I believe from my experience that creative surges from elevation do ultimately lead to burn-out. It isn't a wonder why people who are manic, and untreated, self-medicate with alcohol or any drug to avoid the burn-out feeling. It's just too taxing on the body! (134)

The individual needs to search for a supportive general practitioner and, usually, a psychiatrist with whom they feel comfortable. An open and sympathetic relationship with medical help is central to good back-up, and to find the best combination of medications to keep stable. While there can be problems initially with dosage, combinations and side-effects (unfortunately, annoying side-effects sometimes arrive first and medication benefits can lag behind), communication, persistence and patience will assist in forging a trusting therapeutic relationship.

Bipolar disorder came late to me. I was almost fifty before I experienced my first episode of depression—and this was followed, not by a high, but by a period of relative normality.

I cycled rapidly from the start. My initial period of depression lasted about three weeks, it terminated abruptly and was followed by a three-week normal period, which was followed by another three-week period of depression and so on. I must have experienced at least sixteen mood swings in that first year. I suffered all the usual symptoms of moderate depression—lethargy, lack of enthusiasm, absence of pleasure, sleeplessness, paranoia, anxiety, suicidal thoughts—and my ability to work was severely affected. Nevertheless, I 'soldiered on' but became increasingly apprehensive that my lack of productivity would be discovered. So I was secretive and told no-one about my problem, not my family and not my closest friends.

About a year after my first depression, I had my first episode of hypomania. On this occasion, my mood swing out of depression coincided with some particularly exciting developments at work, and as my mood lifted I became very excited about the future. My self-confidence soared and my sleeping pattern was very disturbed. I talked passionately about the developments, and impulsively planned grandiose schemes to carry the work forward. Eventually I came down from my high and slipped into depression, appalled at the uncharacteristically extrovert behaviour I had exhibited. But that first episode of mania had set the pattern and, ever since then, I have cycled between euphoric highs and melancholic lows. A year after this pattern became established I finally sought help and consulted a psychiatrist. He put a name to my problem—bipolar disorder—and prescribed lithium.

The meds I take act on the lows rather than the highs and make life more bearable. I'm fortunate I respond well to lithium and show no major side-effects. After I first started taking it, the severity of my depression eased a little—not a lot—but sufficient to take away some of the anxiety and sleeplessness, some of the lethargy and lack of enthusiasm, so I was able to work productively. Several years later, my doctor increased my daily lithium dose, and this caused a further decrease in the severity of my depression. Recently, I added fish oil (1 g/day) and there has been a further reduction in my depression symptoms.

These days my relatively mild periods of depression last three to four months. While lithium and fish oil have been very effective in reducing my lows, they haven't done much to change the intensity of my highs. Interestingly, however, it is clear that lithium stops my highs going higher—on those occasions when I've stopped taking it (which I've done several times), the next high has gone very high, even approaching mania. (167)

The first experience, plus the side-effects of the major tranquillisers, took years rather than months to get over. Not that I sank into depression when I got out of hospital, as I was still able to function as mother to my family and work at my normal profession, but more as an automaton, still dazed and distracted. I went on to have six further manic episodes, probably in part due to my inability to view psychiatric drugs as efficacious, experience notwithstanding! I now take lithium to keep my dear ones happy. While being well aware of the risks of toxic overdose, I even increase it in times of stress, family upsets and travel, to reassure them.

Lithium is a metallic foul-tasting drug which sticks to your tongue, is associated with batteries and swimming pool chemicals, and is dispensed, uncoated, by the bucket-load, practically free, by a pharmacist with one eyebrow raised. A great underestimation of its value. I don't know if it stops me getting manic or depressed—it seems to allay irritability—but mainly it comforts and reassures my loved ones. It is my 'other people's happy pill', and whatever its long-term effects, they will be a small price to pay for my family's comfort. (156)

Continuing feelings of elation—escalating beyond boundaries of normality—become an early warning system for my impending madness, plummeting my mind into the darkest of canyons, like a yacht at the mercy of a freak storm. Thoughts cascade through the narrow canyons of my mind, the deep dark depths of eternity, and are lost forever in a whirlpool of turmoil. Ancient boulders are reduced to river pebbles, worn, like the torrents of thoughts wearing away at my mind. There is no resting place, my mind becomes its own prison; there is no escape. Delusions of intergalactic communication and delicious feelings of grandeur replace any need to sleep. The control I have is ebbing away, but my chemical straitjacket—a medication called lithium—will stop an almost certain episode. Any delay now and I will lose the critical insight needed to decide the fate of my own mind.

Later, after increasing the dose of lithium . . . The war is over now. I won. I have beaten my mind at a game of madness. The world appears less bright today, I can't understand what the frogs are saying . . . they just make noise; messages from different galaxies don't get through. I am no longer a significant player in a world of conspiracy: I am nobody, nobody at all. The birds that flew in perfect formation weren't trying to send me a message—my mind is more truthful now. The world in which I had become a leader is gone. I have a new leader now, Lithium, an invisible defence system, shielding my mind from its own self-destructive thoughts, its own creeping madness, restoring sanity.

I don't have the luxury of controlling my highs: they control me. The exhilarating feeling that floods my mind is intense and wonderful. I would love to be able to hold the escalation at a point where I could sense reality, but the reality is I can't. I live trapped in a normal world with a mind that isn't.

I wish I had a story to tell . . . how I manage my elevated moods in an innovative way. The truth is there isn't one. My control is lithium. It scares me, taking a drug to control my mind. But the thought of another episode scares me more. (103)

One major improvement for me has been the lessening of the intensity of my illness. I am faithful to my medication regimen, and I have not experienced full-blown mania for many years. During such episodes I would believe that I was someone I was not, and think some pretty 'out there' things. I now mainly experience hypomania, an exaggerated form of myself. I find it difficult to sleep, and I find myself singing 'Amazing Grace' all the time! I guess I now look like I've taken cocaine instead of an acid trip, except without having to spend any money. (121)

Polar warfare

I take two tablets at night: a mood stabiliser plus antipsychotic that is especially effective for bipolar people who have a tendency towards depressive episodes, and another that regulates my sleep and puts an end to many years of relative insomnia. The only side-effects for me are mild grogginess in the morning and the subtle slowing of my metabolism. Partial morning functionality and a modest belly are small prices to pay for my stability, a sustained state of being that allows me to live my life with a large semblance of direction and control.

I'm not a religious man, but I do thank God or Whoever for finding me these two little tablets, and the shrink with wings who prescribes them, manna from heaven to sustain, to enable me to be. Many view taking medication as a sign of weakness—an easy way out for those who can't 'sort themselves out', who should 'quit being melodramatic', 'be a man' or 'a bloke', or whatever paradigm of emotional invincibility society projects to keep the lines clean and drawn, so that we don't breed a generation of 'sissies'. Let me tell you that not only do Boys Cry, but so too do they retch into their pillows because they're losing it again. There's nothing that exudes as much strength as accepting the nature of one's illness, and not surrendering to the fallacy of a miraculous recovery but taming the beast long before it devours you. Do not listen to the shallow, rejectionist and borderline criminal rhetoric of the pseudo know-it-alls who preach otherwise. It's the Medication, Stupid. My government-subsidised nuclear deterrent against the Stalinists of totalitarian chaos. (162)

Here are some views of individuals who, though they would prefer to manage without medication, have learned that it is not possible. For them, the drawbacks have been frustrating. They have persevered and found a medication or a combination of medications that suits them better. In the long run, it is up to the individual to calculate the medication benefits versus any disadvantages in its contribution to their stability.

There is nothing romantic about being bipolar. It is an incredibly frustrating illness. It has taken me almost two years to get my medication mix right, and I am aware that this may change as I experience highs and lows. Or age. Or for no reason at all. (116)

Treatment with lithium to reduce the severity of my mood swings was not in my best interests because I had to take a large dose to barely reach the minimum therapeutic effect. Once I refused to take it anymore and lasted roughly two years before suffering a clinical depression, with no intervening high. But, even while taking lithium regularly, I experienced suicidal lows.

At the age of fifty-four, I discovered that lithium, for me, was a depressant, and asked my psychiatrist why he prescribed it. He told me it was to stop me going high and doing strange things, particularly spending money I did not have. When I pointed out that my two previous highs had not involved overspending and that I was tired of being slightly depressed and fuzzy in my thinking, he suggested I try something new, a drug designed for epilepsy—sodium valproate—plus an antidepressant. This combination has served me well for the past six years. It has levelled out my mood swings, and I am grateful that I can lead a normal enough life, monitored by my GP instead of a psychiatrist. (6)

It's important to take as much control as I can. I take my medication, working with the doctor to get it as low as possible but still provide protection. I have tried to live without it, under doctor's supervision, but found the old pattern of the third stressor in a row undid the attempt. I will try again sometime. (38)

As considered in Chapter 3, there is continuing debate about whether treating bipolar disorder with medication has an impact on creativity. The severity of the disorder may provide a guide; some people—though inspired by a mood swing—are unable to harness it, and medication stabilises them sufficiently to be productive. Another consideration is that all individuals with bipolar disorder suffer a loss of productivity during depressive episodes—and such episodes almost invariably follow the highs if the disorder has not been stabilised.

The following accounts are from people who are taking medication for their bipolar disorder, who are comfortable with this, and who consider that they are able to access their creativity and continue to be productive.

> I feel that 'creative surges' *have* been dampened by my commitment to taking medication but this hasn't stopped me from achieving two degrees and having a successful career in nursing. Regardless of maintaining the prescribed medication regimen, I still manage to have, in the most part, an outgoing and bubbly personality. (113)

> Yes, I am creative. I write poetry, short stories and am writing my memoirs and I do this while I am on medication. Who isn't on some type of medication? How many people take the occasional aspirin or puff at an asthma spray? But no-one takes notice of this. (4)

> I have heard it said that lithium dulls the creative urge. In my case that is far from the truth. I am much more creative now, or at least far more *productive* now. Prior to being on medication, I would have a million ideas but they went nowhere except into mania, where I raced from one thought to another. Now it seems that the more I produce, the more the ideas come. (124)

> I often hear people say they will not take medications as they don't want to lose their creativity. For me, I was never creative

when high. I thought I was, but I never finished anything. I was too busy being reckless; I had no time left to be creative. I had delusions of how good I was and unrealistic expectations of what I could achieve. I was certain that as soon as I wrote my novel it would be on the bestseller lists and I would be interviewed on talk shows. The reality was I never wrote more than a few pages, and poorly written ones at that. The creativity was all in my head. That is the seductive nature of mania. It made me feel so wonderful but it was only a feeling, and no matter how fantastic that feeling was, it was never going to help me write a book. Since taking my medication, I have had two poems published in an anthology and two articles published in readers' columns in the morning paper. My creativity has been able to flourish. I am still an outgoing person, but without the mood swings. (132)

After diagnosis, and in consultation with a medical practitioner, some people with bipolar disorder are able to manage without medication altogether. This depends on the severity of their condition, how careful they are with self-monitoring, and the extent of their fallback options. The following account is from a woman who is seeking to manage her condition by strategies other than medication. She has retained back-up support, is vigilant and careful with herself and is prepared to go back onto medication if it becomes necessary.

The getting of wisdom

This is not a success story. It's a succeeding-for-the-moment story. It's a succeeding-from-moment-to-moment story.

I can't remember how long exactly since I came off the meds, but now summer is here and the true test begins.

I'm eating less and less, experiencing paranoia more often, and feel my physical, mental and spiritual energy growing. Can I keep it in check? A zinc, magnesium, B6 formula has been my mainstay these past months, and practising 'CBT' (cognitive behaviour therapy) thinking. I've managed to talk myself down a few times so far and I've kept my support crew informed—but there is a tightness in my chest and if I'm not vigilant I know it could easily all fall apart.

This was my decision. The choice I had to make. Stay on the meds, stay in control, and live a half-life, swimming through jam with some soul missing, or risk following what every atom of my being was telling me. I could do it. I had to do it.

I guess my current 'wellness' really started with my support crew. After my last stint in hospital, my mother and I decided to join a support group. There was nothing in our town, so we started our own. A social group essentially, we have a barbecue each week, share stories and information, and offer support to each other in times of crisis. We collect literature on mental health and dispense it among the town's people. We attend Mental Health First Aid and Active Listening (suicide prevention) courses, and whatever else may be helpful. We reduce the stress in each other's lives by helping each other move house and fill in job applications. We water each other's gardens should one of us be 'away'. We attend conferences. Those of us who are more 'well' look out for those of us who struggle. And it has helped all of us.

Luckily for me, as I was still a bit manic while I waited for the meds to kick in, I had enough confidence and energy at the time to talk to people and be proactive about my ideas. My mother helped to keep that energy focused. By the time

I'd started sinking back into the ground, the group was an entity all of its own.

They kept me going that first year, when it would have been so easy to hide in front of the TV and chain-smoke cigarettes. Despite the meds, I was falling into a winter lethargy. Not really a depression this time, just a weird kind of cancerous emptiness. I stopped writing. I stopped drawing. Hell! I even stopped reading, and I've had my head in a book since I learned my ABC! This was not just a creative block. This was something far more sinister. My splendid imagination—that by which I had always identified myself, that which had always been my centre of 'self'—was dying . . . The meds were too much and though I was pacified and unemotional, it was obvious to me and friends and family that I was really no better off. In some ways, I was worse off.

When you've been able to create clever and beautiful things your whole life and then you can't anymore—man! It doesn't just feel like a part of you is dying . . . it feels like it's screaming a hollow, low-pitched, endless sob and clawing madly, like a kitten in a toilet bowl, shredding your organs apart with grief and terror. That's Inside. Outside, the robot walks and eats and sleeps and barely even notices. But my robot had not completely taken over. And my 'kitten' was a fighter with claws of steel.

Hope came in two ways. Zinc, magnesium and B6. That was the first. 'Cognitive Therapy' was the second. So I took vitamins and paid attention to my thoughts. After some time, I felt I was ready to wean myself off the mood stabilisers and antidepressants. Phase One was complete. As I progressed, the doctor was reducing my antipsychotic drug and I was feeling better every day.

I had kept up my interest in all things 'New Age' and was finding meditation and essential oils to be very helpful. Now I also take an essence similar to Bach's flower remedies. It's a holistic approach—from the support group through to the CBT, meditation and natural remedies. And it's working for me—so far . . .

It's not always easy. Some days are harder than others, but I stay vigilant in my thoughts and my practices. I avoid stress and stimulants.

And my Muse has slowly returned to me. My seductress and my saviour. Yes, there are some nights when she has me up until two in the morning madly working on a painting of a nude torso, but I'm okay with that. It's part of who I am to be a bit crazy. I embrace that.

The moment it's all getting out of hand, my support crew will be there. The doctor will be there. The counsellor will be there. And we'll work it out then. If I need the meds again, I'll take them. Maybe a lower dose or a different type . . . I may not always be med-free, but I'm determined to live my life as a whole person, wise or not.

But there has been some wisdom along the way. Some of my wisdom has come from doctors. Some has come from books and leaflets. Some has come from fellow sufferers, but the greatest wisdom has been this—life needs to be managed, not cured, so hang on to who you really are with both hands tight and don't become your illness, or its cure, but the 'self' you can be between them. (63)

The extracts that follow are from individuals who believe that they need to take medication but are less happy with their experience of how it affects them. They miss their previous access to what felt like unbounded inspiration. They experience particularly unpleasant side-effects and/or the mood-levelling effects are too deadening. Some have continued searching for a compromise and have trialled alternative medications or different dose levels or combinations with good effect. They demonstrate patience with trial and error on their way to finding the best solution.

> I'm a flatliner, definitely not positive, but not immensely negative. My medication keeps me flat, it keeps me breathing, but not really living. I feel like a spectator in the game of life. Even when I participate, there is self-doubt; I fear that I am not doing 'the right thing'. When I let go, I fear that I have gone too far.
>
> Sometimes I use alcohol to loosen me from my fears, loneliness and inhibitions—then I often have regrets. I have looked for, hoped for, joy, peace and happiness in this life. But death seems to be the only certain way out of this abyss. Yet I keep plodding on. (62)

> After years of trying different medications, with the most beneficial outcome only ever being that they helped me to sleep, my GP trialled me on olanzapine, an antipsychotic mood stabiliser. Mood-wise I feel more normal than I have in years. So 'normal' that, sometimes, I'd swear that I'm emotionally flat-lining, and this in itself can be a problem. (55)

> I am very interested in the work done by Professor Ellen Frank in the US, where research was conducted to find out how much time people with bipolar disorder spend in an induced depressed state. Because there are degrees of mania, my medication is not so strong that it seriously impairs my functioning. However, I do agree with Frank, who suggests

that psychiatrists are too worried about the manias and keep people with bipolar disorder in a slightly depressed state rather than running the risk of a little hypomania, which might be associated with more productivity and pleasure in life. She goes on to say that she feels clinicians need to be willing to take a few more risks with such people. I continue to debate this with my psychiatrist. (143)

Trading fire for earth

I started to see a pattern (of highs and lows) emerge. Somehow, through all of this, I felt better knowing why I felt this way. My psychiatrist prescribed Epilim. It was working and I was able to get through the days, but as a songwriter I felt empty without my music. I decided that the medication had stolen my creativity in a worse way than any depression, so I stopped taking it. My music returned, painful and confronting. It felt like some nasty ghost had been released and I couldn't control it. This really scared me.

By early the next year, self-destruction had taken over. I was driven. A holiday almost became my last, a friend's liquor cabinet, valium and a swimming pool almost too tempting. My music was overwhelming me.

I scared myself into submission. I swore to myself never to get that wretched again. I made a choice to live, whatever the consequences for my creativity, and medication became a big part of that. To survive, to be in the world, to make some mark, has become so much more important to me than the never-ending descent and rise from the maelstrom that is my raw emotional life.

This time the music didn't leave, and somehow the distance that medication gave me allowed me to process my experience through songs. Now I feel I am able to write music that speaks from all of my experience; my humour, my politics, my cynicism, my passion and my emotions. I can share myself through these songs without the searing pain that characterised the songs I wrote when I was in my early twenties.

I understand why so many artists who deal with their bipolar choose to ride the mania—it really is indescribably intoxicating. We make our choices based on how we each want to live. I've chosen the harder path in some ways, trading fire for earth. I regret it every day, yet know that this is what I have to do to have the life I want. Life on medication is in no way perfect, but it is more settled. I am thankful for these small things. (59)

• •

IN THE SPOTLIGHT
Re-scaling the heights with medication

- Each person is an individual. Each may need medication or combinations of medications that are quite different from somebody else with bipolar disorder.
- Some medications can cause mania, as can some steroids or stimulant drugs. 'Switching' is the term used for the triggering of manic symptoms in response to the introduction or withdrawal of an antidepressant. Some antidepressants are more likely to cause this than others.
- During pregnancy, the use of medications for bipolar disorder is an extremely important issue and requires guidance from an expert. If you are pregnant or breastfeeding—or planning

to be pregnant—check the safety of the medication with your doctor.

- Acute mania and acute depression are treated with different medications. 'Mood stabilisers' may boost other medications in the treatment of acute mania and acute depression, and may also help keep further episodes at bay.

- Maintenance treatment for both bipolar I and II may involve a combination of medications, such as mood stabilisers (lithium and anti-epileptics), antidepressant and antipsychotic drugs, to even out mood swings. Over time, it may be possible to lower the dose. Use a dosette box or some other reminder to ensure medication is not forgotten—and keep a second store at work as a back-up.

- Medication will help most people but, unfortunately, it may not be the first drug trialled or even the sixth, and combinations may be required, with each step requiring weeks or months to evaluate the cost–benefit ratio. A high level of patience is required.

Capturing common concerns, the webpage Bipolar Disorder FAQ (www.faqs.org/faqs/support/depression/bipolar-faq/part3) has valuable consumer-based views on medication: see 'Ten Little Things I Have Learned About Drug Therapy'. To paraphrase:

- Side-effects of medication are common and are often more complex than described by medical advisers and drug companies.

- Some people still experience a breakthrough 'high', even on the best medication regimen. Often the affected individual will keep 'mum' about this, fearing a raised dose of medication, or the risk of hospitalisation.

- There is no 'right' medication combination that works for everyone. If something is effective, then the advice is to stay with it.
- A medication or combination may be effective for years. Sometimes however, even after years, the medication may become ineffective, and a new search has to be instigated. Medications improve all the time, so be optimistic that there may be something even more effective to combat the disorder.
- The mood-stabilising drugs are a way to cope with an illness that, as yet, doesn't have a 'cure'. Stay on your medication!
- Sort out your preferences with regard to control of bipolar disorder. Together, you and your medical practitioner can determine the best level of medication that keeps the disorder in check but doesn't interfere too much with your day-to-day functioning.
- While some people with bipolar disorder (depending on the severity of their condition) decide to manage without medication, many cannot. Regular medication ensures them a better quality of life.

9. Performance partnerships
Professionals and risk management

I rely on the professionals who keep me in their care—they are
my safety net. They help me stabilise my life. Their job is to
take on the burden of helping me get well. It's not a burden
I can allow my friends to assume. (261)

This chapter is about health care professionals. The psychiatrist,
general practitioner, social or welfare worker, counsellor or therapist,
and countless other professionals are essential supports for recovery
from bipolar disorder. Individuals need to seek out professionals
with whom they feel comfortable and who can act collaboratively
to formulate strong wellbeing plans with them.

Additionally, a person who is at risk of, or recovering from,
an episode of bipolar disorder can benefit from linking up with
a 'health proxy', if they can ask a trusted person to take on this
role. A health proxy could be a health professional or an informed
friend who comes to know what the individual is like when they
are well, and who can thus encourage them and maintain their
faith in achieving a rapid and complete recovery. Such a person can

be invaluable in taking change of the externals, such as arranging doctors' appointments and ensuring that the individual takes medication as prescribed in times when they may be too high or too low to plan such things alone. This support can also provide relief for family and friends, and can extend a measure of privacy to the person with bipolar disorder as then they do not have to constantly present all of the details of their illness within the family arena.

> I have decided not to let my bipolar stand in the way of what I want to achieve in life. It is an illness, not who I am. It is just a part of me that I have come to know, even if I can't quite love it. I know that I will have many more bridges to cross with medication and just the day-to-day living with the disorder. I am ready to face them, with a lot of help from my GP, psychiatrist, counsellor, family and friends. I'm very lucky to have so much support. And it is out there for anyone to access: you don't have to live with your bipolar alone. (116)

Taking the wheel

Think of it like the butterflies you'd have at the start of a car race. The power has been turned on . . . Fasten your seatbelts . . . Prepare for take-off! (You can't hear the countdown, but you can definitely feel it within your body as it takes over your entire being . . .)

It's hard not to want to be this person that is about to fire on all cylinders, who is so confident and so capable, revving like a hotted-up engine, a vehicle with illegal modifications— people pay big bucks for this type of stuff! So be prepared . . . There's turbulence to be expected on this trip and possibly a pile-up in store . . .

When my biology and environment are not finely tuned, I find that my entire body and mind awakens and is filled with a surge of energy: from 0 to 100 in two seconds (and it is exhilarating to know that I will veer out of this valley of darkness—if only temporarily). I am possessed of endless physical and mental strength. Suddenly, I have the power of a turbo-charged V8, the confidence of a Porsche, the elevation of a Range Rover, the creativity of a Kombi van and the grunt of a Mini-Minor. I believe I can accomplish anything, do anything—and that possibly I will. At these times I am unconquerable. There is much to do (and very little time to do it in); the world is wonderful—I know my place in it—but most importantly, I belong in it. It is hard for me to believe that I came off the mundane production line, for I am a showpiece.

But . . . I am also unrealistic (like an Aston Martin D39 coupé); and yes, I'll definitely be disappointed to hear that this is not the way I'm supposed to feel. (Isn't everyone like this?! Isn't this 'normal'?!)

However, if I am allowed to go on like this, I will do just that. Go on and on and on . . . Forget the fuel, I could run on solar power; I can stay awake for days on end—scheming schemes, planning plans and establishing a strategy for world peace. I may produce the world's greatest novella, create stimulating visual works of art, or sit in a darkened room full of candles and claim that I have seen the light. (I might even scrub the kitchen and bathroom, not once, but thrice!) No time to stop and rest! There are places to go and people to see! Things to create and discussions to have! Don't stop me now! I'm on a roll! It's all downhill from here!

Deep down though, travelling at this speed, I know that

what I am feeling right now can become unsafe. Even as good as I may feel, I know from previous experience that if I stay with this ride, it will be like no-one is behind the wheel. I don't need computer technology to tell me that all is not as it should be, and I may need you to help me stick to the speed limit, otherwise the crash at the end will be like hitting a brick wall at breakneck speed—with the driver unrestrained, at that.

I can drive myself into mental and physical exhaustion . . .

Sometimes, I feel a bump in the road. Sometimes, the speed-humps may slow me down but they won't stop me. Sometimes I feel the air beginning to come out of my tyres but I can't let it stop me. This is an important trip. I can't be driven by sadness. But I may need help to apply the brakes; otherwise, my chassis (and my interior) will be bent. My pride in tatters. My beliefs shattered. My confidence broken. (I think I can, I think I can . . . but I can't.)

So, this is where you might step in . . .

To our family and friends, our counsellors, our workmates, our teachers and GPs—we sometimes need you to take the wheel. When you see us careering out of control, we may need you to help us over into the passenger seat. This breakneck speed will take us down. If our heads were clear we'd know the rules, but sometimes we just can't see the forest for the trees as they go rushing by . . . But with the correct education and support, we can gauge for ourselves that this trip we are about to embark on is an unsafe one. (Go back! You are going the wrong way!)

With the right education and support, you can help us see the signs through the fog. (This is not to be seen as a mark of weakness but an encouragement and reminder that

we can take control and assert our independence to drive
solo again.) We don't ask you to drive the entire way. We
may just need some direction. We don't want you to be
chauffeur—we just ask if at times like these you can share
the load (otherwise, these Learner drivers may never get
their P-plates!)

Like keeping any machine in top condition—we need to
be maintained. At times, our medication may need to be
readjusted. Things require realignment. Our airbags to be
refitted. We need to have support people with us so when
they see that we may be headed off the beaten track, they will
call for roadside assistance. Whether that means we need to
be impounded remains to be seen!

We may need a major overhaul because we've left our
ignition on. We may want towing into the workshop . . .
So while we recharge our batteries (and check our power
windows, titanium wheel nuts and electronic stabilisation
program) we ask you, please, for your understanding and
support. All of this is a challenge. We haven't chosen to be in
this race. We were nominated without our consent.

Once we are restored to our original, pristine condition,
it is then in the lap of the gods . . . (I can't tell you if we'll
need another service in four months, four years or 4000
kilometres—it's whatever comes first.) Hopefully, we'll come
out with a lifetime warranty.

Please don't judge all our thoughts and actions until
you have test-driven for yourself. With your assistance and
understanding, you can help us re-establish that we have one
owner and are pre-loved.

That's when the race has been won. (119)

In the following excerpt a wife describes the breakdown of her husband, thirty years into their marriage. He had had previous down moods, but his depressions worsened following increased stress due to a promotion. This extract describes his first manic episode after being discharged from hospital on high doses of antidepressants for his depression (which unmasked his bipolarity), his consequent mania, and the effect of a new psychiatrist who continues to work with them to provide top care.

Persevere to find good professional care

When my husband came home from hospital after treatment for depression, he lay in bed, grey-faced, with little change in his mood for almost six months.

However, by Christmas of that year he heard he had won a prestigious architectural award, and his mood lifted— amazingly quickly. It was wonderful to see him with energy and enthusiasm again. He wanted to make up for lost time, and to thank his colleagues for their support during his illness. He began to have a flood of creative and wide-ranging ideas, day and night. I was exhausted. I started drinking my way through the duty-free cognac—for medicinal purposes. What a waste!

When he could not get sufficient attention from me one Sunday, he threw all the garden furniture and pot plants off the back deck. When I maintained my own reality and refused to humour him, he ranted angrily at me all that night.

I got so tired that I couldn't stick to my principle of 'telling it as I saw it'. I said, 'I'm really too tired to follow what you're saying. Can you write it down in detail so you don't forget it?'

Then followed days and nights of enthusiastic noting and architectural diagramming. His then-psychiatrist decided that

Jim had a personality disorder. I now know that this diagnosis is often code for 'Difficult patient—hope he goes somewhere else for treatment'.

Jim became fascinated with many issues and wanted to communicate with 'experts' all over the world. The tone of his emails became sharper and more argumentative. Yet my husband had always been cautious, considered, polite and diplomatic! Fortunately, he agreed to show me all his emails before he sent them—probably because he was very pleased with them. We argued over the drafts. He copied and kept some of the rejected drafts as a kind of vindication of his judgement.

This period of energy lasted about three or four months. Then he began to slow down, and by the middle of 1999 was suicidally depressed. He took himself to bed again. I felt an incredible anger with the world and with Jim. I sought a second opinion with vengeance, and threatened to leave him if he didn't get out of bed and come to the appointment with me. I dominated the session, describing Jim's behaviour in full colour in his presence. I was angry and accusing and very sorry for myself. Jim was silent.

Fortunately, the source of the second opinion was a wonderful psychiatrist, now retired. He treated Jim and me with respect from our first meeting. He said that Jim's condition was biochemical, that we had been 'let down by the profession', that Jim could be effectively treated, and then admitted him into hospital.

Jim was prescribed mood stabilisers, an antipsychotic and an antidepressant that was unlikely to switch him into mania. 'Now,' said the psychiatrist, turning to me, 'about your anxiety levels. I think you would benefit from some medication too, for a while. It would be cheaper and more effective than cognac.'

Jim improved quickly. He took his treatment seriously and was conscientious about attending a cognitive behaviour therapy (CBT) group for three-hour, twice-a-week sessions for six months. He would previously have raised his eyebrows and dismissed this kind of group as 'touchy-feely'. No longer. With the CBT group, he learned to manage stress and depression, be more assertive, and to value himself again. (35)

The following accounts also underline the importance of astute and compassionate professional help. Finding a 'champion' with whom you feel comfortable is essential. It may require some 'doctor shopping' before you find a professional with whom you 'click'. Trust is an essential element in forging a partnership that sees the individual as part of a team that contributes to the best management of bipolar disorder.

Consciousness, chemical equilibrium and holding the hand of the experts kept me on a steady course as I gingerly traversed the jagged cliffs of my bipolar disorder and sought a ceasefire between the feuding armies of my *unquiet mind*. Whilst nowadays I only see my psychiatrist every three or so months, during the earlier period of crises, diagnosis and medication trials he was my pillar, my knight in white-coated armour. Eternal kudos and gratitude to him and his fellow comrades in this perpetual struggle to curtail the plague of Gross National Suffering. (162)

Initially, my symptoms of mania escalated very rapidly and both family and friends, together with my psychiatrist, would intervene. For family members themselves to have me scheduled was a very, very difficult undertaking indeed. In fact, I was admitted to one hospital and went before a tribunal of about fifteen people and still talked my way out of being scheduled! My mood was indeed very elevated, but my son had the wherewithal to have me rescheduled at another hospital. The emotional drain has been enormous. The moral of this is that some family members can be the most accurate in identifying the beginnings of a mood swing.

It took me five psychiatrists before I found one that I could really relate to and who was empathic to my needs and, most importantly, agreed to treat me while I lived in the country. Initially, he, my Community Health team and my GP would see me every week in turn. All were in communication, with my specialist writing to my GP after every visit. This tripartite arrangement of health professionals was absolutely essential in supporting me until such time as more updated medication became available. Even now they support me, but on a more *ad hoc* basis. I have a lithium blood level test every month and a blood profile twice a year. I am now recognising my own symptoms (restlessness, aggressiveness, irritability and increased spending) and increase my medication dosage accordingly. (177)

How many people would buy tickets for the rollercoaster ride of their life, knowing that the ride is faulty? You may start off feeling on top of the world but will end in a mess. Every high for me has ended with no longer being independent, and experiencing an almighty depression from the drugs forcing me down off the ride, the scary hospital experience, stigma, and finally losing the things that make us all happy and fulfilled, such as a job and a living situation.

Luckily though, there are people in the amusement park

who may not get on the ride with you but are there to help you off at the end, help you heal, and hopefully help you to avoid the next faulty rollercoaster ride. These people include my family, friends, doctors, case worker and employment consultant. My doctors and those closest to me are now able to compare what I am like when well to when I am becoming unwell. It has taken many years to get to the stage I am now at, where the subtle changes are obvious. Feedback at an early stage about mood swings can definitely prevent relapse.

Working with different health professionals over the years has helped me to get up-close-and-personal with my illness. As much as I hate having bipolar disorder, sometimes I have realised that I needed to become friends with that part of myself, to move on from it as much as I can. A 'stay well' plan can be very helpful and includes naming triggers which seem to be a pattern from past highs. My triggers include pressure from life changes, money worries, taking on too much, or interpersonal challenges. Techniques such as cognitive behavioural therapy, yoga and meditation have helped me to become more resilient to stress, while I keep my sleep–wake cycle as predictable as possible to shield me from a relapse. (121)

Two years ago I thought there was no hope—with bipolar disorder and a stroke as well—but I found professional people who found hope in me and they never gave up on me. I also started to learn about some of my triggers. Accept the person you are and be proud. You are as good as the person next to you. (150)

Being hypomanic *and* at your peak sexually, it doesn't take much to fall madly in love with your caring, intelligent, knowledgeable doctor. 'Insight', as they keep reminding us bipolars, is a necessity to keep us on the straight and virtuous

. . . I'm cringing with embarrassment, but the evidence suggests
that being a 'biological time machine' is a common calamity
to deal with. Transference is very real and, sadly, must be kept
in the realm of fantasy as much as God must be kept to heel in
the politics of our country. (57)

Slowing down

'Is it right, that sign?' I asked, turning to the nurse. 'Is this a
psychiatric ward?'

'Yes,' she said gently.

'Were they short of beds in the other wards?'

'No.'

It seemed to me that all I needed was a good night's sleep.
I don't know why they thought I needed to be in a psychiatric
ward to get sleep but everyone seemed quite comfortable
with the concept. I was too tired to care.

That first night at the hospital they gave me some
sleeping tablets and, finally, I slept. In the morning, I met my
psychiatrist. 'Call me Leo,' he said. We talked for a bit and
he prescribed tablets. Lots and lots of tablets, I discovered.
'Bipolar disorder,' Leo had said.

I had never known anything like this. I'd never thought of
myself as mentally fragile.

The nurse brought in a bunch of flowers. They were from
the Grade Three mothers. Fantastic, I thought. So everyone
in Grade Three knows I'm in hospital. Probably everyone at
school knows. More flowers arrived. This time they were
from the Wednesday tennis mums. Terrific; between the
school and the tennis club that should just about cover
everyone I knew.

I felt suddenly exposed by the flowers. I was ashamed of where I was and what had happened to me. I didn't want anyone to know that I was in a psychiatric ward with my own psychiatrist called Leo.

Concentration, focus and memory were so frustratingly weak. If I could have read then, I knew I could have escaped a little, but I was grounded in a baffling reality. The other patients all suffered from depression. My mid-winter mania stood out like a laugh at a funeral.

My concentration and focus started improving slowly over the fortnight—I found I could read a small paragraph without stopping.

Finally, at home, I spent another month padding around quietly doing very little. I watched the French Open and Wimbledon. I walked the dog and I slept. I kept finding and reading skinny books with short chapters. I felt awkward and dull, and if I went out I felt obvious. But I kept taking the big white furry horse tablets twice a day.

I watched Parkinson interview Stephen Fry about coping with mental illness. Fry was convinced that everyone in Hollywood wanted to have mania. It seemed you couldn't have creative ability without some history of bipolar. A whole city of people want this, I mused. Suddenly I didn't feel quite that odd. (171)

Not everyone with bipolar disorder—nor relatives and friends—is able to access care and support readily, which highlights the importance of having professional and other support in place ahead of any possible crisis. The style of intervention offered in an emergency situation is likely to be from the police, or the acute care team from a mental health facility. While this is part of the scope of such services, if a plan has been made prior to such a distressing situation, intervention can be more effective and cause less 'bruising' and subsequent embarrassment to an individual in the grip of an extreme mood swing. In some circumstances, respect for the civil rights of the individual makes necessary treatment very difficult to access.

Accessing effective treatment and care is much easier and less intrusive if the person with bipolar disorder has discussed with relatives, friends and workmates how to effect it. It is much more challenging, however, if there is no plan in place, as in the case of a first episode, when everyone can be taken by surprise.

It was the night before Christmas and all the presents were laid out under the tree. My husband and I took in a movie, relaxed, ate bad food, I think we may even have had something to drink—though I must admit I am not a big drinker, there is no need with my illness—and began a typical night in, with one difference: I became completely acutely manic.

My husband did not know what to do. In our four-year relationship he had not seen any of this behaviour. He did the only thing he could do—ring his father, who just happens to be a very good emergency doctor, the type of doctor that comes around to your house when your GP can't be arsed to get out of bed to tell you that you are alright. We got lucky.

In my daze I can't remember being needled to sedate me, but I didn't want to be sedated. My parents were there with their usual worried looks. It all makes me feel like I am the scary little girl in B-class horror movies. However, I'm not far from weighing in at 100 kilograms and almost 180 centimetres tall, so I can pack quite a punch when I am scared or angry. Nothing made sense, but I was scared that night, in my haze. (33)

I had had no previous personal involvement with mental illness until returning from a trip overseas this year. I knew that bipolar disorder was a new name for what was previously known as manic depression. I was also aware of the fact that people suffering from the disorder tended to shun treatment either because they considered it unnecessary or because they simply preferred the exhilarating highs and omnipotence of the manic phase.

My thirty-five-year-old daughter, and mother of two, picked me up at the airport, and I immediately noticed that she appeared changed. Her speech was clipped and her manner dismissive. I later heard from the family that she had been experiencing lack of sleep, agitation and irritability, and had been binge-drinking.

In the weeks that followed she left home and began a downward spiral, fuelled by substance abuse, excessive spending, inappropriate behaviour (due to increased sex drive), and arguments with friends, family and business associates, all of which eventually led to the destruction of her reputation and put her in a general state of confusion and anger.

In total disbelief and with anxiety and helplessness, our family came together seeking strength, support, solace and understanding. To our horror, we found out that my daughter had been diagnosed with Bipolar II Disorder two years earlier, during a depression that followed a five-month manic period. Further, we were told that a decision had been made to try to attack this thing without recourse to medication. She had then descended into a depressive state. We also heard of what we now believe to be the primary trigger of her latest episode: after a life-threatening asthma attack early in the year, she was treated with a huge dose of steroids, which, I now know, can have mood-altering effects, and can trigger mania.

The weeks that followed involved desperate pleas to different crisis teams who could not take any action unless the person was 'causing physical damage to herself or others'. When I was consulted, as her mother, about what I would like to see done, I asked that she be hospitalised, stabilised, medicated and brought to a state of mind where we could communicate with and then care for her. The medical people (her GP and her psychiatrist), however, could offer no help unless she sought it herself. Furthermore, legally, we had no recourse.

Nevertheless my daughter, in her delusional state and believing that her family was hostile, engaged the services of a law firm. The firm was advised about my daughter's illness and inability to think rationally. They were also made aware of her total lack of funds, and consequent inability to pay their fees. The worse infamy is that, despite all appeals to desist, they continued to clock up fees amounting to thousands of dollars.

Eventually, police intervention was sought when my daughter made threats of physical violence to her husband when insisting on having the children with her and wanting access to the family house and car. At this point, and after various reports of further inappropriate behaviour in public places, she was finally scheduled with the help of the police and the crisis team. She spent five days at the mental facility attached to the public hospital. Here she was stabilised and declared fit to return to normal life by the magistrate. This 'new' life saw her renting a unit she could not afford and sharing with a new partner to whom she was pregnant.

As her mother, the agonising journey has involved trying to understand more about the nature of the illness. I was lucky to have the support of a family friend and psychiatrist with whom I had long and informative conversations.

My daughter, after almost six months of unrecognisable behaviour, is now calmer, and visibly more rational. However, she still blames everyone and everything for her current situation.

And the most distressing factor for the family in its supporting role is that there are no clear-cut avenues of thought or action for the future and the threat of similar episodes. I anxiously wonder what each day will bring. My life as I knew it has gone, and I mourn the loss of my child. (8)

To manage the highs of bipolar disorder you must be able to put Mind over Mood. Before I started knowing how to do this, my life was quite unmanageable and chaotic. I would blurt out things that were often quite hurtful but because I was feeling out of control, reasoning seemed out of the question.

After telling my then-psychiatrist that he made an easy buck, I was on my own! (115)

On a knife-edge

The signs of my wife's approaching mania had been accumulating over the past three months and I was helpless to do anything about it. There was the faraway look in her eyes that signalled an inner conversation, the sleepless nights when she would lie in bed with eyes open staring at the ceiling, the hyperactive cleaning, painting the house and going for six-hour walks in the heat of the day. There was the urge to spend large sums of money on unnecessary presents for family and friends, the sudden flight of fancy that might see her buying a ticket back to the UK and then disappearing without telling me where she was going, the loss of a sense of socially acceptable behaviour that would cause her to be sexually provocative in both actions and words, and worst of all the feelings of persecution that caused her to abuse friends or relatives for some perceived affront. The sum total was a person who was dysfunctional, and as time passed this behaviour became accentuated and more aggressive.

I had been to see her doctors and had told them about the changes in her and that I was positive that she was not taking her medication. They made me feel like an idiot and suggested that the problems were marital and not anything to do with her illness. Even pointing to her history made no difference, and I walked away from the hospital with a sense of utter despair.

Over the next weeks we staggered from crisis to crisis. Our bank account was getting low, so I transferred money to another account and told her our savings were gone. Our friends had stopped calling in and I had to ring them to apologise and ask for understanding and patience. Life was starting to run off the road and we were in danger of crashing. Then, one afternoon, I came home and my study was trashed, all my books were scattered on the floor, the stereo system was on its side, filing cabinets had been emptied of papers and my computer was damaged. I looked at it all in disbelief, and sat down and wept. I wept not only for the damage done, but for the deterioration in her condition.

She needed help and I knew that I had to get her to hospital, so I walked to the public phone box and called the police. I explained the situation and, before long, two young policemen arrived, surveyed the damage, asked my wife if she had been responsible and, having had this confirmed, took her off to hospital. She had always been compliant in the face of authority and went without a murmur.

After we'd waited several hours in hospital, two psychiatrists arrived and separately interviewed me and my wife. In the end they said that she did not show any signs of psychosis and they believed the whole thing was just a domestic tiff. I was completely crestfallen. What did I have to do to get help?! My wife had been through the system so many times (seven episodes in ten years) and interviewed on countless occasions, so that she knew what questions they would ask and, of course, had provided sensible, rational answers. She was able to convince two qualified psychiatrists that she was not ill, even though her thoughts were dancing through her head with the choreographed moves of classic mania. She was capable of perceiving fully what was happening and able to erect a façade of normality to avoid hospital, and yet she had no insight into her condition, and vehemently denied that she had a mental illness.

Back at home I was subjected to tirades of abuse and threatened with a knife: 'You had better stop scheming behind my back or I might use this.'

Three days later, she tried to overdose, using a bottle of aspirin, was admitted to hospital to have her stomach pumped, and then transferred to the mental health unit. When I went to visit, she had been put into the high security area because she was verbally abusive and violent towards staff and other patients.

My relief that she was finally receiving treatment was palpable, and, even though I was distressed to see her ranting, I knew it would abate as the medication took effect, and eventually the person I married would slowly return. (24)

I have shared with my parents that I live with a mental illness [Bipolar II Disorder]. This has wrenched memories from the past of my paternal aunt who lived with schizophrenia and eventually died in Rozelle Hospital. I think there is guilt carried all these years about the way her life transpired and deep pain in the love of a sister lost. I didn't know her at all. I think she was kept a secret. I now have her photo displayed at home. She has a twinkle in her eye. I wonder what her life must have been like as a woman living with a mental illness in Australia in the 1950s. (125)

A delicate fire—managing the highs of bipolar disorder creatively

Picture a group of people sitting around a table. They are animated. They are conspiring with their eyes, then all laughing at the same unspoken joke. It makes perfect sense, and that fact seems hilarious. There is no prejudice—though typical learned social concepts would usually be in place. It is a world in which this momentary reality feels sacred, because these people around the table are manifesting their reality, they understand each other. *Perfectly.* The problem is—no-one else does. *Literally.*

The obvious treatment, medication prescribed by professionals for the manic high, is for many an effective way of bringing the peak of mania back to a relative norm. But without teaching other methods of prevention, coping skills and management, the high is made more dangerous and seductive, and may, I believe, also be prolonged. Holistic management during the high times is important, to avoid other problems that may stem from the experience—not least being a resistance to get help in the future.

Sedating medications and the repeated phrase 'calm down' are often the only tools given. The nature of the illness means caregivers or professionals are often patronising. The feeling of being stifled, or having needs ignored, can result in a further resistance of sensibility and an even stronger desire to rebel, and stay high. The after-effects of being treated solely with medication can leave a feeling of being greatly misunderstood. Individuals may also be embarrassed or ashamed of their behaviour, there may be a feeling of having wasted time whilst being ill, interrupting what semblance of life there is to go back to. This can be frustrating and contribute to a sense of helplessness and low self-esteem, ultimately making the recovery process harder.

Just as a routine helps eliminate mess in day-to-day life, instruction and direction helps a person with an overwhelming rush of ideas and notions to narrow their focus and feel calm for a moment—almost as if retraining the brain to concentrate and still the inner drive. It is not easy for 'normal' people to understand the insatiable drive to compulsively 'do' things when you are manic.

Because of the excessive need for some bipolar people to create, therapy such as fine arts or music can be of great benefit. Many can play or respond brilliantly to music. In an in-patient facility, a planned and practised concert may give focus to patients, and cooperation, listening and a chance to express are involved. Knowing that they will get their turn to speak or perform will be enough incentive for individuals to sit and listen for a matter of time. Helping prepare meals on a daily basis is a tool which is essential for life, and an encouragement to participate in normal activity. Keeping the hands busy can allow the mind to slow. Rolling clay whilst discussing interesting topics is a simple but effective meditation for someone who cannot stop moving or talking.

Doing nothing whilst being manic, especially in the company of others suffering from psychiatric illnesses, only serves to intensify delusions, and the creative mind has no other option but to overuse an imagination which is already out of control! Giving patients things to do passes the time constructively and decreases aimless and destructive behaviour. It helps the patient to feel they had some control and choice in their recovery, and limits feelings of helplessness, giving them a sense of worth.

I have been extremely high with mania, and several times it has continued for more than eight weeks. Much of this time has been spent in psychiatric institutions, both public and private, adolescent and adult, where being treated for mania has at times been terrifying, complicated and often more confusing than the illness itself. Whilst in the grip of a manic episode, although the symptoms may offer a feeling of euphoria, it is also excruciating and frustrating to be high—where you know you are unwell, but you cannot filter what's real or what's not. You cannot control your behaviour or stop saying or doing inappropriate things, and you are left to watch yourself from the inside, as though you are trapped behind your own mirror image—it's you, but it's not.

If a manic person is having delusions, allow them to discuss them openly with you. Let them feel safe to tell you, without the fear of fierce rebuttal. However, gently discuss the logical reasons why their chosen delusion is not actually fact. It may be helpful for that person to have a list that they can develop with you about their fears and worries, and to write down anything that can easily be dismissed. They are then able to read it back to themselves, giving clarification and positive affirmation, dismissing needless worries: for instance, 'I am not on the radio', 'I am not being stalked', 'I am safe in my home', and so on. This may be useful in a group situation as well.

Traditional group therapy may not be helpful to manic people, but specifically discussing their illness together may help them identify that they are not the only ones facing such symptoms. It could even help resolve some delusional behaviour.

For someone with bipolar disorder, the grey scales of life (between the despair during depression and the drama of mania) can appear bleak at the best of times. Because of this, that manic feeling, although ultimately destructive, is at times welcomed and run with—like holding the string of a kite. Because it feels so good to fly just for a little while—it can't be so harmful, can it? Boredom and depression itself can trigger a high, where the sufferer feels that they will be better off seeking that elusive high, and go on a lifestyle bender. This may include destructive behaviours such as ceasing medication, drug abuse, promiscuity, dangerous behaviour and the consequent mania. If the increasingly manic behaviours are not immediately addressed, the manic person becomes the kite, oblivious of the fact that he or she will ultimately crash back down to earth. Therefore, treating depression with a proactive lifestyle is just as important as the focus on the manic side of the illness.

So in a situation that seems hopelessly complicated, it is with some irony that I suggest that balance is the simple key. Setting routines that are dependable for oneself. A budget, and/or keeping a diary, eliminates clutter in the head, and leaves space to focus on other relevant activities. Some routine in day-to-day activity is also imperative for maintaining stability. Regular sleep and eating routines contribute to balance and health both physically and mentally. This is a must for bipolar sufferers. Continued contact with a professional such as a psychiatrist or counsellor is essential. And far too often, the spiritual and emotional aspects of a person with bipolar disorder become neglected and are not treated with the same importance or dignity as with 'normal' people, because so much focus goes on the mental and physical side of 'staying well'. Yet, it is just as important to continue with activity that satisfies these needs, and to develop some structured or social routine, in which one's guard can be let down and the mind's emotions can slow in a relaxed and comfortable environment. Again, some direction is always helpful where concentration and focus may be lacking: structured classes are a good idea.

The steps leading up to a full manic phase may seem scary. It can be difficult to approach a person who is becoming increasingly aggressive, defensive, or delusional. The usual questions, such as 'Have you taken your medication?', may be met with hostility, and the situation can slide out of hand very rapidly. Therefore, it is important for carers and family to discuss warning signs, and agree on a plan of action should one become ill. Write down the plan. A great deal of tact is required when dealing with a manic person. One should expect, unfortunately, that the closest person to the bipolar sufferer will be the recipient of the most aggressive and defensive behaviour.

Sometimes, in the early stages of mania, a person may go and seek help but be turned away because of the very fact that they recognise their sliding sanity. An insane system indeed. Prevention is the best alternative!

Importantly, it is imperative for someone with bipolar to remember that 'staying well' means more than just 'not being ill, depressed or manic', but enjoying an active and balanced life and having the choice to be fulfilled.

There *is* something to be learned from bipolar disorder. Everyone experiences extremes of personal thoughts and feelings. But the stories, thoughts and feelings of those with bipolar disorder often give a glimpse into the extreme spectrums of the human psyche. They do and say things we may think and feel, but never actualise. If we listen, we may bridge the gaps to understand, so we may watch the kite fly, but guide it so it does not crash. (108)

· ·

IN THE SPOTLIGHT
Keeping the show on the road

- Research shows that people who enlist health care professionals to help them to manage their bipolar disorder have fewer relapses and better control of their disorder.
- Professional help is best when it is 'pluralistic'—has many aspects—and is not solely medication. A health care professional can also help the person with bipolar disorder to recognise and list early warning signs via mood charts. They can help in drawing up a 'wellbeing plan', a plan of action that is put together when the individual is well. This sets out management strategies that treating professionals, family and/or friends can use if the individual is too unwell to access or manage their own treatment.

- Enlisting professional support lightens the burden on family and friends, and enables the person with bipolar disorder to keep some aspects of their illness at arm's length from their family.

- A general practitioner and a psychiatrist are usually the two professional mainstays for managing bipolar disorder. Obtaining the right professional help is often difficult. Rather than relying on chance, the bipolar individual and/or their family should seek recommendations, and keep looking until they find a professional with whom they feel comfortable *and* who is competent.

- Doctors (psychiatrists and general practitioners) can be expected to take responsibility for the medications and techniques for managing any side-effects, but their capacity and interest—as for all professionals—can be variable. As medication compliance is highly correlated with successful management of the disorder, having a doctor competent in both prescribing and monitoring medication is of central importance.

- Other health care workers can—if trained—enrich the management plan, whether by educating the patient about the geography of bipolar disorder, or by providing counselling or specialist techniques. The support and advice of a psychologist, counsellor, social or welfare worker or other relevant professional can make a big difference.

- Many people (and their families) find benefit in support groups, particularly those that are structured and which focus on practical day-to-day strategies.

- The more that health professionals are 'in the loop' on a regular basis, the more they will be available if there is a crisis.

10. The acrobats' pyramid
Family and friends in formation

As his son, I learned to play the dancing bear to his
erratic tunes. (90)

The highs are easier on you than on those around you.
The lows are harder on you, but easier for us.
[A son who has lived with his father's bipolar disorder
for twenty years] (38)

This chapter chronicles the role of family and friends in the life
of those with bipolar disorder. For those that are 'one ripple out',
it can be a difficult and exhausting support role; sometimes near
impossible. While nearly every individual with bipolar disorder cited
the support of those closest to them with warmth and gratitude, it
is essential that carers maintain their own life, health and interests
as much as is feasible. Burn-out is all too common. Writers also
indicate how family and friends, a warm and attentive audience,
can act as the 'outside insight' for a person who may lose touch with
reality during an episode.

Polar bears

Depression has the 'black dog'. In our home, bipolar has the 'polar bear'. A code term created between my sister and me when she was first diagnosed with bipolar which aptly describes the illness and our experience of living with this 'animal'.

Polar bears look cute and cuddly and, most of the time, my sister is open, funny and playful. Polar bears enjoy company, and my sister has a wide circle of friends, enjoys sport, movies and going out. Polar bears are versatile, living on land and in deep waters, and my sister is managing her illness extremely well, aged twenty-one, having had the illness since she was fourteen, attending university and singing in a local church group.

However, polar bears also have a predatory side, and this is when we see the illness emerge and my sister goes from gorgeous to grizzly.

From gorgeous to grizzly

The early warning signs for us are overreaction, overemotion and extreme irritability. My sister is aggressive with my parents and myself, and favours her friends over us. This is brought about by a lack of sleep and racing thoughts. The racing thoughts are ones of anxiety and worries such as being late, organising her room, meeting people, failing in her studies—all mixed up in her mind. As a result she stays up late and cannot relax.

My sister's illness is quite brittle. Within a couple of days she is in a full bipolar episode, and a few days after the inevitable hospital admission she is back home and in recovery. She has experienced far more manic episodes than depressive episodes. Seeing other friends with depression, the manic episode is actually easier to handle, believe it or not. Although it requires a higher level of prowess and fitness (like when her thoughts become too overwhelming, and she decides to leave home regardless of time of night—so my family and I have had some stealthy midnight strides across the local shire where we live), the mania is highly transparent. Depression is hidden and darker, we can't tell what she is thinking or feeling, and it is far harder to help and takes longer to resolve.

As the episode progresses, we also see a change in clothing: haphazard dressing where she tries to wear everything that she likes—all at once, regardless of weather and venue, like a *haute couture* model! The final indicator for my family and me is the episode's 'theme tune'. My sister listens to her iPod constantly throughout her illness and chooses one song that she will play repeatedly: J-Lo, Eminem, Dido have made up our 'bipolar soundtrack' over the years.

It's all about the strategy . . .

In terms of management strategy, as a family we are fairly experienced in our approach to managing an episode, as my sister has had about six episodes of illness. Once we have noticed the warning signs individually and collectively, we check with her friends to see if they have observed any change in her behaviour. The change of behaviour is usually triggered by a series of 'small' events—a low grade at university, a disagreement with a friend, a summer job rejection. I write 'small', because as a family we consider this to be small; it's a setback and we just need to dust ourselves off and get back on that horse. However, for my sister (and from what I understand it affects all bipolar sufferers), that 'small' event is a huge event, as her stress-tolerance levels are far lower than most people's.

When her friends concur that her behaviour has changed, we invite the local hospital out-patient unit to assess her. Based on this, they will decide whether to admit her and then begin increasing her medication to reduce the mania and calm her temperament. Slowly, her aggression towards the family dissipates as we visit twice daily in hospital and she starts to appreciate us again (due in part to the influx of chocolate and McDonald's smuggled into hospital by Mum, as well as the medication balancing her moods).

Our coping strategy, however, is less orderly. Despite my humour in regard to 'polar bears' and 'theme tunes', the illness is a very sad one and, at times, very difficult to accept. My sister has just reached her twenties and her teenage years have not blossomed as others' have, and opportunities and expectations have had to be re-assessed. My parents, who have provided for my sister and me in so many ways, struggle especially, as this is one part of my sister's life they cannot 'fix' with advice, money or experience. We build resentment towards the illness when she is most unwell, for debilitating such a talented young girl.

However, we try as a family to stay focused and put the 'cuddly' polar bear goal into our minds and know that the aggressive bear is just temporary. We support one another and are blessed with a bipolar support group, loving extended family and friends, accepting workplaces, and the hospital out-patient unit that is on hand for my sister's post-episode counselling and family discussions to prevent the next episode for as long as we can.

The creative bear of brilliance

During every one of my sister's episodes we have seen an increase in her brilliance and creativity, but as a force, it is one that is difficult to harness. She starts painting when she is unwell, and paints with great depth and feeling in her choice of subject. This reveals the issues that have built up inside, forcing the emotional eruption; but often even through pictures we can't see what is the source. Her poetry and writing helps her healing and understanding of the illness, but are closely guarded and intensely private, so for us, we just have to wait till she is ready to open up.

She doesn't get burnt by her brilliance, but curiously doesn't return to these activities until the next episode. When she is well, her brilliance shines in other ways: a sharp sense of humour, a fantastic memory for trivia (she is in a pub trivia team unrivalled in our district), and singing and acting talent that brings joy to all who see her perform. Consider her the polar bear who stars in the Bundaberg Rum advertisement—hilarious and gregarious!

Silver linings to the stormy cloud

I truly believe things happen for a reason. I don't wish bipolar on anyone and frequently wonder why my sister was given this illness—a kind, sweet and clever girl who occasionally becomes agitated and unsettled. Humility is the greatest lesson we have learned as a family since my sister was diagnosed. Celebrating the small wins and setting achievable goals is the reality check that bipolar has given us. We enjoy each other's company more, make time for one another and do not feel guilty about relaxation. Life's pace is much more manageable and we demonstrate that to my sister as often as possible to keep her stress levels low.

As a family, our resilience grows as we overcome each hurdle that bipolar has set us, making us stronger and more united. Others of life's self-absorbing battles, such as acquiring the latest material possession or being first place for everything, are now presented in perspective. Health and family impact now govern my life choices and wellbeing. I give thanks for my sister, my family and all those who touch my life in a positive way, which I doubt I would do if I were not going through this experience.

My advice to any family members of a bipolar sufferer is not to be ashamed or worried about what others think. Be upfront about the polar bear in your family—chances are the person you tell will know someone with mental illness and, in our experience, we've yet to encounter anyone who hasn't shown empathy or a willingness to help and learn more. But most importantly, love your polar bear unconditionally. The calamitous carnivore is fleeting and gives way to the cuddly creature time and time again. So whether your bear's condition is hibernating or active, let them know every day that the fact they are part of your life is a blessing.

After all, just as real polar bears are living in an uncertain environment—with melting ice caps and hunting threatening their existence—so your polar bear needs you to help them survive and succeed in the wilderness of real life. (168)

Relatives and friends can show enormous generosity and compassion to people in the grip of bipolar disorder, provide a safe haven and maintain a steady faith in the individual's capacity to regain their health. As shown in the following excerpts, this can be greatly reassuring to someone coping with a high or a low who feels that they have lost their footing.

You have to feel safe when a high is brewing. I used to get that from my grandfather and still get it from my aunt. Grandfather was never fazed when I turned up at two in the morning, talking sixteen to the dozen. He'd offer me a cup of tea or some burgoo, and the back bedroom. Feeling safe, I'd get some well-needed sleep. His house, where my aunt still lives, is tucked away at the base of a mountain, surrounded by forests. My aunt deals with my disorder by going into what she calls 'clinical mode'. Old nurses never die. It's a way of her keeping enough distance to make sense of what I'm up to without getting caught up in it. I went to her for safe haven during my last high, and channelled my excess energy into sorting out her garden. She's grateful for this. Hey, there are benefits to highs! (38)

A very kind lover who cared for me through one bout of mania has explained the feeling of being constantly on edge. There is a fear of the unpredictable. Expect the unexpected, anything can, might and does happen. Saying 'no, no, no, no!', to the point of exasperation does not work in managing my manic behaviour and antics. Trying to reason with me is futile. The best way for him to manage my illness was by discouraging me and intervening to stop me doing anything impulsive that was too detrimental. This was successful, but took a lot of hard work and brought truckloads of emotional stress. Not exactly fair in a relationship. But he was there and he did it and it worked.

But a lover cannot be with you all the time to monitor or control your thoughtless behaviour. As is known, promiscuity can be a very prominent element of manic episodes. And yes, for me promiscuity has been the biggest problem in every relationship. I have been upfront and honest about this in advance, but that is little compensation for the pain it causes. Unfortunately, I have yet to come up with a foolproof strategy to overcome my infidelities when I'm manic. And, unfortunately, I've hurt a number of truly beautiful people in the process. (41)

My son is nearly twenty now, and for the last year he has been absolutely, continuously stable. I'm still watching for those signals, but—touch wood—they are staying away, at least for now. The joy I feel at having my son back is indescribable. It's like meeting him all over again. We've been able to cut back, cautiously, on his medication, and he is once more slim and full of energy, but it is 'good' energy, not the destructive force which drove him before. I know that his mood could start to escalate tomorrow—that's the nature of bipolar disorder. I can't cure my son of this condition but at least I've come to understand that I have some power over its course. I can fight for him by watching for the danger signals, keeping him in touch with his doctor, and making sure he has the best medication that is currently available. And should I need a reminder of the value of what I'm fighting for, I need only listen to his carefree laughter. (95)

Relatives and friends learn a variety of strategies—effectively 'on the job'—that can bring comfort and support to the bipolar individual. Research indicates that those who have been very ill, with a psychotic disorder, have poor insight both during and after their episode. They often cannot remember what they said or felt during their episode, as opposed to the external 'factual' observable consequences such as the credit card bill and the letter of retrenchment. The common 'disconnect' between them and family members seeking to support them during illness episodes is captured in the following excerpts, as is the patience required of relatives to also gain 'wisdom' about the disorder.

How have we learnt to cope over the years? I don't know. PATIENCE, or maybe because it is very repetitive. You seem to adapt to routine. We do try to be very patient when Mum is talking really fast non-stop about the same topic over and over. Or the times when she's visiting and comes and sits on your bed at the oddest hours—also another sign—because she can't sleep and just wants to talk to someone. Well, I like my sleep, and I try very hard not to lose it.

My sister has a better knowledge of bipolar as she is a pharmaceutical representative for a drug that treats mental illness. Over the years she would always say, 'Mum can't help it, you must be more patient.' But she loses it too, occasionally.

At this stage Mum was living in Queensland. So my sister and I thought we would drive up from Sydney and take Mum to Noosa for a few days. When we arrived, we noticed she was a little high, but we thought we would get her out of the house and give her partner a break anyway. Just twenty minutes into the drive Mum started and wouldn't stop, same old stuff we had heard hundreds of times before, reliving the past, paranoid about someone. 'Mum, we have to concentrate on the road, can you be quiet please?' Of course, she didn't take any notice, so I told her to shut up. My sister gave me a right serve and told me how awful I was to speak to Mum like that and once again said that 'SHE CAN'T HELP IT.' Precisely one minute after that she turned her head while driving and said to Mum, 'Would you bloody shut up.' I gave her a look that said it all. We both started to laugh: what else can you do? Sometimes we all lose it a little.

Mum lost her partner of twenty years a few years after that trip. Death usually brings on Mum's mania, but this time she had a delayed reaction. The first six months of grieving was hospital-free, but in the year and a half since then she has been in and out of hospital three times. But I am so proud of her because she has accepted her condition, takes her medication and recognises when her levels are out and that she is becoming high. We don't know what the future will bring and I know there are some very good medications that treat bipolar. I have to say though, I pray for a cure. Mum has had a tough life and I would love to see her well always. She is a beautiful person. Just a handful when she is manic. **(144)**

The trouble with the highs is that they feel so good. I have to weigh up whether to worry that he's so good or worry that he'll feel so bad in just a few hours or days. As a mother, I wonder if there is anything worse than seeing my adult son cry. His pain is so intense, I wish it upon myself: his tormented eyes, his forehead heavy with depression.

Then the full-on high will suddenly hit. It always starts with his dark glittering dilated pupils. I know then it's a day of fast talking, fast spending and even faster and fantastic ideas. He's feeling great with a capital 'G' and there are the most profound and imaginative plots and stories to be told. He can buy a block of land today, build a skateboard park tomorrow, employ everyone he knows there and get famous. He won't sleep tonight; he will be drawing plans until I beg him to turn out the light.

At first, the laughter is better than the weeping, the excitement better than the anxiety, and the social interaction better than the recluse he's become. But the escalation and the scale at which this force arrives becomes like a rock careering down a mountainside, destroying everything in its wake. It bounces high and wide without stopping, crazy zigzagging and tearing at everything to get to this unknown destination as quickly and as wildly as possible.

I keep one eye on his spending and one eye on the time. Receipts mount up in his waste bin like trophies on a shelf. This one is for a T-shirt costing more than any dress I could ever own, designer jeans and sunglasses at prices you see in the glossy magazines and, my absolute worst nightmare, a motorbike that will give a couple of days' pleasure before being consigned to the shed to gather dust, before being sold for a song.

So now it's midnight and he's at the casino. Do I ask how much he's spent, or take a back seat where I quietly observe? Do I mind my own business? But then what is my duty? I question how much I should interfere. I question if this is OK or not. I don't know. How bad does it have to get to be bad?

I go with my gut instincts, my maternal instinct, and read until I could be a consultant myself. I become expert on biochemical imbalances, drugs and therapies and the best time to ring his psychiatrist. My address book is brimming with names and phone numbers, notes and jottings on ideas and information I have gathered. It's my bible. I daren't leave the house without it—I would feel insecure and unsafe not to have it with me. (30)

Every six months these spikes seem to happen for my wife, but you can never pick it, you can't plan a neat and tidy strategy because anything can trigger it—you just have to know the signs. It certainly keeps you on edge with a constant drip-feed of stress. This last trigger was a family member's marital separation that shafted a sword somewhere deep into her psyche. But it could just be the Christmas holidays, or some other change of routine or life stress. Sometimes the warning signs are her repeating old fears or concerns, some relevant, most excessive: replays, like tape recordings you have heard over and over.

I remember waking one Sunday morning, the sacred morning, the day of rest, *huh*! My wife had taken a handful of tablets, about twenty. Pacing the floor, she was tense, nervous, driven. Her thoughts raced hard, trying to work out her life from beginning to end. That morning I carried her into Casualty with three kids in tow. 'It's all right guys, Mummy's just not well.' They're too young to know yet.

This last spike was a *very* quick one, unlike at other times when it could emerge at the end of a slow build-up of symptoms over several weeks. It was very matter-of-fact. My wife walked into the kitchen and declared, 'The voice is telling me that it's time to die now.' My heart thumped. She was strangely nonchalant, though pacing the floor. The warning signs had been rearing their ugly heads only since the previous weekend: the excessive phone calls to concerned friends and family, the rapid talk, the irrationality, unloading life with its woes and delusions in a tirade of sentences devoid of breathing spaces. Oh the phone bills! But the real hazardous sign was the late night disappearances for mysterious drives somewhere in the city, coming home at all hours, tired and haggard but 'wired'. I hid the keys. You must hide the keys.

The week's tension, the build-up to who knows what, created the spike. The mountaintop where she could be saving the world, marrying someone famous in another country, being a real princess, spending a fortune, booking a first-class ticket or an expensive hotel room, or, worse, wanting to jump off a cliff and end it all. 'It's time to die now.' Yeah, right, as if I would let that happen. I'm the Carer dude!

I rang the hospital crisis team straightaway. They were there like family—the irony was not lost on me. The night nurse stated the inevitable and I brought her into hospital immediately. I didn't panic. She did what I said. And I packed a bag for a possible few days. This time it was two nights of observation plus hits of the drug olanzapine morning and night that brought sleep and rest. Floating her down and numbing it all—where everything can stop. Peace. (20)

My family members are very astute at picking up a change in my persona, a little bit too much make-up, a slight change in hairstyle, too well dressed, and they alert my psychiatrist. At a very early stage, we had a number of family conferences with my psychiatrist for family members to raise concerns and for me to work out an amicable agreement as to when and how they would become involved. One of the outcomes of these meetings was that instead of using that phrase (as I used to become very aggressive when told I was ill), we have a code word for it, which is 'elephant'. If anyone mentions the word 'elephant', I know I'm in trouble! (177)

My method of trying to defuse a potentially serious problem is firstly by remaining very calm myself. I find this to be important. If I react with huge concern to her mood swing, it not only doesn't help my daughter, it seems to make things worse. Susan insists on total attention when she feels needy. By keeping calm in stormy waters, I seem better able to pull her out of her own exaggerated high. So we sit down, have a cup of tea, and she tells me her plan. If she talks quickly

I tell her that I can't follow her unless she slows down. Usually, because she very much wants me to listen, she does. (69)

Along the way I have gained knowledge about the illness. Not only from my sister's bipolar disorder, but I majored in Sociology, with a focus on mental illness, at university. Naturally, I brought home some theories. My sister was more receptive to the one where there is no such thing as mental illness, and she was simply medicated because she was not adhering to society's behavioural norms. My mother was more taken by the theory that once an individual is stigmatised they start acting up and taking advantage of their position: 'I can't vacuum, I am sick.' Me? I'm none the wiser. (180)

When I was younger I didn't really understand why my mum was 'different' from everyone else. My parents divorced when I was two and I lived with my mother until I was ten years old, when my dad fought to get permanent custody of me. I am now fourteen and have learnt a lot about how to handle her highs and lows.

Sometimes I get angry with her for the way she is but, as I have gotten older, I realise that it is something that I have to accept. The people she sees, like her psychiatrist, push her hard to take her medication, but in the end it's up to my mum to decide whether she wants to take it or not.

As a teenager who regularly talks closely with friends, it is sometimes difficult to discuss with them about what bipolar is and how my mother suffers it. My mum has come up to my school sometimes and made a scene, which makes people ask questions. I can't tell my mother a lot of things, like where I work, where I do extracurricular activities and where I meet with friends, because when she is sick she would come and make a scene. I often feel bad because I feel like I am lying to her, but now I think of it as 'withholding information', not lying. (184)

Blessed by bipolar

The road to understanding my dad's illness and his creative side was a long and tough one for me.

My father has had bipolar disorder since I can remember. I guess it happened when I was young enough that it was sort of a way of life and the way he was. He wasn't diagnosed, but there was always something different about him: his mood swings. Now that I'm older I realise more of what he is going through.

His nurse's badge has a photo on both sides. On one side he is smiling and on the other he has his hair spiked up in an overly messy fashion and a smile like some kind of crazy scientist. He says that it reflects the two sides of him: normal him and bipolar him.

My acceptance of his illness wasn't always there. There was a time when I resented him for who he was, or what he had and what he was doing. The hardest time was when he couldn't come to my graduation. I was four weeks away from my end of school exams and my father was in a depressive episode with suicidal ideas. It came as a massive blow to me. I never believed he would actually try and commit suicide. I've never actually asked him about the events of that day; all I know is that he survived. Maybe he went through with it and it failed or maybe he stopped just before he did it. All that matters is that he is alive.

For days after it happened I was so angry. I walked around with a chip on my shoulder. Then, one night without warning it suddenly hit me. I cried until I was exhausted. I didn't cry because of what had happened or because of what he had done. I cried because I didn't actually think that the illness would get the better of him. I always thought he was too strong or he had too much control over his illness to let such a thing happen. I also realised that we couldn't help him, it was out of our hands.

He wrote me a letter (I still have it) explaining that he needed to go to hospital and would come back better, and that he needed to go away in order to do so.

This was the first time that I really told people about my father's illness and also the first time I noticed how much support there was out there. I was given an exemption from my final exams and given special entry into university through a program that helps students gain alternative entry because of family issues like mental illness. The outpouring of understanding from my friends was amazing. I'm so grateful for that.

My brother told his friends that our dad was away, working at another hospital. I guess he didn't think they would understand. I think that's one of the biggest obstacles to revealing mental illness—lack of understanding and knowledge.

The time in hospital was a turning point for our father. He returned and decided never to work full-time again. He worked three days a week and it gave him more time to be himself. He started to act more in the local theatre, made furniture and lead-lights, and shopped at 6 a.m. at garage sales to buy old furniture and restore it. It's not really what he does though, it's the way he goes about it. He gets this idea, creates it and somehow this off-centre idea works.

Every time he goes to a garage sale he picks up an obscure object with the bright idea of turning it into something. And every time it's the same response from us. My mum rolls her eyes, I look at it and shake my head, and my brother just laughs. But, sure enough, every time his idea somehow works out and we are eating humble pie. He once bought an old bedpan cabinet and turned it into a bedside table that has a hidden compartment for jewellery in it—now my fashionable bedside table. It's as if he has this gift that no-one else has to see what something can be.

There is a Missy Higgins song that I first heard when my dad was in hospital—about being 'blessed' by a different view. I thought that was a magnificent way to describe bipolar, as being blessed by it. Bipolar has made my dad see the world through different eyes. (139)

How I involve others in managing myself

The tendency of those experiencing bipolar mania is to think nothing is wrong. After all, spirits and self-esteem are high. It is therefore left to close family members to give the alarm. And, to do that, in addition to ensuring ongoing medication and psychotherapy compliance, self-help will be needed.

One way is in the form of adherence to a plan of attack, constructed whilst in the 'normal' state, and with input from anyone who will be affected. It must be a regularly updated working guide that displays flexibility and adaptability as its key ingredients. It needs to be reviewed every day—written, sung or read. Part of the plan should determine what to do once manic symptoms are detected: for instance, the medical practitioner and hospital preferred; a statement of spiritual beliefs; who has the power of attorney over financial matters, especially access to bank accounts; and who will organise recuperation, including time away from work. It should also document a stay-well plan detailing a healthy diet; the need to exercise; how to avoid stress, and the importance of adequate sleep; medication that must be taken; social support available; and ongoing professional help. And how to self-monitor, so that specific symptoms that occur, for instance, any extra 'sparkle', combined with an increased drive to goal-oriented activity, can act as an early warning signal.

Commitments to regular involvement in self-help groups that teach how to recognise manic symptoms make this easier. In addition it must give chosen people permission to say when predetermined symptoms of manic behaviour are being displayed, ergo, behaviour that is sufficiently different, such as increased social need, activity, ego, talkativeness, irritability, substance abuse and sexual drive. The plan also needs to identify specific triggers. Triggers are extremely personal and are often tripped by stress. Major life changes and events, seasonal fluctuations, deprivation of sleep and illness are prime examples. All cause stress but what is stressful for one is not necessarily perceived this way by another. Once identified, triggers are less likely to occur if family and friends are supportive and there is a good network of social interaction, such as in tennis clubs and churches, with members that focus on the abilities rather than the disabilities associated with bipolar disorder. (39)

As the stories in this chapter show, many with bipolar disorder are clearly aware of the impact of illness episodes on family members and friends. They warmly praise the commitment of such loyal people, particularly because the intervention of family and friends is often received with hostility by someone who is in the throes of a mood swing. It is only after they have returned to themselves that they can appreciate the action that others have taken to limit damage to life, limb and reputation—and the patience and tact that were often employed.

> It doesn't have to be the case that you fail to recognise that your personality is operating outside the boundaries of a normal playing field if you know what to look for. For example, just like in any other game, your team-mates or friends seldom accompany you outside field boundaries. If you remain there for any length of time, they become agitated, offer more than the usual amount of advice, and they are unresponsive to your arguments. You are also besieged by minor annoyances despite a feeling of great wellbeing.
>
> Don't be fooled. Your freedom is an illusion. Being outside the play, you are no longer bound by the well-known set of game rules, but you are still bound by rules—most of them unfamiliar, and with serious ramifications. A sudden increase in legal liaisons is a good sign that you are operating beyond boundaries!
>
> Your friends' agitation and inexplicable unresponsiveness can also suggest it's time to re-evaluate your position, or at least to listen to their advice. And that influx of minor annoyances could be a by-product of increased sensitivity—another sure sign that you might have left the confines of the game. (11)

> Some of my greatest friends have been my family and my doctors—when I was convinced they were there to help me!

To reach that point I needed to forget my ego, as I thought that I would become better if I was left alone to get on with my self-cure, and I had to learn to trust others' judgement of my condition. It was others who saw me creating endless stories until the midnight candle burnt to a cindered wick, and they saw me frustrated because I'd forgotten to do things I should have remembered to do. I was going round and round in circles and working myself to a standstill in this last high. My doctor had given me a 'drug holiday' to give my liver a rest. She was trying to change me from older style to newer medication for my bipolar illness.

My husband was very firm with me when he took me to my doctor and insisted that I was having a relapse. I went along to the psychiatric out-patient unit at the general hospital, where they interviewed me and referred me back to my doctor, who referred me on to a psychiatrist. It was like a game of pass-the-parcel that we used to play at children's parties. Now I am once again stable in my moods. To be able to admit that I have this illness is a major step in helping me to cope with it. I am now on the latest drugs and they are working well. I also see my psychiatrist regularly. **(4)**

There is unrecognised stress on family, friends and carers of a person with bipolar disorder which can take a severe toll on health. It is imperative that carers take good care of themselves and maintain their own friends and contacts to avoid such burn-out.

Many research studies identify carers as being at high risk for stress-related illness. Caring for someone with bipolar disorder can mean loss of opportunity, juggling work and other commitments and generally putting oneself second. Most carers place their own wellbeing low on their list of priorities and never get around to talking about it with any health care professional. Yet, the capacity to care for others is greatly affected if their own health deteriorates.

Without my realising it I had already become accustomed to reducing my (now, unfortunately, ex-) husband's stress levels. He had no concept of financial management, spending on items without regard to affordability. At one point when I attempted to discuss our impending inability to meet commitments, he made it categorically clear he had his own problems and therefore resolution of the situation was entirely my responsibility. It was a welcome relief when, with understanding, he would discuss his urge to spend before purchasing and accept without question 'no' for an answer.

Another aspect we needed to deal with was his, at times, unbelievably intense sexual proclivity. Although always con-sensual, I found it extremely difficult to cope physically and mentally, but chose not to mention it. After reading that this was just another symptom of bipolar, we were able to discuss the issue in a non-threatening way. As a result, without any embarrassment from either of us, I never invaded his privacy, thus giving him the space to deal with it in his own way. (37)

Being 'commitment phobic' I did not marry until my late forties. My husband has been an absolute pillar of strength, sometimes at significant personal cost to his own physical and mental wellbeing. He is my best monitor, providing relevant feedback to my psychiatrist who often states how important this is in my treatment. (113)

After six years on the rollercoaster ride of elevated swings and dark valleys, the pressure and the stress finally affected me. I was diagnosed with type I diabetes. My nervous system was razed—sometimes my whole body tingled. You can't carry the stress. You mustn't! The carer has to be cared for. You must look after yourself! Go to the gym, swim, have massages, saunas, work out, have some fun—get it out of your system as much as you can. If you don't, one day you will break down yourself! You need the reprieve as much as the bipolar sufferer does. This is not wisdom, just essential. (20)

. . . .

IN THE SPOTLIGHT
Family and friends as assistants

- Bipolar disorder is an unpredictable illness that benefits from family as well as professional support. Family support can be fundamental in getting the individual to accept assessment and, subsequently, management.

- Some people with bipolar disorder refuse to seek help all their life. Others resist at first, but ultimately acknowledge that they cannot control the disorder by themselves. You cannot live their life for them and can only assist up to the point when they will let you help. Discussion—within the family, with the relevant health care professionals and support organisations—can progressively shape ways forward.

- A carer needs to look after their own health and wellbeing, or risk physical and emotional burn-out. Carers should maintain facets of their lives that do not include the person that they care for, just as they would do if that person were healthy.

- It is important that the carer allows the person affected with the disorder to develop their own strategies and approaches. They should also know their own limits as a carer. A carer can't 'cure' the affected person and, at best, can only lessen their pain.

- Carers should discuss how to widen their circle of support with other family and friends. When people offer to help, carers should take them up on their offer. This builds a network for both the carer and the person with bipolar disorder.
- Carers need to develop a different range of strategies for coping with the bipolar lows than for coping with the highs.
- Carers' support groups are important anchors, offering education, strategies, lists of early warning signs, advocacy, help in coping with the consequences of both highs and lows, and links to health care professionals.
- As a 'proactive' move, a carer can encourage the person with bipolar disorder to develop a management plan while well—a 'wellbeing plan' that can then be used in coordination with health care professionals if the individual is experiencing a mood swing and is consequently too unwell to manage their own treatment. See Appendix 2 for details.

11. Becoming a ring master
The discipline of self-management

Since I have no desire to revisit either depression or hospital,
I have been working hard at remaining well. (61)

I've chosen the harder path in some ways, trading fire
for earth. (59)

This chapter is about strategies for maintaining control over bipolar
mood swings, 'spotting' swings before they gather force, and
resisting the temptation and seduction of a high. It is helpful for
those with bipolar disorder to rely on systems outside their own
perceptions. To combat the temptation of momentarily lifting
control and then drifting into an irresistible high, most people with
bipolar disorder need to ensure that they have safeguards in place to
bring them back from the edge.

It is possible to move in early to control potential mood swings—
both the ups and the downs. People discover what works for them
as individuals, but common feedback includes filling in a mood
chart (see www.blackdoginstitute.org.au for an example), keeping

a journal, and using the 'outside insight' provided by trusted others to spot early signs of an impending mood swing. Medication compliance is essential for most, so that the back-up strategies for a faulty memory are needed: tactics to ensure that tablets are not forgotten. Medication dosette boxes and reminders from relatives or friends are two approaches.

> I need to remember that pushing beyond my boundaries inevitably results in me feeling less well and behaving less well accordingly. I rely on what is measurable and visible, and I chart or journal how I feel, what I am doing and what I am thinking. This provides me with indicators of where I am moving around in the spectrum of wellness and disorder. (47)

> Because it's difficult to access my own emotional state, I need to have outsiders prepared to play that role. Luckily I have these yardsticks in my life, people I have known for a long time and can trust, and who can point out that things are getting perilous. If they say I'm coming adrift, even if I can't feel it yet, I have to look at what's going on. I am privileged to have a supportive partner, a good son, caring family members and old mates who know me. Without them, my life would be trickier.

> I can still forget my medication. It's no longer deliberate. I just forget. My strategy—I take it in a certain order so I know what I've taken. I still stuff up, but less frequently than I used to. (38)

Everything I can is all I can do

The word 'mania' doesn't exactly come with the prettiest of associations. Should it come up in idle conversation, chances are that mania will be linked to religious cults or terrorist attacks. Mania can be found kicking around with drug-addicted rock stars, or co-starring in a B-grade horror flick. When people think of mania, they think of crowds in death-metal mosh pits. They think of English football fans. They think of department stores during end-of-season sales.

But a very different kind of mania also exists—one with which I share an intimate relationship. That is, the mania that comes with having bipolar disorder. As you know, living with bipolar is all about living between two extremes—mania and depression. Neither of these two 'poles' is a comfortable place to live. The weather's foul. It's lonely. And the days are either desperately long or painfully short.

Depression is always a hard piece of real estate to sell. However, the state of mania is a bit harder to define. Unlike depression, it's not a uniformly nightmarish place to be. In its extremes, it can be just as terrifying. But it can also be exhilarating, exciting and energising. In short—you wouldn't want to live there, but it's a great place to visit.

That's why, when managing bipolar, the highs can be the greatest challenge of all.

Like many people, I lived with bipolar for years before I was diagnosed (or even knew that the condition existed). So not only did I think that highs and lows were a part of life, I thought they were a part of my personality.

Upon diagnosis I struggled with the question of identity, as suddenly a huge part of what I assumed to be 'just me' was explained away by a textbook and neutralised by medication. Even as I adjusted to treatment, I found it hard to separate which moods were caused by my emotions, and which could be blamed on my condition.

Over time, I've learned to raise my own internal alarm bells when I'm sliding into depression, but it's always been hard to pick up on mania. The signs aren't quite so clear. When does an elevated mood or a really great belly laugh turn into a full-blown bout of mania?

As a result, self-awareness is the first challenge I face in the management of my own mania. Thousands of times I have found myself asking: when is it mania, and when is it just me? Unfortunately, it's not one of those questions that comes with a neat little answer. But the asking of it has helped me to get to know myself better—which makes it easier to discern when mania makes me act differently.

So what happens when mania pays a visit? When does a personality turn into a disorder, a mood into an episode? I'm sure it's different for everyone, but for me, when I start talking a little too fast and my mouth can't keep up with my thoughts, it's probably mania. When I reverse my car into a brick wall at high speed because Led Zeppelin's too loud and I'm distracted by a weird-looking tree, it's probably mania . . . When I find myself having sex with the office nerd in the stationery cupboard at 3 p.m. on a Wednesday (as my colleagues walk by outside) . . . yep, probably mania.

I'm not blaming everything on mania, or saying that I'm safe and predictable to begin with. But when a high kicks in, things get a bit out of hand.

The real trouble with mania is that when it starts, it's actually (dare I say it?) pretty fantastic. It's like stepping into Willy Wonka's glass elevator and being taken to see things I've never dreamed of. My thoughts have new dimension, my ideas sparkle, I hear chords of amazing songs that have yet to be written. Sure, things are a tiny bit surreal, but with all

these dizzying possibilities laid out before me, why would
I complain?

Even on a practical level, for me, mania does wonders.
I work faster, sharper, more creatively. Suddenly, my
vocabulary expands, my mind's razor sharp and I have the
energy to work through the night. On top of that, I am also
suddenly the life of the party. I can talk to anyone. Even that
hot guy in the bottle shop. And, suddenly, everyone wants to
talk with me.

Add a dash of mania and I am the best possible version of
myself.

Trouble is, things don't stay like this. The glass elevator is
being operated by a purple-coated madman who isn't just
content with taking me on the factory tour. Before I know
what's happened, we've smashed right through the ceiling. I
find myself with no control, no boundaries and no judgement.
I'm too damned high, and I have no way of getting down.

Self-awareness can help me to minimise the damage of
these crazy rides—and, in an ideal world, it would be enough.
However, for most mere bipolar mortals it's not. That's when
the next key part of management comes in—Other People.

Inviting Other People into my bipolar soap opera isn't
something I ever wanted to do. I am more than a little proud.
When diagnosed, I resented the condition like hell. For me,
it was crucial that no-one saw me differently because of my
bipolar, and in my mind, that meant not telling them about
it. I also believed there wasn't much that anyone could do to
help me anyway, and that it was therefore best for all if
I handled it on my own.

Many years and many episodes later, I now know that I
was wrong. Not only are there ways that other people can

help me, I actually need them to provide this help. For my close family and friends, it has been frustrating to see me out of control—but far worse to be prohibited from helping.

Developing a support network is one of those things that doctors and therapists and Oprah herself all bang on about. It honestly sounds so American self-help-bookish that it makes me cringe. But for once they're right. Yes, even Oprah. I can't stress enough how important it is for bipolar people to develop a support network. It doesn't matter who is in it. It can include friends, family, co-workers, or none of these. It just has to include people who can offer understanding and support when you need it.

When it comes to managing mania, my own support network is invaluable. They're the ones who have come to understand my patterns, triggers and vulnerabilities. And now they're the ones who can see the signs of mania when I can't see them myself.

For example, my friends know that when I start driving like Steve McQueen or insisting on buying a new pair of shoes in every colour (there were eleven colours), I may be getting manic. At that point often all they need to do is give me a bit of a nudge—just so that I realise what I'm doing and can deal with it myself.

Sometimes I need more intensive support, whether it's to pick me up from some far-flung location or to have me as a house guest for a while. However, I suspect that the hardest thing I ask of them is to accept me as I am—and to acknowledge that there are limits to the support they can provide. That, at the end of the day, they can't 'fix' me. There will be times when all they can do is sit there and watch.

Acceptance. I know. We're back in Oprah-land. But

that's the final thing that I believe is key to managing mania. 'Acceptance' sounds like such a generic word. But for someone with bipolar, it can be the most powerful. Because coming to terms with bipolar disorder means accepting that there's just no foolproof way of controlling it all the time.

No matter how hard everyone tries, episodes will happen. No matter how closely we watch the door, there will still be times that mania sneaks in. And when it does, it's no-one's fault. Sometimes these things just happen. All you can do is pick up the pieces and move on—much easier to do when people offer help but not judgement.

Managing bipolar and its highs, for everyone, is ultimately about understanding limits. The limits of what we, as people with the disorder, can do for ourselves. The limits of what other people can do for us. Doing everything within our power, and living with the things that are beyond it. I know I haven't had my last ride in that glass elevator. But I'm getting better at handling the guy who is controlling it—and keeping him *inside* the building. (163)

Apart from loss of insight, which can creep up unannounced despite an individual's best intentions, another reason why treatment may be refused is common to many with long-term chronic illnesses, and that is 'denial'. It is neither easy nor pleasant to admit (even to oneself, much less to others) that one has a serious mental illness. Stigma, despite inroads being made in recent years to eradicate it, is still alive and well for those with mental illnesses. Denial is called a 'coping mechanism' and it results in an inability to recognise or a lack of acceptance of symptoms. The subconscious can usher one past some small glimmers of recognition that all may not be well.

Circadian rhythms are implicated in mood swings, hence there is the need to maintain a regular routine. Our body has a built-in clock to regulate our functioning. Most people can tolerate a certain amount of disruption to their body clock but this can be fraught for people with mood disorders. The body's circadian rhythm is one of the first systems disrupted by a manic or hypomanic episode, hence the decreased need for sleep, increased energy and low appetite which are common early warning signs. Similarly, there are larger yearly rhythms—with some people with bipolar disorder showing a seasonal pattern, and being more at risk of manic episodes in spring and (less commonly) autumn. Intervention to normalise the sleep–wake cycle is usually beneficial—as is avoiding situations that disrupt this cycle such as shift work and flying across time zones.

I reckon staying well is kind of like sun protection. We've all heard about the importance of things like sun block and a hat in preventing sunburn. But these items will not prevent a sun-burnt nose if we fail to apply them in the manner intended. I now know that I need many things to keep well: regular medication, sound uninterrupted sleep each night, a nutritious diet (I do this mostly Monday to Friday), exercise at least three times a week (which I don't do), and keeping my weekly therapy and other clinical appointments. I also have to believe that I am not perfect and to stop always trying to be—it's so, so exhausting. Possibly above all else, I need to like myself enough to want to apply all of these things just for me alone. I will continue to hold this agreement with myself.

My experience of bipolar has changed me. I've had to grow up. I still rebel against 'better judgement' and I hope I always will. It's a part of who I am, and makes me feel alive. But maybe as I continue to grow to an acceptance of my illness,

I can look forward to channelling my passion and energies into more creative pursuits that invoke less harm on others and me. (125)

Early to bed

I can't tell you how to manage your illness, I can only tell you how I manage mine, but 'Early to bed, early to rise' is a little bit of wisdom that I've adopted to manage my bipolar highs. I don't go out at night. Okay, that's not strictly true. I go out at night three, maybe four, times a year. The rest of the time I'm at home and in bed at seven o'clock. It might sound boring, and how we hate that, we bipolars! But I don't have real highs anymore and that's been worth what it has cost. Because I don't have real highs, I don't have to manage them. I don't have to regret them. I've lived consciously this way for four of the last five years since I was diagnosed with bipolar disorder. I also take an antipsychotic but not a mood stabiliser.

Before you say you couldn't live like this, consider what people go out at night for: in one word, 'entertainment'! And entertainment is one thing people with our condition don't need. Entertainment is loud, fun, stimulating, puts you on a high. Pubs, pictures, parties. These are the things that get you on a seductive high. It feels good. And how we are addicted to that.

Personally, I have enough stimulation and excitement simmering in me that I don't need any external triggers. My husband watches television in the evening. That too, is something I'll pass. I don't need murder, mayhem and bright images of disaster in my life. If I want to know the news, I can read a newspaper. Much less dramatic. And since we only have two rooms to live in, I go to bed and read, write in my journal, meditate, think and dream.

Because of heavy medication, I bed down between eight and nine at night so that I can get up between the same hours next morning. Staying at home and avoiding stimulation has calmed me and slowed me. After a few months of this routine, the highs and lows evened right out to a pleasant state of feeling good and looking good most of the time.

My husband is retired, and I no longer feel the need to rush around in the rest of my life either. I don't have the busy lifestyle I once had, with volunteer jobs and meetings. Those things lose their interest and I don't have to be busy 'doing good' anymore. I was never as indispensable, or even as important, as I thought I was.

Since I've been diagnosed I've been loud, aggressive, in-your-face, witty, smiling, and oh so clever, though I don't think I ever reached the true heights of 'charming'. I was like that for about a year before I began to hate myself for being a show-off and what my husband called me, 'a smart-arse'. Thankfully, the love of my life told it like it was often enough that I had to believe him. It was the only really sensible thing to do.

I began to read books about bipolar disorder. The one thing that kept cropping up in all the literature was the need to 'regulate the sleep–wake cycle'. I noticed if we had a night out, however low-key, and, say, got to bed at ten o'clock, I would have a night with little sleep, followed by a day dragging myself around, worrying about it, more sleeplessness, the next night, fatigue, mood swings, arguments, feeding addictions—coffee and alcohol—and the inevitable depression. Not really responsible living. So we stopped going out at night. It does take a while to even out, but as you withdraw from the stimulation, life becomes surprisingly pleasant.

I *was* uncomfortable for a long time when I first adopted this routine. I cried, I missed the lights and laughter of going out. But if you spend enough time alone you meet yourself. You can't run away. You grieve for the stupid things you've done, but you know you can always start again. Early next morning.

It's been four years now and it's been good. My husband's watched a lot of television. I've read a lot of books. I've prayed, hoped and dreamed of living as a 'normal' person rather than someone who is 'different' (superior?) and who claims special privileges (excuses?) because they have an illness.

In the last four years I've had eleven or twelve hours a day to do all that I need to do—housework and self-care—and to do what I want to do—develop myself as a creative person. I've knitted bags and hats and scarves. I've done art—paintings, drawings, collage and mosaics. I've learned basic auslan, and Kantha, and I've trained as a barista. I've written, and self-published, a poetry book. This year my mood drop-in centre hosted a one-woman photographic exhibition for me as part of mental health week, and I won an art encouragement award for a lino print the same week.

These things come not from the erratic and spasmodic energy of 'highs' but from the slow walk that I'm able to manage now in my daylight hours. They are the things I dreamed of accomplishing when I first lay in bed at night and began my journey to wellness.

This small wisdom—stay home at night—is offered for you to consider as a way of managing bipolar highs. 'Early to bed, early to rise' has given me happiness and riches that looked unlikely when I was given that awful diagnosis of bipolar disorder. (16)

Reading the signs

As a relative latecomer to bipolar disorder—around my sixtieth year—I have probably not managed to develop many strategies for dealing with the highs, but those I have may be of relevance to other people with the condition.

During the manic episode my behaviour rapidly escalated to become very noticeably abnormal and socially unacceptable. I left the house and went to the local shopping centre and talked to anyone who crossed my path, demanding their undivided attention and asking constant questions. I was very uncooperative when my wife tried to persuade me to calm down and come home. Even though I never became physically violent, there is no doubt that the police would have needed to intervene to get me to hospital if a good friend had not come to my assistance. This friend, in whom I have always had great confidence, was willing to talk with me, agree with me, humour me and generally cajole me— over a five-hour period—and eventually get me to hospital. I feel that this strategy of employing someone, not a family member, not someone too close, not someone who I saw as a threat, to help me, avoided a lot of trauma which I would have had difficulty dealing with later. It possibly also avoided physical violence in which someone (most likely me) could have been hurt.

I am fortunate to be able to visit both a psychiatrist and a psychologist regularly. The psychiatrist manages my medication, talks to me about my mood and general physical state in relation to the medication, and helps me to understand how I can make the best of the situation, weighing up side-effects in relation to wellness. I find this helps in managing my attitude to side-effects and developing behaviours to minimise them. For instance, I am conscious of maintaining a healthy diet and I do regular exercise to avoid putting on weight and I avoid alcohol and other drugs which may interfere with the prescribed medication. The 'other drugs' are not a problem for me, as I have never been personally involved with them and neither have my friends. Avoiding alcohol, however, is not so easy. Personally, I don't miss it, but I never cease to be amazed at the reaction of other men. Our social lives seem to be very driven by alcohol and I am constantly pressured, both subtly and overtly, to 'just have one, just one won't hurt you', 'be in the shout', and so on, by good friends, sensible, intelligent people who are all aware of what I have been through and what treatment I am having. I acknowledge that it is hard to totally ignore this, especially as it happens very frequently and I do sympathise with younger people for whom the pressure must be even greater. One strategy I have used which worked quite well was to wander around at a New Year's Eve party with a wine glass filled with dark grape juice—no-one batted an eyelid!

I believe another strategy is to try to live your life as normally as possible. I know that to do this, one needs the support of family and friends, and I am fortunate that I am accepted, warts and all. They include me in all the activities in which I wish to participate, and they understand if I indicate that I think something might be too stressful at a particular stage.

With the psychologist, I have been working on cognitive behaviour therapy (CBT). I have found this very helpful, as I believe I had developed a lot of bad 'life habits' during the long period when I suffered from depression and anxiety.

I feel very comfortable with her, and she has helped me to understand the thoughts I was having, and to work on changing some of them. She has also helped me to work on a daily timetable which keeps me active both physically and mentally without overdoing things. I enjoy it. I am also exercising to improve my breathing patterns and my flexibility so that I can be more relaxed and deal with the stresses of life more easily.

While I was in hospital and still high, someone suggested I keep a diary of daily events. I did this amazingly well, even though I have very little recollection of doing it, and I actually enjoyed it, so I have kept it up ever since. The daily entries are not necessarily extensive, but I have kept a record of my moods. I find that being able to compare how I have felt from day to day, week to week, has taken the guesswork out of assessing my wellness or otherwise. The fact that I know now that I have felt quite well for five months is starting to restore some of the confidence I had lost and I think it is helping me, along with the CBT, to understand my feelings better. (61)

Knowledge is power

If you could feel gloriously alive, at one with the world and buoyantly optimistic, why would you ever wish it to stop? It is an incredibly hard thing to swallow that these blessed feelings are actually part of an illness, known as bipolar disorder. Yet once true acceptance has occurred, wellbeing can then be achieved by careful ongoing management, effective communication and awareness.

Knowledge is power—an old saying—but one that is true for bipolar disorder sufferers. Learn as much as you can about your illness from your psychiatrist, from reading, from doing a course at any hospital that provides one, or contacting your local community health centre. Empower yourself so that you know what you are dealing with—the many faces and variations of bipolar disorder. Each episode you have may be different, so you need to prepare yourself for all possibilities.

Management of the highs involves accepting that every high will be followed by a low, and that low will be proportionate to the high. Therefore, it is not worth it for your general wellbeing to let a high keep escalating. You can learn to recognise your warning signs and then take steps to cut the mania off in its tracks. You can learn to become mindful and aware of your daily thoughts, emotions and activity levels. If your thoughts become fast, your positive mood increases or your energy levels rise, you will recognise these and heed the warning.

Each of us has many warning signs but one of the earliest is changing sleep patterns, usually involving not being able to get to sleep due to racing thoughts or requiring less sleep. If this occurs, it should be a red light flashing and immediate steps should be taken. Such a change should be notified to your psychiatrist, who may authorise medication changes over the phone, especially to normalise sleep patterns. Also, be aware that some antidepressants may increase mania, so they will often need to be decreased dramatically, in consultation with your psychiatrist.

You can also help yourself by decreasing all stimulation from talking, television and radio, and deliberately and consciously slow down everything you do—from eating to moving to talking. Avoid indepth conversations, making lists and frenzied activity. If you have practised mindfulness, you can use this to alter your behaviour. I've also found yoga and pilates to be helpful because they take you away from your mind, back to the body. Meditation or relaxation tapes can also be very useful. I have found a deep relaxation called 'Yoga Nidra' to be especially calming, and able to take me into a deep, restful breathing state. It does this by focusing awareness around each and every body part, bringing you into the present time, rather than racing on ahead of yourself.

You may find it helpful to start a journal where you record your fluctuations, your highs and what you did about them, what worked and what didn't. This then becomes part of your knowledge bank that you can refer to later. Every high episode or averted high builds your experience and expertise in managing this illness.

Learning balance in all things might sound boring at first but it's what I've found is necessary to prevent manic attacks. Most important is ensuring I get regular sleep and have a regular bedtime. However, I also don't overdo things and don't load too much on my plate for any one day. If I do feel pressure building in my mind, I cancel things and consciously slow down my day.

Prevention is definitely better than cure. However, effective management also provides for the worst-case scenario. You need a Management Plan written out and kept in your house in case your high keeps escalating. Have emergency numbers at the ready—your psychiatrist's, your local community centre, and public and private hospitals. Declare your wishes now so that you will feel less violated and controlled during and in the aftermath of an intervention.

I have written out a note to myself and done a tape with my voice of reason so that my loved ones can give these to me if I'm heading for danger territory.

I have three people on my support list—my husband, my sister and my best friend. If I need them, at least one will be there for me in a manic crisis. They have seen me in full-blown mania before and know the signs. If my husband tells me I'm talking too fast or in a sing-song voice, I trust him and together we turn to the Management Plan. We've learnt the hard way—from two enforced hospitalisations—that the sooner we can put our Management Plan into operation, the greater the likelihood of success.

A note to family and friends dealing with a manic person: it is easy in your concern for a loved one to step in and try and parent them. This will only lead to escalation. They will feel controlled and may react with irritableness, defensiveness and even aggression. Don't argue. Don't control. Instead, seek to work with your troubled companion. I was fortunate to have a doctor who understood this and successfully worked 'with' me when I was extremely manic. She suggested we do a Deal. I was to talk for five minutes then she would talk for five minutes. We would take turns. She recognised that I needed to be heard, not silenced, and that it was hard for me to stay on one topic. Therefore she asked if she could gently redirect me if I strayed and I said 'yes'. By using this Deal she worked with me, a very ill, manic patient. I felt cared for—rather than controlled, overpowered and violated. If this could be achieved with even an extremely manic patient, then it could be used very successfully in the early stages of a high. The Deal is therefore part of my Management Plan.

People experiencing a high do talk a lot and talk over others. I have seen other manic patients and believe a core need is to be heard. Therefore, when doing the Deal, I suggest you offer to 'Listen' first. To Listen does not mean just biding your time and jumping in the second their time is up. It means actively listening, nodding and taking on board what the person has to say. Don't write them off as out of their mind just because of their altered behaviour or zigzagging thoughts. In two severe manic episodes, I felt the same person, just trapped in my altered body.

It is often difficult for a person experiencing a high to know how they appear or how their behaviour has altered. When it is your time to speak, focus your concern on this. List what you have noticed is different. Point out the warning signs on the Management Plan that have been reached and tell your loved one you fear the high is escalating dangerously. Communication of this information will be more likely to have the desired impact than controlling, silencing behaviour. Of course, there is a chance that your companion has become too ill, too high to take on your warning. You will then need to contact their psychiatrist or Crisis Team. At least, when the episode is over, your loved one will feel less traumatised because you tried to work with them, rather than against them.

It is important to realise that a manic person is under extreme pressure, almost to breaking point. It is not just their behaviour that has altered but the world they find themselves in. I could only cope in my manic episodes by focusing on the next priority and then the next. My senses were overloaded. In particular, everything was too stimulating for my vision and too deafening for my ears. To expect me to behave normally under such strain is unrealistic. I mention this only to shed light and to say that while you cannot walk in my shoes, some compassion and accommodation needs to be made in dealing with me or any other bipolar sufferer.

Manic episodes are extreme but even they can be dealt with if caught early enough. Other highs, the up-mood swings that don't escalate into mania, can be managed by regular, close contact with your psychiatrist, by developing your knowledge and awareness, and by effective communication with family and friends when warning signs are apparent. (109)

The next excerpt offers similar advice to relatives, while also taking a wry look at the temptation to escape the ordinary, the flirtation with the high and the wrestle to get the disorder 'back in the box' and under control again. (Note: It has been twenty years since this writer's last major episode.)

Peace prevails

The enquiry, 'Have you taken your medication?' can really get up your nostrils, particularly when it's asked every day. It's a question that can only be met with hostility because it is so patronising. It presupposes that you cannot be trusted, that you need constant surveillance, because it's never uttered without the accompanying eyebrow-raised, head-tilted scrutiny. It always stimulates a learned response: the contraction of the muscles in your upper back, causing your shoulders to pull back and your head to rise. Then, every fibre of your being musters the energy needed to force you to silence the desire to scream, 'You are not my personal policeman!'

And silence it you must, because to scream is to provide the very proof that medication is still needed. So you reply with a cheerful smile and a, 'Yes, with my orange juice'.

Ironically, the only time that you can cheerfully deal with The Question ('Have you taken your medication?') is when you've deliberately chosen to stop taking it. For very good reasons, of course. It's been some time now since your last episode, you're in control now, and the medication takes away that edge you tell yourself you'll need for the essays due in the coming month. And, of course, it can't be good for you to take such strong drugs for too long.

You may know deep down in your heart of hearts that the resulting sense of wellbeing—never, never, never let it be called euphoria—could be put down to the defiant childishness the disorder seems to engender, but you choose to see it as your body having been purged of poisons and psychotropic drugs. You see yourself freed of the bondage of the daily grind of medication morning and night—even though you still must keep up the necessary pretence. But it's all right, because it's no longer your personal policeman, but you, who is now in control. Past experience has taught you all the symptoms, and this time you will not make the mistakes you previously did. You even find the enquiry, the tilted head and raised eyebrows quite easy to deal with. Indeed, life is easy to deal with!

Work becomes effortless. The management of house, career and university study becomes a series of simple tasks that dovetail seamlessly in the time–space continuum.

You are able to move from task to task easily and readily. You're up early, dressed and ready for a walk. After breakfast it's off to work, then back home, dinner and to the study. You just knew it would be like this! And as an added bonus you're losing weight—weight that your doctor told you was no fault of your medication, but you knew he was wrong, didn't you?

The assignments that had previously put such a strain on your time become a joy. *A Doll's House* by Ibsen, that bleak Norwegian playwright, is enlightening. From a space more than a century and a hemisphere away, this dramatist speaks to you, directly to you. He understands what it is to be female and to be treated as a child. He speaks to you of rebellion and freedom from the shackles of what others say is best for you. He knows and rejects the stultifying, artificial demands of society and the constraints of conformity. Oh, you are enjoying this essay. In your mind's eye, you can already see that 'A' grade.

As you go about your daily mundane tasks, Ibsen's protagonist, Nora, is there with you. As you deftly bypass questions about your medication, you think of Nora hiding macaroons from her censorious husband. You understand how she feels cooped up in that doll's house of an existence with a condescending husband who tells her he knows what's best for her. Nora's world is there with you. Duplicity is a necessary part of life for each of you. You can see why some things have to be kept from husbands and doctors. You're in the zone. Never before have you felt so inspired. This is the one that will nail a course Distinction.

You don't mind the first night that you wake at two in the morning and cannot go back to sleep. With a quiet giggle, you remember a Dr Seuss book: you simply can't turn your 'thinker-upper' off. That gives you time with Nora. For the next four hours you plan this perfect essay. In the dark you experiment with structure and quotes. It's all so exciting and at six you're up and ready for your run. You take Nora with you, for now she is impossible to leave behind. Like Nora who wildly dances the tarantella as a symbol of her freedom, you run with abandon as well. At work, colleagues look askance as you tell them of Ibsen and his enlightened, ahead-of-his-times play. You make connections with your work, your life and Nora's dilemma. You see added significance in even the songs you hear on the radio on your way to and from work. You can see life—see it all with a sparkling, resonating clarity.

It's during the third night of absolutely no sleep that you gain some insight. And now you know, don't you? You know that you have your very own version of the tarantella going on inside you head and it's a dance you cannot stop. Round and round you go in a frenzied mental version of *The Red Shoes*, and you are destined to continue to dance like a dervish unless you do something quickly. You take a double dose of antidepressants at midnight just to get some sleep. That should do it!

But it doesn't. Your husband, who's seen many variations on this theme, calls the doctor who suggests that you be brought immediately to Sydney, and so begins another movement of this fugue. Gone is the brash overconfidence. You beg forgiveness for your stupidity, but your husband does not want to hear, for hasn't he heard it all before? Tight-lipped, he goes through the bedroom, throwing your clothes into a bag, packaging up your assignment, readying all for the trip to the hospital.

If only hospitalisation were the cure. It takes days before

the antipsychotic drugs begin to have the desired effect—sleep. And then you have to deal with the involuntary leg shakes. You desperately want visitors, but when they are there you're acutely embarrassed. Nurses watch you lest you sink drowning in a dangerous depression. But you're past caring.

Days meld into weeks and finally you are brought to a state of relative normalcy. You know how to behave in a socially acceptable manner and you beg to return home to family and job. Your husband comes to pick you up. The trip home is silent—for what is there to say?

Home and work prove demanding—too demanding. Fears and hallucinations have you walking the streets, pacing the floors. Your concentration is so poor it is difficult to string a sentence together both verbally and in writing. You tell your boss that despite the month's sick leave, you will need to take your holidays and re-enter hospital. You contact the university to seek an extension, noting grimly that your Ibsen essay earned you a 'C–' and a comment that it was not up to your usual standard. Then you ring your doctor and agree to—no, beg for—ECT (electroconvulsive therapy).

You vow that this will be the last time you ever return to a psychiatric hospital; that you will do everything in your power to stay well . . . and you do. You do it step by little step. You faithfully take your medication. You talk willingly with your husband of the many and varied symptoms that ring bipolar bells; and then you ring your doctor and discuss your symptoms and up your medication when necessary, and then ring back and report on your progress. That's what it takes and you do it because the alternative doesn't bear thinking about—the rollercoaster rides into suicidal depressions and out-of-control, off-the-wall highs. You find that you can content yourself with the little highs of setting goals, achieving them and the raising of the bar just a little higher.

In the more than twenty years since that last major episode, you have only stumbled the once, necessitating a short stay at a local general hospital—not a psychiatric unit. Life has provided many hurdles to test your levels of sanity and strength, but a loving husband, a supportive doctor and a powerful determination have prevailed. (117)

As the writers in this chapter have shown, management strategies are most successful when they are created by the individual—with guidance from doctors, family and friends—and tailored to their lifestyle. The actual strategies employed should be whatever works best for the person with bipolar disorder.

These are ways you can prevent or manage your mania:

- Display or have easily accessible the list of your warning signs of mania. Give copies to your family and friends.
- Keep a calendar, write down your mood each day and reflect upon it to recognise the pattern of your moods.
- Relax and meditate. When feeling stressed and uptight, take a deep breath and let it out slowly. There are groups you can join that can help you to de-stress: pilates, yoga, tai chi.
- Exercise is a great way to 'burn off' excess energy. Try swimming and walking. Wear yourself out so you will sleep better.
- Schedule regular visits with your doctor or psychologist, or ring a mental health hotline and talk about how you are feeling.

- Get a massage or a facial—you have to keep still for that and it will help you relax. Aromatherapy is great too.
- Get a friend to hide your credit cards or ATM card. Direct debit your bills. Go grocery shopping with a friend and stick to the shopping list.
- Join an arts and craft group or a creative writing course, so you can be creative but only for a few hours at a time. If you do it at home, you may not eat or sleep for a couple of days.
- If you find your job is too stressful, take a holiday or change careers.
- Keep a diary or a personal organiser so you can focus and keep track of what you need to do. Don't overcommit yourself.
- Stick to a routine during the day with lots of breaks to relax and be still. (102)

My tools are medication, meditation, faith and creative work. Getting the medication right was very important. Having a certain stability from medication allowed me to work with other strategies. As I was recovering from my episode, I was back at work caring for people with intellectual disability. Working with people who were less fortunate than me, and who I had to be on deck for, was important in managing my condition. And I was inspired by the way in which they made the most of their circumstances.

I try not to let delusions get on a roll. I find meditation is a very helpful technique for stilling the mind. The delusionary 'high' thoughts can be very exciting, especially when contrasted with those feelings of worthlessness that I have during depressions. When the feelings of heightened and unrealistic self-importance come on, I try to talk to myself: 'Come on mate. Pull your finger out. Who do you think you are, Jesus Christ?'

I think having a faith is important. I am not a religious person but I've invented a sort of higher being that I can talk to. I've named her. I have a little chat with her every night as soon as I get into bed. She likes me and cares for me. We are kind of cheeky secret partners in life. I thank her for the day with 'I think we handled that pretty well' or 'We slipped up a bit there, eh'. I ask her to care for my boys and all my family and friends. Then I say, 'May I wake with a clear mind and a warm heart.'

If I was asked to state my most important management tool, I would have to say it is my creative work. It is work that I have discovered rather late in life. I make sculptures, collages and assemblages using found objects. To do it well, I have to stay well. What started with a friend doing art therapy with me has become a passion. For me, the beauty of working with found materials is that it doesn't require great technical skills as is the case with, say, painting or drawing. **(124)**

Goodbye Hollywood (Part 2)
My ten lessons

Lesson 1 was not to alter my medications or self-diagnose. I did this thinking that the meds would still be effective at a lower dose, to lessen the side-effects. How wrong I was, and of course I went down in a heap. Luckily my friend took me to my psychologist and then straight to the doctor. I was already in a position where I couldn't and wouldn't do these usually simple tasks. The self-injury was quickly corrected and a few days later all was well again. What a great lesson I taught myself, and something I will never do again without first speaking with my doctor.

Lesson 2 showed me the importance of having friends whom I trusted, and who knew me well enough to notice any mood changes. I was regressing fast and my friend prised out what information she could from me, made appointments with my psychologist and the doctor, and took me there.

Lesson 3. While well and healthy, it is crucial to communicate with trusted family and friends to set plans in place for when mood changes occur.

Lesson 4. Shop around for a doctor. I was not going to compromise my wellness with a doctor who made me feel insecure and a burden on their practice because I have a brain dysfunction. I had appointments with three doctors before finding one with whom I felt comfortable.

Lesson 5. 'Negative' is not in my vocabulary. I now read only positive literature, happy light-hearted books. I see positive movies, and the DVDs I watch are always G- and PG-rated. I choose programs from the TV guide and I don't watch news reports or current affairs. I listen only to ABC radio news, which I find much less invasive than TV. I buy Friday's newspaper to get the local entertainment guide which always has free, fun, different and interesting events.

Lesson 6. This is the duty of care I owe to myself in making these considered choices in my life that give me a sense of achievement and self-worth.

Lesson 7. I find it imperative that I live in a calm environment and keep stressors to a minimum, with strategies in place to handle difficult and unforeseen situations. Sleep is crucial and I always have mild sleeping tablets on hand to get me through any sleepless periods.

Lesson 8. Worry time. As soon as a matter becomes a concern and ruminations unfold, I say, 'No, not now. That goes to Worry Time.' This is time that I set aside each day to deal with any problem that has arisen. This 'positive action', as I describe it, enables me to keep functioning in the present and deal with the problem at my time, 4 p.m. It works, because the action part of it gets the problem out of my head and gives it somewhere to go until the appropriate time. I then deal with the concern as an exercise, jotting down all the particulars on paper or writing about the situation.

Lesson 9. I create goals that are small and achievable, not ones that are against lifelong habits—as much practice is needed to change the latter. So, for instance, if I feel that I am watching too much TV, I begin by reducing this by half an hour. Writing down a list of goals is great as it's satisfying to tick them off, no matter how small they are, and say, 'I've done that. I've achieved my goal. Good on me.'

Lesson 10. I nurture myself. I'm learning to say 'no', and to be my own person. I am thankful every day for my 'reprieve'. I no longer beat up on myself for not having a job. When I'm asked, 'What do you do?' I answer, 'I live Life.' My job is me and I can now live with that very comfortably. I am beginning life for the first time in fifty-five years.

I have read masses of self-help literature over the thirty years, but now it seems as if I am reading it for the first time. I describe it as seeing and reading from the heart.

I have always tried to remember the life lessons shown to me during my depressions, but the 'highs' never allowed me to participate for extended periods. This quasi-confidence is always waiting in the wings, even now. I am always on guard against the two triggers, stress and lack of sleep.

> I respect where I have been and my choice is not to
> go there again. The correct diagnosis has finally given me
> medication to be able to live life in wellness and I am not
> going to abuse that privilege. I never want to see the black
> side of my illness again, only the back side! (178)

• •

IN THE SPOTLIGHT
Maintaining skills and techniques

- In many cases, the first mainstay to remaining well is compliance with prescribed medication, together with awareness and acceptance of the condition.
- Three other key strategies for remaining well are recognising and attending to early warning signs of a possible episode, developing wellbeing plans to maintain psychological wellness, and education—the person should know themselves and their disorder. These objectives can be achieved with counselling, support and the continuing update of their knowledge about bipolar disorder.
- To remain well the person should be open with their health practitioner, and be willing to consider observations made by family and friends about early warning signs. They should seek help before the temptations of a high become irresistible.
- The individual should fashion a comfortable day-to-day routine. They should be self-protective, avoiding stress and the sorts of people who create it, and limit or moderate any excessively stimulating situation.
- Developing good sleeping patterns is important. The sleep–wake cycle is a central plank to wellness, and, if it is disrupted,

the individual should rapidly implement their proven methods for reinstating it, using medication if necessary.

- Not only should the individual develop pre-emptive and episode strategies with family members and friends, the latter should be aware of the need to work as an alliance—and to respect the many needs of the bipolar individual during an episode: for instance, to be heard rather than silenced and controlled.

The following points are a summary of key issues identified in relation to developing wellbeing plans by Sydney psychologist Dr Margo Orum (in *Bipolar II Disorder: modelling, measuring and managing*, Gordon Parker (ed.), 2008).

1. The individual needs to develop a 'fine-tuned awareness' of their own early warning signs and triggers, and seek information about the illness—i.e. 'know thy enemy'.

2. A strong sense of ownership and stewardship of their illness is helpful, and often easier for those who have had psychotic manic episodes because the awareness of the impact of their 'craziness' on family and friends is often highly motivating.

3. The difficulty in moving to a wellbeing plan reflects the 'basic psychological logic that anyone compelled by ill health to live by new restrictions will naturally feel ambivalent'.

4. Ownership of the wellbeing plan will be more likely if the individual judges that it will serve their preferences and interests in both the short and the long term.

5. It is helpful to involve the individual (rather than only the managing practitioner) in identifying both the costs and the benefits of the illness, using Motivational Interviewing techniques. People are more persuaded by their own deliberations than by those of others.

6. A wellbeing plan works best when developed during a time of 'wellness' but shortly after an episode.

7. Involvement of trusted family members and/or friends is desirable, if possible or feasible.

8. Commitment to a wellbeing plan is 'essentially a commitment to personal growth'.

Dr Orum's template and strategies provide a very practical approach. (See Appendix 2.)

• •

12. Practising the art
Bipolar disorder and the getting of wisdom

*See yourself as a survivor, taking small but steady steps
through this unusual life of ours. (5)*

*Change from victim to victor. Grow beyond the confines of
the illness by learning about it and yourself. (10)*

This chapter presents the positives that are gained from knowledge
and mastery of the ups and downs of bipolar disorder. Many of the
writers in this book say that they would not be as inspired, nor as
inspiring, if their bipolar disorder was suddenly 'cured'. They feel
that, despite all the downsides, they have been granted a special
way of seeing the world that remains with them even when they
are stable.

The first piece of writing documents the experience of a woman,
now in her sixties, who has lived with mood swings since early
childhood. It charts her gradual recognition of the disorder, her

increasing skills in its management and her current resourcefulness and resilience. It is an understated piece, marking a life led with dignity. It illustrates the plurality of the supports which underpin her control over the disorder. It was written by a family member who sought, on behalf of the family, to honour her and her graceful accomplishment.

The staircase

There's a girl standing at the bottom of a staircase who thinks to herself: 'There's something wrong.' She's only eleven years old, but already she's discerning, already she owns the survival skills that will see her through life. It's difficult to tell where she picked up these skills. Certainly not from her mother, who told her about Santa, the tooth fairy and periods, but never broached the subject of mental illness. But now, staring up at the darkness from the bottom of the staircase, she realises this feeling has nothing to do with somebody else. This type of unease has everything to do with her.

She dismisses the feeling, carries on through her teens thinking that everyone feels and sees the world as she does. She is driven, energetic, passes exams without studying. A slim, attractive brunette, she flutters from one boyfriend to the next. She finds sleeping difficult, some nights near impossible, yet she remains alert, retains the glow in her face. She makes endless trips up and down the staircase, spending weeks, sometimes months, on the highest step or the lowest rung. Rarely does she pause for breath on the steps in between; her mind knows only how to plummet to the bottom, and how to propel itself to the top.

The teenager can arrive at the top step in an instant, without warning or furore and, once there, she never wants to come down. But the top step, like any high place, is not without its dangers. At this altitude, the teenager can get wedged in a moment, lucid and unmistakably real, when she thinks she is a saint. Then she formulates a plan to travel to the Speakers' Corner, to stand on a butter box and proclaim to the strollers, the joggers, the dogs playing on the grass, how the world should be run. You can't tell her anything when she's standing on the top step, not a single fact that will challenge her opinion, for then the anger sets in, the aggression takes over, and the attractive brunette turns into a fireball. The danger, then, is not that she could fall and hurt herself, not even that she could fall and topple someone else. The real danger is that from the top step, the mania tricks her into thinking that there is nothing wrong.

Years pass, bringing with them a handsome suitor who soon becomes a husband, and three sparkly-eyed kids. She doesn't know it now, she won't realise for some time, that she already has the most vital survival mechanism in place: a family who loves her unconditionally. She tells herself that she is too busy being a mother, maintaining one household and renovating another, to make trips up and down the staircase. But, still, the mania persists; it is mangled like a bad car crash, with the debilitating lows.

At thirty-five the mother slides down the banister and hits rock bottom, her body lying crumpled in a heap. When suicidal thoughts prevent her from catapulting to the top again, she finally acknowledges, in the most timely and haunting way, that something is terribly wrong. Suddenly she is afraid of her next thought, petrified of her next move.

'Whatever you do, don't leave me,' she pleads with a friend.

And so the friend stays, sitting beside her on the bottom rung, until the mother is hospitalised for an illness she has always sensed but never been able to grasp.

It isn't until the mother's third hospitalisation that she is diagnosed with bipolar disorder. When the doctor explains the symptoms of the illness to her, it is as if someone has turned on the lights and the mother can see the staircase. She is relieved to see the staircase. She always sensed that it was there, but finally she has tangible, undeniable proof. Now that she can see the stairs with her own eyes, she is confident that she can travel up and down them with her own feet, rather than her mind. She is keen to get going then, to get back to her husband and children. But before she takes off on her latest adventure, the doctor prescribes her lithium, which keeps her—give or take a few steps—towards the middle of the staircase. The mother returns to her home, to the family who loves her, with awareness by her side. Now that she has been formally introduced to bipolar disorder, she can recognise its symptoms and curb its urges. Her movements have grown cautious; she knows to slow down when she is close enough to read the sign at the top of the stairs. 'Warning!' screams the diamond-shaped sign. 'High step ahead.' Underneath the sign, in much smaller print that only the astute can read, are the words: 'euphoric mood, excess energy, surge of ideas, impatience and irritability, fast and furious speech, decreased need for sleep, distracted mind, flirtatious libido, and overzealous wallet'.

The mother adopts a set of strategies to control her ascents up the staircase. She knows she likes to shop—she has a credit card statement and a husband to remind her—but now she has the insight to choose where she spends her money. She exchanges designer boutiques for St Vincent de Paul and the Salvation Army, where she can buy clothes as bright as her mood, for a fraction of the price. She begins a diary, loses herself in books, spends more time in the garden; she does anything that minimises stress. After dinner each evening, she walks to a neighbouring suburb with her husband and, on returning home, she lies down to sleep, even though sometimes she has enough energy to power the whole street.

On Sundays, the mother frequents the local church, for she believes faith keeps her focused. She has a doctor she can trust, whom she can contact at any time; someone who not only considers the patient's life when giving advice, but the lives of her husband and children. She knows no self-pity and exercises little hesitation in seeking help for her problems. She takes pleasure in the simple things in life: brunch with a friend, a family dinner, a trip to the Blue Mountains. Every Monday evening she meditates in a room full of friends, her mind always returning to her via a different road from the one it departed on. But above all—when she is literally 'above all'—she tries to look at the humorous side of life. For, if you can't laugh at the top of the staircase, you may as well slide down the banister.

Despite the mother's strategies, the mania can still take hold of her, suddenly and ferociously, and whisk her away towards the top of the staircase. It is during these high-flying episodes that she relies on her family the most. They remind her to take her medication, three times a day, even though the mania is hollering: 'I don't need drugs, life is wonderful up here!' But by now, the family can see the staircase clearly, especially the steps towards the top. Gently, they persuade the mother to take her medication, and the family meets her midway up the flight of stairs.

Now sixty, a doting grandmother, a treasured mother-in-law, she has collected suitcases full of wisdom on her many trips up and down the stairs. She imparts her wisdom to others, not standing on a butter box in the Speakers' Corner, like she once envisaged, but within the walls of her own home. Her wisdom is the quiet kind, the type that lurks in the tone of her voice, in her off-hand comments and heartfelt advice. Wisdom, she believes, is the by-product of living with bipolar disorder. For each time she has plunged headfirst into pain, she has resurfaced with a few scars, and a little more insight. Surviving the pain has propelled her forward, encouraged her to grow, and, having experienced more pain than most other folk, she now stands ten foot tall.

Almost twenty-five years after she first discovered the staircase, it is still brightly lit, the polish worn away by years of pedestrian travel. Yet, the strangest thing is happening to the staircase. Every day, it becomes a little more crowded. Her husband, her son and two daughters, her grandchildren and her in-laws are making the journey up and down the stairs alongside her, just to keep her company. This is the beauty of the staircase: anyone can see it, if they truly want to. (148)

As people with bipolar disorder reflect on their experiences, many state that they have come to know themselves in a way that would never have been possible without having had their illness. Most value this highly. Many writers noted how they had developed and accessed reserves of compassion and wisdom. The vagaries of their disorder have often meant that they have had to forgive themselves and learn from each episode. The majority observed also that they had come to value people and relationships more, to not take things for granted and to appreciate more of the fabric of their lives and the everyday pleasures.

Fellow survivors, although we may all suffer from the same illness, we all have different chemical make-ups, have had varying life experiences, and react differently to medications. There is no panacea for an illness which diagnostically has five categories, all accompanied by diverse characteristics. Our journeys are as different as are our attempts to control bipolar disorder. However, I believe that knowledge is essential to empower us to comprehend that part of our life causing us such trauma and heartache. Knowing our triggers, having a support group and taking baby steps give us ways of coping and accepting that are necessary to distinguish between us, as people, and the illness. Internet support groups and medical research can be so overwhelming, but if one takes the time, when able, to sift through so much information, hopefully it is possible to come across a site, an explanation, or sometimes even just one word, which for that day allows our journey to continue.

For those of you who have not yet realised it, I am in a 'hypo' state at present, due to a change in medication. Were I not, you see, you would not be reading this. At least I am aware, but it has taken much time, hard work and anguish to reach this point (loss of family, friends, two marriages, and medications until I rattled as I walked). I find my rainbows in every day and knowing that you are all out there, struggling so often, but surviving each day. That's what keeps me going. (5)

I understand that to keep healthy I need to maintain a routine, minimise stress, use my support networks, take my medication as prescribed and have an honest and open relationship with my psychiatrist. I refuse to be controlled by the disorder, and I understand completely the damage that being manic can cause to my life. It has been a long and difficult struggle to make it this far. Every New Year I hope that this one will be better than the last and again this is my wish for this year! Would I change what has happened to me? I wouldn't wish it upon my worst enemy, but I wouldn't change a thing—I think I'm a better person for it. (105)

The orientation of my life and my illness comes down to making a few simple choices that, admittedly, I have been granted the opportunity to make.

One of these choices involves choosing the kind of work that allows me to keep all this in balance. The work I have chosen allows flexibility, it allows the management of my own time and means I can take into consideration my moods. This flexibility allows me to experience dignity and job satisfaction, and an opportunity to contribute. It allows the best possible outcome for the responsibility of my work and also, more importantly, my life and wellbeing.

Secondly, I have chosen to be in control of my life, and where this is not possible have indicated to others the situations and circumstances where I will need support. I allow others to care for me and my wellbeing, they help direct me into making the right choices in my life. They too make a commitment to my overall health and wellbeing and without them there are times when I feel my life would spin out of control.

Without the mystery of this in my life, perhaps writing this would not have been possible. Or perhaps only possible in a fictional sense, not my real 'lived' experience. Perhaps it would have been written without passion. A passion to tell the world, this is how I live, I own it, and countless others support it— some without knowing it. I believe it is possible to be a 'highly functioning' human being. By highly functioning, I mean feeling I have something creative to offer, that only I can offer. A human being satisfied with self and her contribution to the world in which she lives. I am just one with an extra burden to bear, a burden that if harnessed adds to my attributes.

My articulation of this experience is just that, mine, and in no way undermines any other's experience. It is my attempt to feel deeply and live courageously and have ownership over my life and illness. At the end of the day, what keeps me surviving and keeps me well, despite all the adversity I sometimes feel, is that I believe I am a young woman who has been granted an incredible depth to view the world in a way not possible by many others. These are skills only learnt in the 'school of life' and this undertaking allows depth, empathy and clarity— in a world that so desperately needs it. It needs us—unique individuals who face adversity not with weakness and fear but with STRENGTH, COURAGE and OPTIMISM. (44)

Everybody experiences mental illness differently. Each time I have a manic episode it brings different symptoms, so I have to adapt the remedy to what is going on at the time. If I had kept on the lifestyle path I had in the past, I would have ended up permanently in a psychiatric ward, or dead. The life I have today is something I never dreamed possible. I have a job. I'm getting married next year, and we are looking at having children, so I have enlisted the help of a psychiatrist to help me do this safely. And, yes, it has been hard looking at and working on myself. It took five years, but I've never been happier or more stable. (53)

The experience (of coping with my husband's last mania) has enabled me to develop resourcefulness. Our marriage is more honest. Our family is better integrated. My stepdaughter, I believe, respects me for not abandoning her father. She feared I would. We are more relaxed in each other's company. Amazingly, the high had the most therapeutic side-effect on the relationship between my stepson and me. My stepson showed strengths I never knew he had. He visited his dad daily. We are bonded through surviving this most distressing experience and our mutual love of a husband and father. In crisis, I know I can rely on him because he was our most constant supporter. (106)

Hitting rock bottom

An upside to having bipolar disorder is that I have accepted I need the help of others. In the past, I just wanted to celebrate life with family and friends. However, I have seen in the dark times the truly amazing gifts I have received from people in my life. Now I know that the relationships I have with other special people in my life have made me realise how connected we really are.

I guess what I have learned in this journey so far is that no matter what is happening in my life, I can still enjoy the moments along the way. It is really important to enjoy the adventure and be a part of each day, even though there are some really difficult ones. I used to avoid going to parties when I wasn't working because, of course, the first question is often, 'What do you do?' Now I think that because of my illness I won't always be working but that doesn't mean I can't still enjoy my life. I think it is so important for recovery to be part of the world, even though it has been scary for me sometimes as I felt I was a loser in society's terms.

I can proudly say now that because the bipolar card has many challenges, I feel I have become a better person. When you have been in a psychiatric ward time after time because of the highs, it is impossible to judge anyone. Many people I have met haven't had a lot of support and I know how much support it has taken for me to come out of what has felt like a wilderness. I have met many patients with big hearts. I think that being sensitive contributes to the susceptibility to an illness such as bipolar. I would not want to give away my sensitivity which allows me to perceive the world in a certain way, or the challenges of living with bipolar disorder which have shaped me as a person.

And one positive to hitting rock bottom is that there is no need to fear it because it has already happened! The last ten years for me has included hospital episodes and the transitionary periods back into work and life. Right now I am job hunting so that I can hopefully enjoy my work and the people I work with, have money again to pay rent and then possibly start to achieve the personal goals that I have for myself. (Since writing this I have found a job. Yippee!) (121)

We often look at other successful families and sometimes it appears they are skimming the surface of life, when by necessity, we have had to plumb greater depths. My wife claims a further advantage of having bipolar disorder is being able to experience increased positive emotions and feelings. For example, it is apparent she has a greater ability to express and receive love, and her vibrant personality and conversation has contributed to her popularity and has provided her with many opportunities in life. Perhaps this is why so many successful people have bipolar disorder. (129)

Being challenged with Bipolar I Disorder has funnily enough been a kind of blessing. It's forced me to *stop* and observe my life in a new way that works *for* me, not against. A way that is more mature in my dealings with relationships, stress and anger management, self-love and self-worth, and acceptance and forgiveness of others and myself. I've learned to eliminate the need to feel *victimised*, I've learnt to take responsibility for all my actions and outcomes, to leave other people's problems to them, to build social networks (where before I lived more isolated), to remove my own sense of the stigma of mental illness, to not take life so seriously, and especially to be kind and gentle with myself at all times! (134)

I am not the person I was, or thought I was years ago, but who is? I've grown in many ways and truly believe that in some way I owe my thanks to a diagnosis that forced me to look deeper. That perspective has been a long time coming—ain't that the truth! (146)

Losses to the illness have been spontaneity, self-confidence and simplicity (incarceration and scrutiny aside). But I have gained experience of love and caring to a degree I wouldn't have thought possible, both near, and from strangers. In a life with a former scientific focus, I also count as gain the derailment to philosophical interests and above all, literature. (156)

Nearing my twenty-fourth birthday, I've come to believe as true that no tablet or ladder-to-salvation can ever hope to totally train the tumult of life's tumble-dryer to the rhythms of his or her own desire. All one can really do is get a tight grip and hang on. Hold on with all the grit and feistiness your Darwinian knuckles can muster. I'll never be the *same*. As before. As the majority. As those constrained by the rigid elastic of the sanctified square. I'm at peace with the demons and stark truths of my path, two poles swapping the bane of war for the art of love. The child of their union—permanent residence in the Land of the Sane. (162)

I would be lying if I said there was no cost to last year's episode of mania. Shortly after 'landing', the inevitable months of depression ensued. Thankfully, because of early intervention, it was nowhere near as bad as previous post-mania depressions which had all ended with crash landings leaving a trail of carnage in their wake. I had, somehow, for the first time, mastered the art of landing. I definitely won't garner any of the respect that the astronauts do. If anything, I'll have to share my stories under a pseudonym (like here), in case large parts of the population start treating me as a second-class citizen.

But despite the hefty payment, I reckon it was worth it. Like astronauts I discovered new planets. Only these planets were simply different versions of planet Earth: new ways of looking at our world, new ways the world could be. Given the present mess the world finds itself in, alternative ways of understanding it might not be such a bad thing. (173)

I am lucky that my self-worth, dictated by genes, star sign and unshakeable faith in God, has helped me to come to terms with this illness. I know that even better medication will be developed which will be one of the single greatest factors in helping people with bipolar disorder. I have maintained all my old friends in the big city, and all my new friends in the town of my birth. They all treat me as a normal person. I have worked hard at maintaining friends, calling them, remembering birthdays, meeting for lunch and movies, and for the past sixteen years I've often stayed with people when I'm in the 'big smoke'. I have admitted openly that I have a mental illness, but that it can be managed. I have shown that I can lead a normal life, managing a business, a bed and breakfast, and keeping up with four married children and 6.5 grandchildren. I am president of the local garden club, teach scripture each week and sing in the church choir.

I was invited by Rotary to address a number of meetings in the area about my illness. I was really frank, and in fact probably shocked some people by what I had suffered (including being widowed with four young children) and the strategies I had used to overcome such adversities. Many people came up to me after the meeting and said that they had no idea that I had this illness and they had no idea of the adversity and consequences. So, I guess if I have helped just two or three people, then maybe that will spread a little more and people will become enlightened. (177)

So create your own wisdom, collect your own truths and strategies to carry you forward. Create a suit of armour; use this to shield you and your journey will be better for it. Such armour does not slow you down as you might think; it is well-fitted like another layer of skin. It will help you with your purpose and deflect unwanted and unnecessary occurrences that may trigger a changed mood state, an unwanted dip, climb or turn. I leave you with these words, and wish you the best of luck! (159)

A part of the human race

It is good to be in my sixties and to be 'countercultural'. The last five years have been the healthiest and most contented of a life that has been otherwise coloured by serious episodes of misery and turbulence. I have had a bipolar condition, probably since my early teens, which was not diagnosed until I was in my forty-first year.

I say I am 'countercultural'. Many of my peers are just beginning to struggle with chronic, debilitating illness, whereas I have been living with my 'friend' for so long it is almost familiar enough to be ignored. It demands more attention at some times than others, but my life is tidier and richer for my learning not to be mesmerised by it. I am a woman who has an illness, rather than a diagnosis. 'Margaret Ordinary' who has a bipolar condition, not 'Margaret Ordinary' who is bipolar.

The contentment of the last five years basically flows from the 'getting of wisdom' rather than a narrow focus on managing 'highs'. My life is much more fulfilling because I know what I need and I now have more assertiveness to say so—I sense a greater maturity in myself which is also affirmed by close friends. Life as a whole is more manageable, so there is relatively less stress to deal with. And, as a side-effect, I seem to be having fewer, less disruptive highs.

Probably we with a bipolar condition are psychologically frail. But we, too, need to negotiate our life tasks, even though they might be a bit more difficult, perhaps, for us. Human development is a bigger, more integrating task than just learning strategies to lessen the impact of a particular illness. In this area, I have been lucky. I have had good opportunities for personal growth, and people around me who believed in my capacity to face challenge. Some of them thought I was a bit of a slow achiever at times, mind you! Personal development is also important even for managing a stress-related illness like bipolar disorder. Failure to negotiate life stages leaves people stuck in uncomfortable, stressful conditions.

There are countless examples of human resilience which bring observers to silent awe. They are displayed by people who could have been suspected to be without resources. I have joined the rest of the human race in facing and doing my best to negotiate challenges as they present themselves. I hiccuped my way through various 'seasons' of parent–daughter relationship: submissiveness, independence, equality and, finally, nurturing them. At eighteen, I resocialised into a strict convent culture, which has been constantly changing ever since. I have faced and changed the original lack of wisdom in my choice to be a teacher. I was eventually able to grow beyond miserable dependence towards mutuality in relationships. Learning to value and express my creativity has, itself, been creative of my sense of self. I have taken the risk of living alone after fifty-five years of various kinds of group living. I have explored and integrated expressions of generativity appropriate to my uniqueness as Margaret Ordinary first, religious woman second.

It is with a great sense of thanksgiving that the 'getting' of these and other wisdoms has left me in a life space of such unexpected contentment. Gratuitously, also, bitter intensities about victimhood have evaporated, and gratitude is a constant companion now. On the authority of this week's *Sydney Morning Herald*, I have apparently joined the ranks of contented women over fifty-five!

From early teens to age forty-one my life was significantly marked by the pain of an undiagnosed, poorly understood mental illness. Since my first hospitalisation in 1985, I have learnt some life skills that are specific to managing my bipolar condition.

Good, clear knowledge gave me power over the condition. That knowledge included general information, clearly applied to my personal experience. For the first time my symptoms were objectified as a medical condition rather than a failure to be any sort of decent human being. I learnt about the validity of mental illness diagnoses and welcomed the appropriateness of psychiatric drugs.

The psychiatric help I have received has been patchy, but sometimes good. As I have gotten older, I have become more assertive about seeking and maintaining good GP and psychiatric support. I value such sounding-boards in times of crisis, but, more importantly, in negotiating personal growth.

I have continued to seek good spiritual information through reading and through a competent 'spiritual director'. My image of God can be distorted by both mania and depression. My membership of my religious order is important to me because we challenge each other to be idealistic, realistic and authentic. I have significant relationships within and outside the group.

A protective attitude that I have found helpful is to remember not to take responsibility for things that are none of my business. A personal tendency to 'fix' others can be very stressful, and lead to exhaustion, not to mention delusion!

My stomach, and its resident butterflies, is an infallible barometer of tension. Being aware of such physical symptoms is very useful to me in being comfortable, and in the last resort, in preventing mania. My most common cause of tension comes from not balancing solitude and gregariousness in my life. There are also other balancing acts that can benefit from attention: inactivity/hyperactivity; being self-contained/self-disclosing; self-discipline/ spontaneity, etc. All of my major highs have been the result of a strong external stressor (e.g. my parents splitting up) during which it would have been much better to seek early counselling. (I 'know' and have been through the proximate warning signs of my highs many times. But, by the time I am experiencing them, I often deny that any of this is leading to a high. My real protection lies in good, early self-knowledge and well-developed habitual stress management.)

Within the structure of my religious community, an arrangement has been made to quarantine the resources of the group from the financial indiscretions of my highs.

A few good friends know the warning signs of my highs, and they loyally try to tell me when I am getting into danger. They are women of stern stuff who usually bear the brunt of my denial and anger, endure my absence from the relationship while I am off being 'mad', and then forgive me for my arrogance when I am available again.

The capacity to maintain friendships in spite of my disruptive, even frightening behaviour is what sustains me most in living with bipolar disorder. I belong to a group of religious women who all knew me in a fairly detailed, if superficial, way before I had a particularly public manic attack. They know that there is more to me than my illness. (Humanly they find the silence of depression easier to put up with than the unpredictability of highs!)

My eventual capacity for openness and appropriate self-disclosure has widened the circle of people who know there is more to me than any medical condition. They join with me in debunking the thing. You can't be a victim of something you send up! On a more important note, shared vulnerability is most often a source of intimacy. Sharing simply any of my vulnerabilities (including the bipolar diagnosis) has led to like responses, leaving me and others standing together on 'holy ground'. These experiences have been part of the 'upside' of being bipolar, or part of the upside of taking the risk of other self-disclosure.

There is another positive side-effect of having a bipolar disorder. It led me for the first time to experience the truth of myself as a woman who is both flawed and gifted.

I am grateful for the blow-out of my worst manic attack being so extreme that I was forced to get psychiatric help. I had to 'call things by their right name', a process I often resist at first. Naming my weakness, instead of using so much energy denying it and trying ineffectually to control it, freed energy I was able to use for the first time to live with much more happiness and health.

Acceptance of myself as both flawed and gifted was deceptively simple in the freedom it gave. I am part of the flawed and gifted human race, not a misfit after all! **(46)**

• •

IN THE SPOTLIGHT
Becoming expert through practice

- A person with bipolar disorder can grow beyond the confines of the illness by learning about it and themself. They can aim for quality of life, not just managing the disorder. 'Bipolar' is a word, not a sentence.
- Having bipolar disorder can help a person to identify what's important in life—to reflect on what has been learned, and to develop a larger and more philosophical view of the world. The individual should visit their ghosts, make peace with themself and their past, and start every day afresh.

- Bipolar disorder does not define the individual. It is an illness, like any other. Those who matter don't care, and those who care don't matter.
- As for dealing with other lifelong illnesses, tools for contentment exist. They include promoting optimism, feeling and showing gratitude, cultivating hope and spirituality, and being 'mindful' rather than rushing through life. Once the individual has learned to pace themselves, he or she can outpace the condition.

Though no one can go back and make a brand new start,
anyone can start from now and make a brand new ending.
Carl Bard (1907–1978)

Appendix 1
Perfecting the routine:
More bipolar control techniques

For further resources, please see the Black Dog Institute's website: www.blackdoginstitute.org.au.

This section offers a representative set of strategies found useful by the writers in this book—collating and summarising some of their management approaches detailed in the previous chapters. You may find something in the following pages that you can incorporate to assist you, or someone close to you, to achieve better balance.

Meditation and exercise

I meditate to relax an overheated mind. The centring influence makes this the most effective non-medical tool I have found. I believe that meditation has been responsible for the permanent improvement in my mood stability. I exercise, doing repetitive and low-impact sport like swimming, spending time in a dreamy, calm state, where thoughts barely register and there is only the automatic movements . . . a brief respite for the brain. I try to practise mindfulness, keeping reactiveness in check, thus lessening the chance of careless deeds and words. I don't have any alcohol, avoiding any substance that could increase disinhibition. And when I get it wrong, maybe not working as hard as I need to keep my mood stable, or a swing just happens and I can see no triggers, I try to forgive myself, put it behind me as soon as I can, and start again. (9)

Normal meditation is impossible for me during a manic phase, but sometimes a fast-walking one helps. You just need to be mindful of each step you take, and, when your thoughts wander off, simply (she says with a chuckle) come back to focus, without judgement and try again. Also set little mind-focus goals: read one page or street sign like it's the most important piece of information in the world. (161)

Exercise. I thought I hated it but began to realise that I actually liked it if it was the right kind and had lots of variety. After much experimentation in the gym and falling off step blocks and fighting from sinking to floor level on the stair climber, I discovered my own style. I swim laps at the local pool which leads me to a meditative state. I learned a martial art which has the added bonus of helping me to feel strong and in control, a boon for dealing with a disorder that leaves you at times feeling so out of control. I exercise along with home fitness DVDs—because if I don't and the outside-of-the-house lessons or workouts get overrun with appointments, bad weather or just plain not feeling too well, then I find that my momentum slows to inertia. I need to keep moving to keep those endorphins flowing and to keep feeling well. (47)

I was experiencing rapid cycling for which I was prescribed drugs which evened out the cycles but made me incredibly sluggish and sleepy, as well as ravenously hungry—and my weight ballooned. Then I started swimming again, something I hadn't done since I became depressed in my late teens. I also stopped drinking so much, and my weight began to drop. I started a business, which gave me a purpose—I simply couldn't stay in bed on bad days and pull a 'sickie'. If I didn't work, no money came in.

I did my first 'long' swim in January last year. It was 1.5 kilometres, the longest I have ever swum continuously. The water was cool and clear and felt fantastic. I felt completely in my element and knew I was alive. The drugs had neutralised the highs and lows but, for me, they'd made everything a dull shade of grey. The bright white light was back. I'd found my new drug.

I train at 6 a.m. Even on a good day, I'm rarely jumping out of bed with enthusiasm at that time. But on a bad day, I feel I can't move a limb. My husband gives me a friendly kick out of bed (he knows what's good for me even if he doesn't know what's good for himself). I turn the alarm clock off so that he can have some extra sleep and I force myself to swim. Nine times out of ten it makes me feel better.

Occasionally I get a panic attack or I'm suddenly claustrophobic in the water. I then count down from one hundred in threes. It concentrates my mind on something sane and rational and, eventually, instinct takes over. (138)

I am doing yoga, which is great for staying on the 'high' side of life. There is a part of me that misses that manic high and my doing yoga is a way for me to get the buzz of the natural high without the mania and the pain that goes along with it. (104)

Sleep routines and the biological clock

To help with drifting off to sleep, I assemble onto an iPod a collection of soothing music to last the night. The radio, even when turned low, is likely to have a sudden change in sound that disturbs you just as you're drifting off to sleep. I used to eventually manage to fall asleep by lying close to my husband and listening to his heartbeat. Years later, I suggested to my psychiatrist that he make a recording of a normal heartbeat and place it in a pillow, along the lines of the recordings made of the sounds within a mother's body to help newborns sleep. (6)

Permanently employed nurses are expected to work combinations of early, late and night shifts and have little control over their rosters—I work all 'earlies' or all 'lates', with no switching between. (65)

'The rotisserie' is a technique I have personally developed for times when I am in an elevated state and need to get to sleep. Beginning by lying on my back, relaxing, I tell myself that everything will be as it was in the morning. I concentrate on feelings of being safe and comfortable. After lying in this position for ten minutes, I rotate ninety degrees and lie on my right side. For ten minutes in this position, I repeat processes of meditation and then roll onto my stomach. By rolling every ten minutes I find it easier to relax and discover the most comfortable sleeping position. (157)

I use melatonin regularly to help even out my daily sleep–wake cycle. When I say melatonin, I mean prescription-strength melatonin, not that homeopathic garbage. It is pricey, but I find it worth a trip to the compounding chemist. I also take sleeping pills sporadically when I feel I need extra help settling down. (158)

I like to listen to soft music when I'm elevated and can't sleep. I make sure it's music without words, or I end up thinking too much about what the singer's trying to convey. Music soothes the mind and allows me to focus on slowing down my breathing which is fast and erratic at this time. Even working on a jigsaw puzzle can sometimes take my mind off stuff I don't need to be worrying about in the middle of the night. This can tire me and is a safe activity I can do without too much thinking. (26)

Forgive yourself after an episode

One of the challenges that I work towards is being guilt-free about the consequences of my disorder: to be comfortable with who I am, whether well or unwell. It's all a part of me. (120)

My advice is to: **Think slow, talk slow, act slow.** Learn from previous experiences and try to be more responsible next time. Bipolar isn't responsible for all your psychological issues. Explore counselling without the illness being a central theme. Confide in yourself. Admit it's hard to leave the dragon, but adults shouldn't spend too much time in story land. It's way too much fun for grown-ups! (57)

Anger management [is] vital in a family comprised of a menopausal mother and two adolescents—hormones ping off the walls. I have a feral temper and no impulse control. When the children were little, I instituted a strategy whereby once I had regained control (usually not having the faintest idea what I had said), each of them had to tell me if I had said anything that had really hurt, and we worked through it. I apologise a lot; the apology I consider one of the most useful parenting tools in existence. (154)

Diet and vitamins

I take omega 3 supplements every day as well as a multivitamin. I exercise a minimum of one hour per day. I have strict sleeping patterns and routines in my daily life. I also minimise stress, a factor that can trigger my manias. I've learnt not to take on too many commitments—it's better to do a few things well than a large number badly. It's also OK to speak up when I am under stress and drop commitments if needed. Better to fail at one or two things than to crash and burn altogether. I follow a low-GI diet (so that varying blood-sugar levels don't affect my mood), limit caffeine, avoid other stimulants such as guarana and sinus tablets with pseudoephedrine, limit alcohol, and avoid artificial food additives such as colourings and sweeteners. (65)

Once I began exercising and I started to feel good, I needed to figure out how to maintain the healthy good feelings. How could I make my body look and feel even better? I cannot expect my body to run at peak performance if I am running it on junk. I hear you groan, 'Not rabbit food!' But having been the proud owner of a rabbit who enjoyed a nightly slurp of ice cream alongside me, I know that rabbits do not have a boring diet, and they certainly are interested in the good side of life if one allows them to be!

However, we could take a little (lettuce) leaf out of the rabbit's proverbial book and think of food and what we need most and least of. Obviously, a nice high vegetable content with high-performance foods including whole grains, raw nuts for snacking, and smart carbohydrates, balanced out with smaller amounts of lean meat, and dairy. Keep food flowing (but not overflowing) throughout the day. It keeps away the feelings of starvation that seem to launch in on me when I have a stressful day. (47)

Self-calming activities

Write down a list of non-high-producing things that you can do to use up excess energy. (143)

My tactics (in the case of suspected mood elevation) involve staying home, avoiding overstimulation and, if possible, sleeping. I usually can't sleep, but lying in the dark, burning lavender oil and listening to quiet music, is almost as good. I can harness my manic energy for tasks such as housework. The repetitive nature of cleaning doesn't allow my lack of judgement to cause too much damage—though, mind you, I have broken many plates in my time. To remove the risk of blowing large sums of money, I have invested the majority of my savings in a term deposit account that I can't access. (65)

Successfully managing the highs of bipolar disorder, for me, is the art of 'emotional husbandry'. Current literature suggests 'internal and social rhythm therapy' is helpful to bipolar sufferers. It seeks to establish regular daily routines and attitudes that encourage people to deal with their schedules in an organised manner.

Some suggestions that have worked for me:

- In summer, I ensure that I maintain my intake of water and salt so that my serum lithium levels don't become compromised. When I am feeling emotionally coiled, I shower often, or go down to the local pool and plunge myself repeatedly in deep water until I feel that I am out of my head and back in my body.
- I almost exclusively use secondary lighting in my flat. Overhead lighting irritates me and puts me on edge. Lots of secondary lighting enables me to manipulate the ambience in my environment to keep myself more centred.

- I've become ritualistic about where I put my valuables (e.g. wallet, keys, mobile phone). Lost valuables drive me crazy.
- I use music and dance to 'debrief' myself emotionally. If strong emotions are threatening to take on a life of their own, I often 'dance out' in the privacy of my home.
- If I begin losing sleep and experience other signs (feeling 'speedy'), I usually put myself back onto a low dose of antipsychotics, as agreed with my doctor, until I can see him.
- Rope in a multidisciplinary team with diverse psychosocial approaches in combination with pharmacotherapy.
- Book long appointments with your primary health carer so that you have adequate time to exchange information. Bipolar disorder does not play out in a vacuum. The socio-environmental context of a person's life is a potential minefield of triggers that could precipitate mood escalation.
- I have often felt paralysed by the need to talk with someone about my bipolar exploits who would not judge me for my transgressions but help me to make meaning of my experiences. I found that counsellors help enormously in this respect. Counselling sessions were safe forums for me to unpack and explore important personal, social and existential issues. Family and friends are thus spared from taking on this, often daunting, responsibility. (111)

The simple art of distraction has proved itself as one of my most helpful coping strategies. At times when previously I would have taken diazepam or painkillers to pass the moment, I now know that doing weights for just three minutes can burn off that nervous energy. I've learnt not to be afraid to call or SMS a friend when I really need another person to ground me.

Similar to things you shouldn't do when intoxicated, you have to learn your limits when you're manic or upset. Obviously there are times when it's not safe to be driving. However, sometimes a long drive with the right music can be just what you need to readjust your mood and affect. The key to these distractions is doing something that you will be proud of later. I've found it far more helpful to channel that energy into short bursts of exercise or creativity than to self-harm or self-medicate. (55)

Chill out. When the passion and the politics are gaining too much momentum, I let go of saving the world via letters and petitions, turn off the radio and slow down with a swim. Relaxation with some soothing and gently inspiring music takes one to a simmer. You may think you are selfish and going against your father's Protestant work ethic, but this is what you need. (67)

What helps us ride the highs without getting out of control? Our house is never normal: so what is normal? We have a bipolar male high school student, a depressed female university student, a bipolar mum going through menopause and an estranged suicidal father who keeps popping up. It is a challenge to cope with the things life throws at you when you have bipolar disorder and have to manage the intense highs.

My mantra is ROUTINE: Rest, OK to be me, Understanding, Trust, I can accept help, Nurture and Empathy. (137)

Self-nurturing

Don't hesitate to take sick leave. Just because you haven't broken out in a smelly green rash doesn't mean you're not going through a serious episode of illness. Switch your mobile phone off. Ignore your email. The world won't crash to a halt, I promise you. **(173)**

Trusting that my emotional state will not be trivialised takes courage and it gives me comfort to know that there are a few people I can turn to when I need it most.

Other tactics include sending myself text messages with encouraging words, or writing my thoughts in a journal to stop them incessantly going around in my head.

Learning to be my own friend, trying not to be overly critical of myself and forgiving myself for past indiscretions and mistakes also helps.

Reading inspiring books, and writing out inspiring phrases and sticking these on my bedroom wall assists me to remember what life is supposed to be like, as I have a tendency to forget when my mind is racing or numb.

Asking myself 'Is this what's best for you right now?' also helps. **(142)**

I find self-nurturing activities are important. Things such as warm baths, reflexology and massage, listening to quiet music, practising relaxation techniques, using aromatherapy and candles, and reading books and magazines with serene images are really helpful. Mild exercise, such as long slow walks and swimming, maintaining my hobbies and looking after my spiritual wellbeing are other strategies I employ. **(143)**

Managing psychosis

Dr Meg Smith: I had to learn to disbelieve the evidence of my own senses.

My tips for managing psychosis—mostly you need someone you can trust and a mantra that grounds you until you are given help. I have a strategy where I ask myself, 'Where am I? What am I doing?' I listen to my answers. If no-one is able to help you, there are resources such as a counselling hotline which is open twenty-four hours a day.

I find that if I take off my shoes and literally feel the ground beneath my feet that helps me. Also, I have a 'magic' rock that I feel protects me. (Yep, I see fairies too!) I carry it around, and when I feel scattered, I roll it around in my fingers to keep focused, just feeling its texture—much less painful than the rubber band or ice cube trick. (161)

I came up with a cricket analogy on how to talk and listen to others whilst having racing thoughts: 'Let the thoughts go through to the keeper.' (118)

Diarise the brain waves, maintain a consistent routine, make a deliberate pause before action. (127)

'Outside insight'

For me, the most useful and successful strategy for lost insight into my condition is the appointment of 'minders'. These are people who see you frequently, either at work or home, and are able to observe your behaviour on a regular basis. They must have your respect. They are selected by you and have agreed to fill this role. They have to be tolerant, patient and loving people who know you well. They must be able to put up with your erratic and excessive behaviour—such is the nature of 'bipolars'—without intervening, until it becomes 'over the fence'. Then they 'lower the boom', and you ignore their advice at your own peril. One day during my last high I planned and carried out a program welcoming two sets of visitors to my town. This involved me making the journey between home and town five times in the one day. It also included conducting sightseeing and providing meals. Ridiculous! This led to a 'boom lowering' action. (131)

How do I know whether this 'happy' is 'normal happy' or the beginning of that sinister manic devil getting its grip? Was that sleepless night just like anyone else's when they couldn't settle, or is it a sign of something more ominous? Has some switch flicked? Has something triggered the beginning of a manic episode? This constant vigilance, this need to 'watch myself' and 'read the signs', is wearying. There's no easy answer, no sure-fire way of striking the right balance between vigilance and obsession. So, I have learned that I must give permission for those who know me well to speak up if they see something that smacks of the mania. I have an understanding, informal, but in its own way, contractual, with those closest to me—my daughter, friend, sisters and doctor who know the signs. They know that they have permission to quietly caution, to gently ask, if they see the slightest hint—of that fast talk, rapid-fire ideas or disinclination to eat. (43)

Journalling

The trick to managing a high is to recognise and manage the feelings. The feeling of the high itself is not to be feared or buried. But the behaviours and actions resulting from a high should always be closely scrutinised, reflected upon, and controlled. How? In the short term, a journal is a great focus. It can be done by hand, or word processor, or audio taped or by adding in the visuals via a video recorder.

By recording one's thoughts when one is high, it is always possible to come back to them and analyse the feelings in a more considered way at a later time when one is more 'balanced'. This provides insights into how the high felt and makes episodes a little easier to recognise.

Conversely, one can record one's 'voice of reason' so that it can act as an anchor or boundary at the beginnings of a high. (166)

Managing finances and decisions

Money can slip through the fingers quite rapidly! At one stage, my affairs were put into the hands of the Guardianship Board, and I must say that those years were the most demeaning, deflating and miserable years of my life. I had no control of my finances and dealt with a faceless body who did not seem interested in my welfare. I now have a method whereby my cheque accounts are linked by computer to my accountant and the amount of money I spend on the business is sent to him by computer. These records are then sent to my office, where my secretary decodes them and this allows my accountant to assess what spending is tax deductible. I do not find this intrusive and it really assists me with my business management. I also avoid making major decisions, and do not take on extra activities.

I have a margin loan as an investment and this is managed by an adviser who, together with me, decides the investment strategy. Should I wish to draw money from this source then her seal of approval is required.

I have a cheque account where my accountant and I are the joint signatories. This protects funds that I may, when my mood is elevated, squander. I do not have any credit cards, but a debit card with a finite limit. I do not have access to my internet banking codes. (177)

The wellbeing plan

My main strategy for identifying an oncoming episode and what to do about it was developed with my counsellor, and has been invaluable to me. It is a contract (called a 'wellbeing plan', or 'advance care directive') that has different sections for episode periods. In the 'mood elevation' section, I wrote down what I experience during a manic episode, how to recognise it and what to do. Because I wrote it myself, I can relate to it more than to a booklet telling me what to do. I then signed this contract, and I will use it when I need to. And if things become unmanageable, I will contact my counsellor. Yes, this makes me accountable, but it is more than that. I see it in writing in front of me and I know what to do because it has worked in the past. (53)

Declare your wishes now so that you will feel less violated and controlled in the aftermath of an intervention. I have written out a note to myself and recorded a tape with my voice of reason so that my loved ones can give these to me if I'm heading for danger territory. I have three people on my support list—my husband, my sister and my best friend. If I need them, at least one will be there for me in a manic crisis. They have seen me in full-blown mania before and know the signs. (109)

I structure the experience. Using a timer and making myself do other chores or activities for a few hours before going back to my creative outlet is a great help. While I'm doing these other things, I can still think about what I'm involved in and my next steps for my current creative activity. It stops me getting too caught-up and obsessed. (193)

Appendix 2
The safety net: A wellbeing plan

It would have been easier to have a clearly spelled-out plan stipulating that 'If I do this, you need to do that'. Friends and family would certainly have had calmer, more rational lives. We did not have these mechanisms, so there were fractures which have not yet healed in the wider family. (114)

Framing a wellbeing plan

Adapted from Dr Margo Orum (2008)

Setting up strategies to remain well. The most effective management plan to manage future highs and depressions is one that the affected person contributes to. People are always persuaded more surely by their own deliberations than by those of others, and when there is ambivalence—such as family and clinicians, for instance, presenting one side of the argument only—this can add fuel to the other side. Being encouraged to express both sides of his/her ambivalence helps the person to weigh up the pros and cons of strategies for managing the illness.

The clinician should prepare the ground for a plan; supply relevant information and psycho-education about bipolar disorder; help the patient work through or, at least, address possible ambivalence that might sabotage a plan; and examine any relationship difficulties that might need to be taken into account. In most cases, where possible, the involvement of helpful family members or friends is desirable, especially those who may well be involved if episodes break through in future. The person should choose those people he/she trusts most, and preferably those who are in daily (or almost daily) contact so that they have the opportunity to notice very early warning signs. Phone or email contact can sometimes serve quite effectively as early warning detection—mostly in conjunction with regular professional help, or additional arrangements with a trusted workmate if there are concerns. Such arrangements must be the choice of the person with bipolar disorder, though, or else they become more like surveillance than a safety net.

Debrief what worked, and what didn't in the past and in the lead-up to, during and immediately after the episode/s. How were family or friends involved? What was most difficult for the person about the way others acted or spoke at the time? What did they do or say that helped the most? Does the person see their input at the time differently than now, being somewhat recovered? What did they do themself that helped or didn't help?

Identify the early warning signs. The person can be asked to identify any possible early warning signs in his/her thoughts or behaviour leading up to the time when clear signs of an episode began to appear. After this, family members or friends can add observations for the plan, and the clinician also can add comments.

Look at high-risk activities and triggers. These include excessive stress at work and/or home; getting too little sleep (hypomania), or too much (depression); stressed metabolism (with irregular energy/sleeping/eating patterns); excessive alcohol; suddenly stopping prescribed drugs without consulting the psychiatrist; excessive caffeine-rich drinks late in the day (that can disrupt sleep); doing intense emotional/spiritual workshops (gentle growth is fine); being in any intense, accelerated learning environment where there is challenge to old beliefs or sudden change to foundational beliefs; acting on impulses, if they arise from possible hypomania; and flying overseas where crossing different time zones may disrupt sleep–wake rhythms.

Specify how the feedback will be delivered. The person with bipolar disorder should be asked to specify who they would prefer to provide feedback of early warning signs. They need to work out the wording of the plan so that it is less likely to be irritating. They may tell the family member or friend selected for such 'outside insight' whenever their own private monitoring has picked up some very early warning signs, and use their help to monitor things further, until they are back in control. It is important that feedback is comfortable and not too intrusive, and in writing.

Acknowledge how difficult it is to receive feedback. It
will nonetheless be very hard for the individual to accept
feedback. They are likely to feel stripped of dignity and,
especially, of their credibility as an equal. If the person with
bipolar disorder denies that there is anything wrong, whether
correct or not, this can all too easily sound like the lack of
insight that typifies the early stages of hypomania. Thus the
individual must be prepared to at least consider the possibility
that signs may be present, even when they feel strongly that
the family member or friend is mistaken.

Intervene at the earliest possible moment. If the
individual can muster the willingness to act upon the family
member or friend's feedback by taking the agreed safety
precautions just in case, at least initially, they are well on
their way to managing their illness. Likewise, the individual's
own self-monitoring may pick up some early signs, to which
they need to respond with similar willingness to consider
the possible implications. Catching signs at a very early stage
generally means that safety precautions are quite minimal
and do-able.

Specify what safety measures will be taken, and by whom.
When early warning signs appear, the individual could
respond by reducing their work pressure, perhaps take a day
off, cancel stressful appointments, or take extra contingency
medication, as arranged with their psychiatrist. If they have
not been sleeping well, they may take a sleeping tablet, or get
some exercise to help with sleep. If they have been forgetting
medication, they may need to ask a family member to help
them remember for the next week or so.

As a basic precaution when they travel overseas, it is advisable to take some time off from work before and after the trip to allow their body to adjust.

• •

Wellbeing Plan

Date: _____

PLAN A

We, _____

Person X (who has bipolar disorder) and Person Y (entrusted by Person X to note early warning signs),

agree to work as a team as shown below, in a bid to minimise or stop future episodes of bipolar disorder. I/we also commit to continually seek out wellbeing attitudes and activities that will keep bipolar at bay, and boost enjoyment and quality of life in the long-term.

Early warning signs, triggers and risk factors that we agree warrant action are: _____

_____

_____

If Person X begins to notice any of the above, he/she agrees to take action such as: _____

_____

_____

If Person Y begins to notice any of the above, he/she agrees to take action such as: _____

_____

_____

PLAN B

If, due to the illness, Person X refuses to act as agreed above, he/she acknowledges the following actions may then become necessary:

_____

_____

_____

Person X

Strategies that I will commit to in order to prioritise my continuing wellbeing are:

_____

_____

_____

_____

Signed:_____ Signed:_____

       Person X   Person Y

• •

REFERENCES

Access Economics, for SANE Australia, 2003, *Bipolar disorder: costs. An analysis of the burden of bipolar disorder and related suicide in Australia*, Melbourne, Access Economics, for SANE Australia, p. 6. Available at: www.accesseconomics.com.au/reports/bipolar.pdf.

Andreasen, N.C. 1987, 'Creativity and mental illness: Prevalence rates in writers and their first-degree relatives', *American Journal of Psychiatry*, 144 (10): 1288–92.

Bleuler, E. 1924, *Textbook of Psychiatry*, authorised English edn (4th German edn), A.A. Brill (ed.), Macmillan Company, New York.

Csikszentmihalyi, M. 2002, *Flow: The Classic Work on How to Achieve Happiness*, 2nd edn, Random House, London.

Farrelly, E. 2006, 28–29 October, 'In Search for a Cure for Paradise Syndrome', *Sydney Morning Herald*, p. 28.

Goodwin, F. and Jamison, K. 2007, *Manic-Depressive Illness, Bipolar Disorders and Recurrent Depression*, 2nd edn, Oxford University Press, New York.

Jamison, K. 1995, *An Unquiet Mind: A memoir of moods and madness*, Alfred A. Knopf, New York.

Jamison, K. 1996, *Touched With Fire: Manic depressive illness and the artistic temperament*, Simon & Schuster, New York.

Jamison, K.R. 1995, 'Manic-Depressive Illness and Creativity', *Scientific American*, February, pp. 62–7.

Logan, J. and Fieve, R. 1976, Talk given at an American Medical Association meeting, Chicago.

Lombroso, C. 1889, *The Man of Genius* (from English translation of 1891), Scott, London.

Milligan, S. and Clare, A. 1994, *Depression and How to Survive It*, Arrow Books Ltd, UK.

Orum, M. 2008, 'The role of wellbeing plans in managing Bipolar II Disorder', in *Bipolar II Disorder: Modelling, measuring and managing*, G. Parker (ed.), Cambridge University Press, New York, pp. 182–92.

Parker, G. (ed.) 2008, *Bipolar II Disorder: Modelling, measuring and managing*, Cambridge University Press, New York.

Schou, M. 1979, 'Artistic productivity and lithium prophylaxis in manic-depressive illness', *British Journal of Psychiatry*, 135: 97–103.

Solomon, A. 2001, *The Noonday Demon*, Scribner Book Company, New York.

Wigney, T., Eyers, K. and Parker, G. (eds) 2007, *Journeys with the Black Dog: Inspirational stories of bringing depression to heel*, Allen & Unwin, Sydney.

Dealing with Depression
A common sense guide to mood disorders
by Gordon Parker

'This unique book, written by one of the world's leading authorities on depression, focuses on a way of thinking about the complexity and diversity of the mood disorders that is both easy to understand and "rings" true. Well-written and thought provoking, it is essential reading for all whose lives are affected by depression.'

Michael Thase, Professor of Psychiatry, University of Pittsburgh

Most of us get 'the blues' at some point in our lives, and some people find that they just can't shake them. How can you tell when you or someone you know is suffering from depression that needs clinical treatment? How can you find the best treatment for your depression?

Dealing with Depression is a brief, user-friendly guide to depression and mood disorders for sufferers, their families, and health professionals who care for them. Professor Parker explains that contrary to popular belief, there are many different types of depression, each benefiting from differing treatments.

He outlines the advantages and disadvantages of drug and non-drug treatments, and offers advice on matching the different types of depression with their most appropriate treatment. He shows that while depression may be severe and disabling, it can be treated successfully providing it is diagnosed and managed properly.

Covering everything from a typical 'blue mood' to severe clinical depression, including mood states such as bipolar disorder, *Dealing with Depression* is one of the most comprehensive and accessible guides available for the general reader and health professional.

ISBN 978 1 74114 214 3

Journeys with the Black Dog
Inspirational stories of bringing depression to heel
edited by Tessa Wigney, Kerrie Eyers and Gordon Parker

Depression can be a dark and lonely experience: sharing with a friend can make all the difference.

In *Journeys with the Black Dog* many people share their stories of living with depression. Personal stories of first symptoms, the path to getting diagnosed, the confusion and frustration, and all the many ways of keeping depression at bay—whatever it takes.

Written with raw honesty and sharp humour, these stories demonstrate it is possible to gain control over depression. *Journeys with the Black Dog* is genuinely inspiring reading for anyone who suffers from depression and those who care for them.

'These stories provide inspiration, wise counsel, and hope.'
Anne Deveson, AO, writer, broadcaster and filmmaker

'A wonderful book for anyone who has been depressed or who wants to understand depression better. It is insightful, compassionate and invaluable.'
Kay Redfield Jamison, Professor of Psychiatry, The Johns Hopkins School of Medicine

'A most important addition to the growing library of books on depression. It is written by those who have lived and experienced depression for those who want to learn more. It cuts deep and speaks to the soul as well as the intellect.'
Professor Geoff Gallop, former Premier of Western Australia

ISBN 978 1 74175 264 9

Living with Bipolar
A guide to understanding and managing the disorder
Lesley Berk, Michael Berk, David Castle and Sue Lauder

Living with Bipolar provides essential and practical information for people with bipolar disorder, their families and friends.

Two leading research psychiatrists and two psychologists, all with many years of experience in mood disorders, explain that this challenging illness can be managed. While there is no cure, it's possible for people with bipolar disorder to live well.

Many people seeking help with depression are diagnosed with a form of bipolar disorder, usually Bipolar I or Bipolar II. The authors explain the causes and triggers, both medical and psychological treatment options, and ways of preventing relapses. Drawing on the experience of their patients, they also show how to develop successful personal strategies for identifying and coping with symptoms, and emphasise the importance of a healthy lifestyle.

'A "must have" companion for those with bipolar disorder and their family members. It contains an excellent description of symptoms, early warning signs, and much more to understand and cope with the disorder effectively.'
Lakshmi N. Yatham MBBS, FRCPC, Professor of Psychiatry, University of British Columbia

'Written with passion, warmth and insight, this is a great reference for people living with bipolar disorder and their families.'
Tania Lewis, educator and consultant who has lived with bipolar disorder for over 20 years

ISBN 978 1 74175 425 4